SEEKER
A SEA ODYSSEY

—— A memoir ——

MIROLAND IMPRINT 19

**Canada Council   Conseil des Arts
for the Arts   du Canada**

**ONTARIO ARTS COUNCIL
CONSEIL DES ARTS DE L'ONTARIO**

an Ontario government agency
un organisme du gouvernement de l'Ontario

Canada

Guernica Editions Inc. acknowledges the support of the Canada Council
for the Arts and the Ontario Arts Council. The Ontario Arts Council
is an agency of the Government of Ontario.

We acknowledge the financial support of the Government of Canada.

SEEKER
A SEA ODYSSEY

—— A memoir ——

Rita Pomade

MiroLand
publishers

MIROLAND (GUERNICA)
TORONTO • BUFFALO • LANCASTER (U.K.)
2019

Series editor by Connie McParland
Cover design by Rafael Chimicatti
Interior design by David Moratto
Photos by Bernard Pomade
Guernica Editions Inc.
1569 Heritage Way, Oakville, ON L6M 2Z7
2250 Military Road, Tonawanda, N.Y. 14150-6000 U.S.A.
www.guernicaeditions.com

Distributors:
University of Toronto Press Distribution,
5201 Dufferin Street, Toronto (ON), Canada M3H 5T8
Gazelle Book Services, White Cross Mills
High Town, Lancaster LA1 4XS U.K.

First edition.
Printed in Canada.

Legal Deposit — First Quarter
Library of Congress Catalog Card Number: 2018962090
Library and Archives Canada Cataloguing in Publication
Pomade, Rita, author
Seeker : a sea odyssey : a memoir / Rita Pomade.

(MiroLand imprint ; 19)
Issued in print and electronic formats.
ISBN 978-1-77183-351-6 (softcover).--ISBN 978-1-77183-352-3 (EPUB).
--ISBN 978-1-77183-353-0 (Kindle)

1. Pomade, Rita--Travel. 2. Ocean travel. 3. Seafaring life.
4. Autobiographies. I. Title. II. Series: MiroLand imprint ; 19

G540.P66 2019   910.4'5092   C2018-906117-0   C2018-906118-9

For Silvia Luna,
my beautiful, intrepid granddaughter

In memoriam:
Gladys Muriel Karolak
A childhood friend who preserved and returned
every letter I sent her throughout the journey

Tennessee 2014

———

"You know your mother," my sister
says, "a bit irresponsible."
"My mother isn't irresponsible,"
my son replies.
"What would you call her?"
"A seeker."

Contents

Oceans

I have a feeling that my boat
has struck, down then in the depths,
against a great thing.
And nothing
happens! Nothing ... Silence ... Waves ...

—Nothing happens? Or has everything happened,
And are we standing now, quietly, in this new life?
—JUAN RAMON JIMENEZ 1881–1958
Translation Robert Bly

THE PHONE CALL

~~~~~~~

November 2015: Montreal

> *Twenty years from now, you will be more disappointed by the*
> *things you didn't do than by the ones you did do. So throw off*
> *the bowlines. Sail away from the safe harbour. Catch the trade*
> *wind in your sails. Explore. Dream. Discover.*
> —H. Jackson Brown Jr.

"Hey Bernard, Roland phoned a short while ago. Something about a friend of his with a yacht in Tunisia that he wants you to sell. He says to get in touch with him."

We're talking by Skype. Bernard, my ex-husband, lives in Mexico. I'm in Montreal. We talk almost every day. Skype collapses distances and there's no sense that he's away — just a feeling of expanded space around me. It's a good feeling. I show him the cats, go for a coffee, and take a short phone call. He leaves the computer to grab a snack while he waits for me to get off the phone. We have an easy relationship, though it wasn't always that way.

"Are you interested?" I continue when he's back in his seat.

"I'm thinking about it," he replies. "Roland's already sent me an email. The guy really wants to get rid of his yacht. She's a 50-foot ketch and well-equipped. He's offering a big commission, but there's no market in Tunisia. Tahiti is the place. If the owner is willing, I'm in. Are you coming with me? We can do it again. Better this time. Rita?"

I feel the excitement in the way he says my name. Years ago we sold the ketch he named *Santa Rita*, but he never lost his love of the sea, and I am woven into the threads of that love.

I'm intrigued by the idea, thrilled he wants to go on another voyage

1

with me. In the eighties we sailed from Southeast Asia to Europe. Now I'd have a chance to explore the Pacific. The offer is tempting. But I'm not sure. Back then we were dreamers, free-spirited and totally self-sufficient — or so we thought. The rawness of sea life brought out our strengths, but it also heightened our weaknesses. In the end, I had to go off on my own. He had to do the same. But those six years at sea were the most extraordinary and influential years of my life, and I could never have made the journey without Bernard. Together we discovered a world we never knew existed.

I think about my creature comforts. How my stomach no longer turns when I see a squall line move across the sky. How I don't jerk awake every two hours for my turn at the helm. How I don't have to hustle for work from port to port or wonder if Bernard could ever love me as much as the *Santa Rita*. I'm happy with my space. Sometimes I lay awake at night and think about my good fortune. Yet — to sail again — to relive that adventure from a more stable and aware place ...

My heart wants to say yes, but —

"I don't know," I tell Bernard. "Let me think about it."

I write my childhood friend Gladys about Bernard's proposal. She's been living in Belgium since her twenties, but we've kept in touch. She writes back saying: "Maybe this will help." In the packet she's sent me are the letters I mailed her through the six years of our adventure. I open the letters, touch the postmarks, finger the stamps — each gesture a touchstone to memory.

Chapter 1
SUCH STUFF AS DREAMS
ARE MADE OF ...

~~~~

October 1969: Mexico City

> *I have no reason to go, except that I have never been, and*
> *knowledge is better than ignorance. What better reason*
> *could there be for travelling.*
> — FREYA STARK

A great sense of adventure and curiosity about other cultures brought Bernard and me to Mexico in the mid-sixties from different parts of the world. He was a French geologist hired to find water for the Mexican government. I was a ceramicist in a potter's studio, a free-lance reporter for a magazine called *Mexico/This Month*, and part-time English as a Foreign Language teacher. On weekends, I read palms — a skill I had learned through reading books. Having walked away from an abusive marriage, I was trying to support my two young sons in a foreign country. Both of us were dreamers and open to new experiences. It was inevitable that our meeting would spark unexpected possibilities.

We met at the home of Leonora Carrington, a well-known surrealist painter who was as famous for helping to smuggle her ex-lover, Max Ernst, out of Nazi Germany as she was for her artwork. Leonora had a weakness for handsome young men, and Bernard filled the criteria with his rugged features, alert green eyes, and irreverently coifed head of thick, dark auburn hair. He was tall and lithe — the perfect escort for the parties Leonora used to attend at Diego Rivera's home. They weren't lovers, but it pleased her that others thought they were, since he was a good thirty years younger. Bernard, a young underpaid

Cooperant (the French equivalent of a Peace Corp worker), took full advantage of the arty parties, replete with free food and flowing booze. I viewed him as a lightweight rake, and made a point of ignoring his overtures of friendship during Leonora's 'by invitation only' Sunday salons.

But all that changed one afternoon when we bumped into each other at the La Merced Market in downtown Mexico City on a miserably hot day.

"Feel like a beer?" he asked, after the obligatory cliché of "fancy meeting you here."

He sat, looking cool and relaxed, at one of the many food stalls inside the market. I slumped, overheated and tired, onto an empty stool beside him. "Why not?"

Over a generous plate of *sopes* — thick rounds of corn *masa* slathered with beans, cream, and salsa — and cold bottles of San Miguel beer, we talked about Mexico. We discovered a shared love for this vibrant country with its diverse indigenous cultures still intact, its extraordinary shifts of landscape, and its warm and gracious people. Suddenly, my mood changed. I started to talk about how Mexico's heart had been ripped out the year before.

"When I arrived in the summer of 1966," I said, "Mexico City was the best place in the world to live. Many writers and artists from Latin and South America made the city their home — some in exile from their own countries, others by choice. Their presence brought interesting people from around the globe, attracted by the creative ferment that had exploded in the country. I came on vacation with my two young sons, but couldn't bring myself to leave. I sublet my apartment in New York, and believed I'd live in Mexico forever." My chest tightened. "That was before the massacre."

Bernard shifted in his seat, giving me his full attention. He had come at the end of 1968, almost two months after the government's brutal crackdown on students demonstrating in the Plaza of the Three Cultures. He had heard what happened, but didn't know the city as I had known it. It was now 1969, but the repressive measures of the Diaz Ordaz government had not abated. Many in the foreign community, accused of instigating the students, were still being deported; the less lucky ones, jailed and tortured. Others left the country of their own accord. The dynamic euphoria that had marked the city evaporated overnight.

"For weeks after the crackdown," I said, "I saw kids taken from their homes. The secret police roamed the streets with walkie-talkies to report any sightings of suspicious young people. Several teenagers hid in my home until they were able to procure forged passports to leave the country."

Wanting to help the students, I remained in Mexico. After, I couldn't muster the energy to leave. I hadn't realized the extent of my trauma until I started relating my story to Bernard. I was grateful that he listened without interrupting.

"I was in the Plaza the night the students were killed," I said. "A journalist I'd met at a party recognized me. He grabbed my arm and pulled me down an alley. While we were running, we heard the first gunshots and the tanks rolling in. I learned the next day about the hundreds of students slaughtered, their bodies never found."

Bernard looked stunned. He hadn't known the full story. The government had covered its tracks well for those who arrived in the country after the carnage.

"I believed as a child," I said, "I could make anything I wanted come true. But I've lost that spark."

Our conversation veered toward childhood dreams. Bernard related a half-buried boyhood dream that began on the Loire in France. He had built a raft to sail the river, but couldn't rig it so that the sail turned. His makeshift vessel raced downriver with no control until it crashed into the river bank. "I told myself I'd have a real sailboat one day."

The idea caught my interest. I had no sailing experience, but an early desire to explore. My family spent summers in a small cottage colony beside the Hudson River in upstate New York. Left to my own devices, I had wandered with no restraints, exploring every cranny of my limited world. I scooped-up frogs from hidden springs; walked in step with the fishermen who brought up buckets of striped bass and catfish from the nearby river; forced down oily eel grilled over an open pit that a fisherman offered me, refusing to deny myself any new experience. I dared myself to befriend an old bull tied up and alone in an open field, though I was warned he had a bad temper. I trailed after the local handyman — a tall, angular fellow who made me think of the tin man in the Wizard of Oz. He told me he came from far away, but wouldn't say from where, though I asked many times.

Learning at five years old that China lay at the other side of the world, I tried to dig my way there with a toy shovel; only to abandon the project two feet down and two summers later, when an underground spring flooded my port of departure. The China memory lay dormant until my conversation with Bernard. It resurfaced with a new-born energy that manifested itself in the form of a yacht and a desire to sail. What better way to see the world than from our own boat. No hotels. No limited stays. No heavy backpacks ...

I fell in love with the idea, and shortly after, I fell in love with Bernard. His raw sensuality awakened my senses. His wry humour kept me endlessly entertained. He even listened with interest when I related my dreams, and he let me interpret his. Most important, his rapport with my sons Stefan and Jonah filled me with gratitude. When Stefan needed an antibiotic shot, and I couldn't bear poking a hole into my son's tender skin, Bernard took over with a deft hand. When Jonah broke a favourite toy, Bernard was there to repair it for him. When Bernard moved in with me, it cemented the reality of our one day sailing the world. We shared our vision with the boys, who were then four and six years old, and eager for the adventure.

Over the years, my housekeeper, Laura, and her boyfriend, Benjamin, had become my friends. "We'll find an island and come for you," I promised her. "Benjamin can build us a house, and you'll tend the garden." It was Laura's dream to have her own garden, and I envisioned us eating home-grown produce around a large, rough-hewn table that Benjamin would build. They'd settle there permanently. For us, it would be a refuge after long journeys.

The two of them were as excited as we were to start this new life. Laura, who had been raised on a farm, didn't feel at home in the city. Work brought her north from a small village in Oaxaca, but every vacation she went back and took my boys with her. "They need the fresh air," she said. "And some good armadillo tamales that only *mi abuela* can prepare." Benjamin was a construction worker, but work was hard to find. When he did find employment, there was never any security or protection. I wanted to share what I thought was a better life with them—perhaps as a way of coping with all the injustices I had seen.

We remained in Mexico three more years trying to save the money for our adventure, while the government continued its propaganda against foreigners. When someone wrote "Gringo go home" in the dust of Bernard's car, we knew it was time to leave. We also knew by then that the pesos we were earning weren't sufficient to support our goal towards building the boat.

Bernard and I opened an atlas on the kitchen table and looked for a suitable country where we could prepare to start our project. With Bernard's background as a geologist and my years of teaching, we had the good fortune of being able to pick our country. It was the early seventies. Life was full of opportunity. Borders were easier to cross, and work was abundant everywhere.

The pencil came down on Canada—sane, democratic, stable, a high standard of living. Bernard had spent time there in 1966 and 1968 mapping the unexplored North for the Quebec government and was excited to return. He liked the fact that he could speak French in the province. I was happy that I could speak English. We would work hard and earn good money. We promised Laura and Benjamin we'd return for them when we were ready.

Chapter 2

GOING FOR GOLD

———

1973: Montreal

> *Your beliefs become your thoughts. Your thoughts become your*
> *words. Your words become actions. Your actions become habits.*
> *Your habits become your values. Your values become your destiny.*
> — GANDHI

Bernard and I arrived in Quebec with nothing more than an assortment of skills, two young children, and a vision to build a boat. Through a girlfriend living in Guam, we learned that Taiwan was the place to build a first-class yacht with a fibreglass hull, beautifully worked interior, solid teak deck, and most important, cheap labour. She'd seen many boats coming into the Guam harbour, and the Taiwanese-built ones were always the best and most elegant.

Bernard researched the shipbuilding market and his findings matched her observations. "The prices are good," he said. "What do you think?"

"I'm all for it," I said.

Bernard got a job on a dam site in the far north of Quebec. I looked for a school I liked for the boys and then got an apartment nearby. Once we were settled I found a teaching position during the day, and re-established my palm reading business in the evening. We lived on my salary and saved Bernard's to pay for building the yacht. During a respite from work, we drove to New York City to buy equipment — a VHF radio and a depth sounder.

"I'll never forget your help in this project," Bernard said during a break in our shopping spree. "I owe you."

"No, you don't," I replied. "This is a joint venture."

Back in Quebec, Bernard read books on the technical aspects of sailing. I read cookbooks and techniques for storing food on long journeys. I also went to an astrologer who assured me I wouldn't drown at sea.

I had never sailed.

"You'd better see how you like it," Bernard advised.

On a warm summer day, we joined friends on their yacht and sailed for a few hours on Lake Champlain. A light breeze eased their ketch through rippled water with no more than a slight tacking of the sails. Lively conversation and an endless profusion of succulent treats filled the hours. After a few glasses of good Chardonnay, I told Bernard: "No problem with sailing. I'll do just fine."

Instead of investing my time in sailing lessons, I decided to invest it in building our savings. I didn't want to be too old to sail by the time we had enough money for this adventure. One afternoon in a neighbourhood magazine store, I found an article on gold in an investor's magazine. I sent away for a newsletter that sang its praises and was seduced by the editor's enthusiasm. Fast track to the future, I thought.

"Totally irresponsible," my businessman uncle blustered, when I asked for his advice. "Get yourselves a home before you start fooling with what you don't know." I was deflated but undefeated. Gold felt right.

I got out the yellow pages and discovered that, at the Guardian Trust on Rue St. Jacques in the business district of Montreal, I could buy and take delivery of gold. The first time I walked into the building I was scared and thrilled. I couldn't believe I was doing this. I was going on nothing but my faith in a contrarian newsletter.

Sometimes I bought South African coins called Krugerrands. They carried one standard ounce of gold and wouldn't have to be assayed when exchanged for other currency, a practical consideration when travelling. At other times I bought small bullion pieces. I was awed by the refined delicacy of one ounce bullion and had even for a time thought about putting a piece on a chain to wear around my neck. Pure gold was beautiful. But my practical side prevailed, and I opted for investing more in Krugerrands than bullion. I stashed my hoard in a cloth pouch that I kept in my underwear drawer.

After a while, my confidence grew, and I started to dabble in mining stock. For the most part, whatever I bought went up, but there were some minor corrections.

"You're losing my money," Bernard shouted at me during one of those dips in the market.

I wasn't that sure of what I was doing, but I had to think fast to defend myself. "Don't worry," I blurted out. "The day we're ready to leave, gold will go through the top." I have no idea why I said that except that I wanted to protect myself from what could have been a terribly irresponsible decision on my part. If we lost it all, I'd think about it then.

But I didn't have to. When I started buying in 1974, gold was $250 an ounce. The day we left Montreal, gold shot up to $850 an ounce. In today's dollars that would be about $2,582 an ounce. We heard the news on the radio. "Gold has gone through the top," the announcer said. I couldn't believe it. Those had been the exact words I used to defend myself.

"We have to stay," Bernard urged. "We can't let it go. Let's buy more."

"No, no," I pleaded. "We've got to go. It won't stay there." Bernard was sceptical but he listened.

Saving for the yacht took seven long years. By the time we left, we had accumulated twelve ounces of gold bullion and a bag of Kruger-rands. Our stash took up less space than a pound of butter, so Bernard carried it to Taiwan in a beat-up old-fashioned doctor's satchel that had belonged to his father. We sold the mining stocks. I cashed in my school pension and retirement savings plan, and bundled my assembled liquid capital with Bernard's cash savings into a combined checking account to await its transfer to Taiwan. Once our streams of income were combined, we discovered we could build the yacht without touching the gold.

The gold bullion and South African coins kept us going for a long time at sea. There wasn't a country that didn't recognize gold as currency.

Point 1 : Taipei-Kaoshung

Point 2: Hong Kong - Macao ...

Point 3 : San Fernando-Manila

Point 4 : Puerto Galera

Point 5 : Palawan

point 6 : Kota Kinabalu

Point 7 : Borneo-Labuan-Bru...

Point 8 : Singapore

Point 9 : Malacca-Port Klang...

Point 10 : Indonesia-Sabang

Point 11 : Thailand-Phuket

Point 12 : Sri Lanka-Galle-Col...

Point 13 : India-Cochin

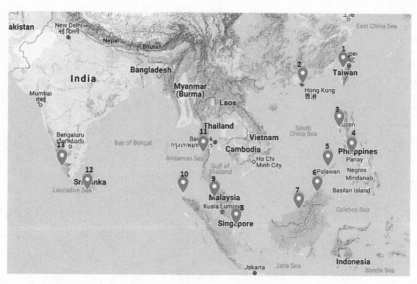

From Tapei-Kaoshung to India-Cochin

Chapter 3

WEST MEETS EAST

Winter 1980: Montreal/Taiwan

Imagination is life's preview of coming attractions.
— **ALBERT EINSTEIN**

Late December Bernard answered an ad for a drive-away car to Edmonton, Alberta. From there, we planned to take the train to Vancouver where a friend would drive us to Seattle for our flight to Taiwan. Three of us set out: Bernard, my son Jonah, who was sixteen, and me — each with one suitcase, plus the doctor's satchel with the small stash of gold and South African coins.

Stefan, now eighteen, was enrolled in a two-year junior college in Quebec that included the last year of high school and the first year of university.

"I'm not going," he announced after some deliberation. "I'd rather finish school."

I felt anxious about leaving him behind, but respected his decision. The years it had taken to save for the yacht was a long time in a child's life, and his desire to stay behind wasn't unreasonable. Earlier I'd received a letter from Laura who had also backed out of the adventure. She and Benjamin were now married with children, and had a small farm in Oaxaca. In the time it took for us to put together the money for our vision, they had moved on with their lives. First Laura and Benjamin, and now Stefan's backing out of the adventure brought home with a jolt how many years had passed since we'd first dreamed of this adventure.

We found Stefan a room in the house of a friend, whom I knew would look after him. Jonah had a half year to go in high school and was looking forward to the adventure of sailing. I contacted the Quebec government and was told that, because I had teaching credentials, he could get his high school diploma if I tutored him. They offered to send his sealed exams to a local high school in whatever country we were in. His high school guidance teacher suggested he apply to Middlebury College in Vermont before we left.

"They're interested in applicants who've been raised unconventionally," she told me. "It demonstrates to other students that alternative ways of living can be successful."

On January 2, 1980, with Stefan's and Jonah's immediate futures settled, we left Montreal in the car we were to deliver to an address in Edmonton. By the time we reached Ontario snow started to fall. Once in Saskatchewan, the storm intensified into a full-blown blizzard with zero visibility forcing us to crawl through a landscape so flat we couldn't distinguish the highway from the surrounding fields. It was clear why the car's owner had chosen to fly, but I didn't regret the drive. I got to see a large swath of Canada I didn't know, and who knew when we'd be back.

Our delivery in Edmonton was timed to catch an Amtrak train to Vancouver the same day, the ride over the Rockies being the highpoint of our cross-country trip. But as soon as we boarded, we were again hit by a blizzard. Snow billowed up through the toilets and settled in small mounds alongside our seats. Black porters in white jackets spent most of the journey shovelling heaps of it through the train doors far into the night. The visual impact and rhythmic movement of the men held us spellbound and kept our attention for a good part of the trip. In Vancouver, we stayed overnight with the friend who drove us to Seattle for our flight to Taiwan. I was winter weary and looking forward to the balmy clime of Taiwan.

* * *

We arrived in Taipei mid-January and stepped off the plane into a bone-chilling morning.

"I thought Taiwan was sort of a tropical island," I said. I flipped the hood of my parka over my head and held it clutched under my chin.

Bernard shoved his toque down over his ears. "We should have checked the weather."

For the next month, I shivered in my parka and complained about the humidity. Jonah took it all in stride and wasn't bothered at all. Neither were the Taiwanese, who left doors and windows open throughout the day to "let out the cold air." I learned to stay warm by drinking mugs of *ching cha,* meaning hot water, served in offices, shops, restaurants, and even railway cars all through the winter. I still drink *ching cha* to stay warm in winter.

There were no heating systems, not even fireplaces in Taipei homes, but many were equipped with braziers or gas burners embedded in the centre of tables. During the winter, families sat around the tables to absorb the warmth from the central fire. I discovered this cozy way of eating when Theresa Chen, an artist who owned a gallery in downtown Taipei, invited Jonah, Bernard and me for a Mongolian hot pot dinner. Theresa did Chinese water brush painting.

"Can you give me lessons?" I asked after visiting her gallery a few times. Her patience with my beginning efforts endeared her to me, and we became friends. Before I left Taiwan she gave me one of her paintings — chrysanthemums and a butterfly in flight.

"A symbol of transformation," she had said. Her gift hangs in my living room as a reminder of her insight into the voyage I was about to take.

It was during one of my painting sessions that Theresa invited us for the hot pot dinner. As this was our first exposure to brazier style eating, she taught us the protocol in three succinct phrases. "Pick up. Toss in. Take out." She demonstrated each step with a leaf plucked from a mound of greens.

A chafing-dish filled with a simmering broth bubbled away at the centre of the table. Thin slices of meat, shrimp, fish balls, tofu, greens, and noodles were placed around the brazier in flat dishes. Each of us had a bowl and chopsticks. Towards the end of the meal, we cracked raw eggs into our bowls and ladled the broth over them. The final product was delicious and the group participation made for a congenial atmosphere. I suddenly noticed how warm and comfortable I felt, and started to understand community.

In the countries we eventually sailed through and among the sailing crowd, a sense of community was the glue that held people together. Before I ventured on this journey, I thought of myself as an individual outside the social order and prided myself on my uniqueness. Slowly, I began to value the unifying strength of community. And from the gradual understanding that we're all connected, I started to embrace the connectedness of all things. The dawning of that perception started with the hot pot dinner in Taipei.

Anthropologist Marcel Mauss in the early 1900s studied the Inuit in the Canadian north where he observed that families lived independently during the summer, but as soon as winter set in, they coalesced into larger groups. This pattern of living was so basic to their cultural way of life that, when the Canadian government built Western style homes for them, the project failed because the communal lifestyle of the people during the long winter months wasn't taken into consideration. The Inuit of Alaska once built structures called kashims for use in the winter. Communal activities took place around a central hearth used for major feasts.

This connection between food and huddling for winter warmth has to be lodged somewhere in our ancestral memory because several years later, during our stay in the Larnaca Marina in Cyprus, a group of us organized what we called a "wintering in" once a week to get through the island's marrow-chilling months. Each week a different yacht was "it," and everyone arrived with items for cooking. The galley stove served as the central hearth, and the local flat bread took the place of bowls. Snug seating arrangements are inevitable on yachts, so body warmth was in good supply, and the feeling of well-being and comfort matched the Taiwan experience.

We weren't often invited to communal feasts, so I paid close attention to how the people managed when alone and discovered the local *chiao tse* stands. These savoury minced pork dumplings arrive with winter, accompanied by huge pots of bubbling hot and sour soup. Small stools placed around shared tables permit the chilled passer-by to warm chest and belly while taking in the heat of a neighbouring stranger. Jonah and I made frequent mid-day trips to our neighbourhood *chiao tse* stand, as much to treat our palates as for pinching a bit of body heat from strangers.

While exploring the fabled marble mountains of Hualien, several hours by bus from Taipei, Bernard and I discovered an area dotted with hot springs. On the tatami-covered floor of our sparsely furnished room was a raised platform with cotton-padded quilts. After drinking several cups of hot tea brought to us by a silent woman on padded feet, and soaking in the hot springs under the chilled air, I sank into the thick quilts and fell into a bottomless sleep. The hot baths and padded quilts were not culture shock but a cultural discovery that softened the discomfort of winter.

We bought a pair of the thick quilts as soon as we returned to Taipei. Every morning we aired them out for the following night as we had seen the Taiwanese do. They were remarkably efficient for soaking up humidity, and served us well in chilly ports. I couldn't bear to leave them behind, and dragged them back to Montreal when I returned.

"You're nuts," a friend interjected as she watched me hoist up the thick, bulky quilts from the cardboard box they had travelled in.

"Maybe," I replied, "but you never know when the heating will go."

I had learned to cope with the Taiwanese winter, but not the conspicuous absence of coffee. An Australian at our rooming house informed us that in the American enclave of Tien Mou we might find a small jar of Nescafe in a specialty shop. He added: "Could be pretty expensive." Like us, he was in Taiwan for a yacht and on a tight budget.

"I'm sure we'll find something along Chung Shan Road," I said. Chung Shan Road was a main thoroughfare that cut through the length of the city. "There's got to be a coffee shop somewhere."

Two hours into our walk, Bernard and I found the one coffee shop in all of Taipei. Two grave employees in white lab coats greeted us. Watery, brownish liquid slipped through a series of convoluted glass pipes that snaked around the room. The brew at the end of this process resembled a dirty puddle, and tasted the way it looked. From that point on, we decided to immerse ourselves entirely in local culture.

Most mornings, we drank hot soy milk served from huge vats sitting on carts that were stationed throughout the city. Sometimes, we frequented the smaller cafés where older men came for their morning soy accompanied by their pet birds. The cages hung on nails in front of the cafés, and the birds socialized outside while their keepers did the same inside. We'd go in the morning, have our soy milk, and listen to the bird song. When I left Taiwan, I couldn't find my morning soy and suffered the same sense of deprivation I did when I gave up coffee.

In 1980, there was little tourism in Taiwan, and few people spoke English, but I wasn't going to let that stop me from exploring Taipei. On one of my excursions, I forgot the card with my address written in Chinese. I had been told never to leave without it. This was a necessary precaution in a city where streets meandered, and the western alphabet was unknown. Though I hadn't a clue how to read the destination of the bus I got on, I was certain it was headed in the direction of the market. After a while, I found myself outside the city. I got off the bus and questioned the locals.

"Taipei?" I asked over and over. Happy, smiling faces nodded obligingly and repeated "Taipei," but no one seemed willing to help. A wave of fear rushed through me. I crossed the street and prayed that the same bus that went one way would take me back along the same route. Then, I hoped that if it did, I'd recognize where to get off. I stood waiting with the sky starting to darken. If I ever got out of there, I knew I'd have to take Mandarin classes.

Finally, a bus stopped in front of me. I got on board and stared out the window afraid to blink for fear of missing a familiar landmark. To my relief I saw Taipei come into view. I guessed at my stop and panicked that I could be wrong. When I got off the bus, my legs felt like soft rubber. And then I recognized our rooming house a few doors down from where I was standing.

"We've got to take Mandarin classes," I told Bernard.

"I don't have time," he replied.

His answer surprised me since he spent a lot of time yakking about nothing with other yachties in the rooming house. I thought learning Mandarin would be more useful.

I turned to Jonah. "How about you? Would you like to take lessons?'

He looked up from the schoolbook he was flipping through. "Sure," he said. "It's got to be more interesting than this."

The next day I took Jonah with me to the Daily News Language School, not knowing that the school catered to graduate students from universities around the world. Our teacher had never taught beginners before. For almost two hours a frustrated instructor shouted at us. "*Zhe shi shenme? She shi shenme?*" She pointed out the window and repeated over and over: "*Chuanghu, Chuanghu.*" We sat there dazed. Finally, we managed a breakthrough. *Zhe shi shenme* — What's this? *Chuanghu* — Window. I learned that day why no one helped me when I was lost. Unlike western languages, we learned the voice doesn't go up to state a question. *Me* or *Ma* stated in a flat, even tone at the end of a sentence means a question is being asked. The people in the country-side didn't understand I was asking directions for Taipei because I didn't say the tag to denote question.

The school had no idea how to teach us, and decided to start with children's primers. I learned to say "little white rabbit" and "mama is good" but these phrases didn't get me far on the street. On my own, I acquired a limited survival vocabulary that made a big difference in my integration into the society. I learned to count, which meant I could read numbers on a bus, and I picked up some basic words for shopping. "*Duo shao?*" I'd say at the market, meaning how much? The shopkeeper would fire off some unintelligible price. "*Tai kwai.*" I'd reply, meaning too much. A few more words would be thrust at me. I'd nod my head, hold out a relatively large bill, and pretend to count my change. I'd then look up and smile my approval. Sometimes I caught the numbers thrown at me, and on those days I felt a short-lived sense of empowerment. I learned to count quite well by the time we sailed out, aided by the fact that I was our sole shopper, a responsibility I enjoyed.

Bernard picked-up very little Mandarin in the time we were there. He was totally focused on building the yacht, and the boatyard owners spoke English. Years later he regretted the fact and took lessons for a while, but it was out of context, and he eventually dropped the course.

"I never looked at the culture," he told me later. "I missed half my journey."

Chapter 4

GETTING OUR FEET WET

1980–1981: Taiwan

> *What each must seek from his life never was on land or sea.*
> *It is something out of his own unique potentiality for experience,*
> *something that never has been and never could be experienced*
> *by anyone else.*
> —JOSEPH CAMPBELL

During our stay in Taipei, our main contact was the small band of yachties who came to build their boats in the local shipyards and found common ground in their anger and frustration. Taiwanese workers had little knowledge of how to make a safe vessel, and shipyard owners didn't care whether a boat sank once they'd been paid. Taiwan and China were at war. When a yacht sailed out, she became a foreign vessel and wasn't allowed to return. This absolved boatyard owners of all responsibility for their yards' shoddy work.

Having observed the agitated state of our fellow yachties and the dishonesty of the shipyard owners, Bernard began to have doubts about building. Yachties came, built their boats and left, while Bernard tried to make up his mind. Always a cautious man, he took his time studying each shipyard carefully.

Meanwhile, I was becoming acclimated to a rich and interesting culture. To pass the time, I taught English in the evening at the Taipei American School, auditioned and was hired to act in a series of English second language films for Ming Chuan University's Women's Business College, continued with my private classes in Chinese water brush painting with Theresa Chen at her gallery, and went every day with Jonah to our Mandarin classes at the Daily News Language School. I managed to advance to my third children's pre-school primer, and knew I could carry on a conversation with any three-year-old who was a little slow.

At one of the local galleries, I met the owner, a young American who introduced me to his American girl friend. Katharine was doing graduate work in Chinese culture and worked at the National Palace Museum. Through her I had the privilege of being present at a private auction where refugees who'd escaped from mainland China sold their family heirlooms from dynasties as far back as the Han. In a small dusty room inside a derelict office building in downtown Taipei, priceless works of art were displayed one at a time while a group of Taiwanese gentlemen, Katharine and I sat around a large, circular table cracking sunflower seeds between our front teeth and sipping tea.

I felt uncomfortable seeing these priceless objects shown under such shabby conditions. The grass-script scrolls, brilliantly glazed ceramics and hammered bronze pots belonged in a museum. I thought about the many generations that had possessed these items, and the family stories behind them. I wondered if the bidders felt justified in taking these objects from the refugees. Did they feel superior at not being in that position, or grateful that it was not their personal patrimony up for grabs? And then I thought ... Who am I to judge?

On free evenings, I went to Sun Yet Sen Park and soaked in the energy of another culture, a people seemingly different, but so alike in matters of the heart. Families cuddled their children, watched them play, and praised their efforts. Young women waited for their lovers or husbands to return from work, ran to embrace them, and walked off arm in arm. Elderly couples shuffled around the park tenderly holding hands. I was moved by the display of tenderness that made up the tableau of the park, and thought of my students who would cross the street with me after class to make sure I got safely to the other side, sometimes insisting on taking me for *shao shung,* dog meat, an expensive delicacy that I politely refused.

Years later, I met a business woman in Montreal who had spent the odd week in Taipei negotiating contracts for her company.

"They're a cold people," she told me. "Racist. I never felt trusted and was treated rudely."

Her perception of the Taiwanese people reinforced for me the value of "slow" travel with no agenda or time frame. Spending time in the countries where we dropped anchor brought home how much more alike than different people were, and made me sensitive to sweeping statements about other cultures.

On occasion, I went to calligraphy exhibitions with Alice, one of the students in my evening English classes. All the scrolls looked alike to me, while Alice enthused over some and dismissed others. I asked her to give me lessons in exchange for extra English. She was thrilled to do it and refused the exchange.

Alice looked at my first attempt and seemed dismayed. "From the heart," she said. "You're not writing from the heart." I tried again thinking about that place in my heart, but I failed to impress her.

"Not the head," she said. "Think of the brush as an extension of your heart. The energy flows from the heart through the arm, into the hand, and onto the page. You must write with your heart."

And then I got it. My characters started to live, to have energy. The writing was a moving meditation, a centering. The more I practiced, the more integrated I felt with the world around me. I could now go to exhibitions and see the difference in work done from the head and work done from the heart.

I impressed the teachers at the Daily News Mandarin School with my writing. They were amazed that a beginner from the West could manipulate the ideographs of Chinese characters so well. I didn't tell them I was practicing daily to make strokes from the heart. They thought I should exhibit. It surprised me to what extent Alice's coaching carried over to the way I practised my strokes in the school exercise book.

I could write like a native but never learned to speak well. More importantly, I understood the loss for this society when they were forced to move from brush to pen — a slippery first step from connection to alienation. Ballpoint pens were on the verge of being introduced into the school system, and parents were upset. They complained in letters to the newspaper that it would be the end of their culture. I thought their cries reflected a need to hold on to the past, and later discovered it was a well-founded fear for the future.

All this was taking place before the arrival of the computer. Today that connection between head and heart is more threatened than ever. Like the last generation of Taiwanese parents, I believe the death of the brush should be mourned. And in my own culture, I feel the loss of the pen to the computer. Each new generation of technical development seems to take us further away from our heart centre.

Jonah, being a typical sixteen-year-old, was far less diligent in his Mandarin homework than I was. "You'll never learn without studying," I'd say. "Why bother taking classes?"

"Don't worry about it, mom," he'd say, usually as he was about to fly out the door to meet his friends. He had found a girlfriend who sat in one of the art galleries, and through her, a group of Taiwanese youth his age. He gave English lessons to some of his newly acquired friends and made a bit of spending money for himself. He also enrolled in a class on scroll mounting and won an original woodcut on rice paper in a raffle at the class. By the time we left Taiwan, he was fluent in Mandarin.

The three of us lived in separate worlds. Jonah had his gang of friends that he spent time with, and when he wasn't with them, he studied for his final high school exams that would be sent to Taipei from Quebec. I worked, continued with my cultural interests, and befriended a number of my students. Bernard went every morning to the various boatyards, and showed no interest in what Jonah and I were doing.

With each passing month, tension grew between Bernard and me. He harboured fears about the seaworthiness of Taiwanese yachts and the possible insanity of our adventure. His growing unease worked on my nerves, and I looked for ways to distance myself. His frustration with the situation erupted in unexpected barbs. Over dinner one evening, he snapped at me without provocation. "This isn't a life for you. You'll miss your friends." I was too taken aback to answer. He also berated Jonah for no reason. "Why don't you read more about sailing than those damn novels?"

"It's for school," Jonah said. He didn't let Bernard get to him. I resented Bernard's picking on us to relieve his tension. But instead of facing the issue head-on, I focused on my life in Taipei, while he became more morose. We had so much at stake in this adventure that neither of us dared talk about it for fear of exacerbating the situation.

To ease the pressure, Bernard, Jonah and I spent evenings at the Taipei Night Market, an experience we could enjoy together. The market was always packed body-to-body with shoppers in search of anything from tiny firm-fleshed eggplants and foot long string beans, to men's cotton striped pyjamas for warm days and women's pink silky nightgowns for special events such as weddings and eating out in fancy restaurants. Night clothes for bedtime were not part of the Taiwanese culture.

Most fascinating were small stalls of medicinal herbs and shrivelled animal genitals for men in search of sexual prowess. One night we stumbled into a crowd of men watching a mongoose pitted against a snake. Men jostled and pushed for a clear view of the spectacle. Invariably, the mongoose won. The handler held up the dead snake for the bidding war to begin. Hordes of enthusiastic men outbid one another for small plastic cups filled with freshly spilled snake blood to increase their virility. I felt like vomiting and was happy to move on. Along the edge of the market we passed venereal disease clinics alongside brothels to accommodate whatever the victors in the bidding war needed. Taipei has since been cleaned up, and all that's left is the name "Snake Alley" and a few streetwalkers.

Another escape was Sunday breakfast at the Taipei Hilton. We'd sip bad coffee and absently stare at the handful of pasty faced westerners in their well-pressed suits who were in town to discuss business with their Taiwanese counterparts.

During one of our visits, Jonah looked over at a neighbouring table and whispered: "Isn't that Spiro Agnew?"

Spiro Agnew had been vice-president under Richard Nixon, and had to resign his position in 1973 due to charges brought against him for bribery, conspiracy, and tax fraud. I couldn't believe that the person Jonah was referring to could be that man. In my mind, Spiro Agnew was under a rock somewhere hiding in humiliation.

"No," I said. "It just looks like him."

Jonah kept staring in that direction. "I'm sure it's him."

Neither Bernard nor I took him seriously.

"Go ask him for his autograph," Bernard said, teasing.

Jonah took up the challenge and walked over to the table. A few seconds later he was back with the signature of the fallen vice-president scrawled across a napkin. It made our day.

Chapter 5

THE DIE IS CAST

~~~~

Spring 1981

> *Travel does what good novelists also do to the life of everyday,*
> *placing it like a picture in a frame or a gem in its setting, so that*
> *the intrinsic qualities are made more clear. Travel does this with*
> *the very stuff that everyday life is made of, giving to it the sharp*
> *contour and meaning of art.*
> — FREYA STARK

When Bernard decided to build at the Shin Hsing Boatyard, we made our fourth move to Shilin, a suburb outside Taipei. The new lodging shortened our travel time to Danshui, the small town where the boatyard was located. Mr. Feng, who knew Bernard from visits to his ship chandlery, offered to rent us a furnished apartment above his shop. It had been vacant for years and derelict, but the location was good. We grudgingly accepted. A metal frame with bare springs, covered with a sheet of plywood on which lay a thick quilt, served as our bed. Jonah's bed was a series of folded and stacked cartons covered with a similar thick quilt. The remains of giant cockroaches were pressed between the layers of cartons and littered the grimy tile floor. I forced myself to focus on the old TV that actually worked and the useable bathtub. I pictured us already on our spiffy yacht in order to deal with our new lodgings.

I soon learned the bathtub was more a necessity than a luxury in Taiwanese homes. Tubs are filled with potable water before the coming of a typhoon since no one can predict the duration or damage a typhoon will leave in its path. During one of those intense storms, a foot of water covered the floor of our second-story apartment, and I came to appreciate our grubby plastic furnishings as well as my rubber flip-flops that floated from room to room. I also came to appreciate the courage and resiliency of the Taiwanese people.

The day of the typhoon, the metal gates of Shilin's small shops banged shut in unison. The scraping noise of the gates reverberated throughout the neighbourhood, and then stopped as though on cue. People vanished off the streets. Even the ubiquitous flying cockroaches and ever-present geckos disappeared. I experienced a silence so complete, it seemed as though all sound had been sucked out of the universe. My body had the sensation of floating in space.

Then without warning, a terrifying howl ripped through the stillness. The wind seemed to have held its breath and now expelled itself with a force that could annihilate the planet. The sound carried with it an angry deluge of rain and whipped-up wind that moved so fast we later found microscopic holes in the windows where sand particles had cut through. Within minutes we were standing in water, but had no idea how it entered the apartment. The typhoon lasted a full day. The second it was over, the stores rolled up their metal gates at precisely the same moment, and it was business as usual. Taiwanese shopkeepers never took a day off except for Chinese New Year and typhoons.

Most mornings, Bernard, Jonah, and I took the Danshui bus through small communities along the banks of the Danshui River to the Shin Hsing Boatyard. Even though the boatyard hadn't started work on our yacht, we went to see the progress on the boat ahead of us and to pressure the yard to move faster.

We rode through Kuang Do, revered by Taiwanese as sacred earth where mountain and water meet. Here cemeteries and temples crowded each other for space, and funeral processions dominated the highway, their vehicles smothered in plastic flowers. Cylindrical coffins carried the deceased with photos mounted high on trucks — the last viewing for public and mourners alike. Mourners in sackcloth and white hoods followed behind. I noticed through the bus window that the bodies of the dead were laid in circular family plots with stones carved to fit the circle. The circular plots, set against the dark green of the surrounding hills, reminded me there was no linear time in the universe, and that all of nature was circular from birth to death to the turning of the seasons.

Kuang Do was the highest point on the highway to the boatyard, and as soon as the road curved round the bend, the Taipei Yacht Club came into view. Once the private dock for Chiang Kai-Shek's personal yacht, it was now under the domain of the Taiwanese army. The burnt-out frame of the clubhouse and the piles of rubble blocking the entrance were a daily reminder that yachting was strictly an export business and not an island sport in Taiwan. A few small yachts were anchored in front of the derelict clubhouse, the meagre reward of years of pressure by persistent members of the foreign community. This bit of neglected property would become my home base for two months after the yacht was built.

Past the yacht club rice fields spread out on both sides of the highway, and the rice farmers glided through the paddies, ankle deep in water, their heads bowed in concentration. In the distance their brick homes, passed on from generation to generation, sprawled out in various directions, depending on the whim and the size of the families that inhabited them. In the year that we travelled from our home in Shilin to the boatyard in Danshui, I never tired of this section of the road because of the serenity of the scene.

Though Bernard hired the Shin Hsing Boatyard in May, by mid-July the yacht was still nothing more than a promise. He had chosen this yard because it was small, but they were also slow. I watched impatiently as the boat before ours crawled to completion. It annoyed me that the Australian building ahead of us came to Taiwan three months after and would be leaving before.

"I wish you had made up your mind sooner," I blurted out in a moment of frustration. Bernard had a different perspective.

"I can study his construction and learn from his mistakes." I couldn't argue with that.

The Australian was a dynamic fellow who had done a lot of cruising on his motorboat before making the switch to sail. It was the first time he had ventured this far from home, but he was full of self-confidence and absolutely sure of every decision he made. His wife was a hairdresser.

"We're having a beauty salon built into the yacht," he told us. "Bronica will have no trouble getting clients."

He invited us aboard to see the two special chairs he had ordered to be installed. Bronica matched her husband's bravura. She talked as though she was raised on the sea and spiced every conversation with nautical terms.

"She's a real sea adventurer," Bernard informed me. "You can learn from her."

Learn what, I thought. *She's all talk.*

The boatyard kept promising a starting date and then ignoring it, but this gave us plenty of time to design and redesign our craft to our exact needs. The time spent plotting our dream yacht was the happiest for the three of us. I loved the idea that we could pick the model we wanted. Many of the yachts people asked for looked like modified cruise ships with wide bellies and big behinds — great as houseboats but uncomfortable for sailing. We decided on a 45-foot Peterson ketch, with its streamlined shape and narrow rear end. The Peterson was built to slice through the waves in a smooth ride. Its graceful shape appealed to my eye. The fiberglass exterior would be easy to clean, and the teak deck and interior defied water damage.

We arrived in Taiwan just as the furniture industry died, and carpenters now turned to the boatyards for work. Each interior was a work of art. We decided our finishing touches would include galley and bathroom counters carved from the dark green marble we had admired on our trip to Taroko Gorge in Hualien. Its marble mountain had tunnels with small tables and seats carved into the stone. Windows cut through the marble looked out on mountain peaks dotted with red-roofed shrines. The scene was so pleasing that I wanted to capture some of its hobbit-like feel for the yacht. To go with the green marble, we chose deep red, water resistant velvety upholstery from a sample book the shipyard lent us. I visualized how luxurious they would look against the teak cabinets and polished teak floors.

With the boatyard picked and the yacht designed, I had more time to hang out with my students and work on my acting assignments. Jonah had completed his final exams, sent from Quebec to the American School in Taipei. Now seventeen and a high school graduate, he turned his full attention to teaching English to his new friends. We continued with our Mandarin classes because I refused to admit defeat. I loved the music of the language, even with my tin ear. I believe Jonah continued with me because we had found a delicious curried chicken and rice wagon just outside the Daily News Mandarin School, and it was our habit to eat there after class.

Bernard had nothing to do until construction started and decided to make a trip to France where he had money waiting for him. I suggested he take a side trip to Montreal before he returned, so he could check up on how Stefan was faring. Reading between the lines of Stefan's sporadic correspondence, I felt he might be regretting his decision to remain behind. I wanted to make sure he was okay.

After Bernard left, Jonah went daily to the boatyard on his own to learn about construction and put pressure on the owner to start building our yacht. He took on the responsibility without being asked, and thrived on the challenges it presented. It gave me some reassurance, knowing that the following year he'd be entering Middlebury College in the United States, a country he hardly knew.

On August 4, 1980, the shell of our long-awaited yacht emerged from empty space, taking its shape from nothing more than some buckets of liquid plastic that hardened to form its skin. It seemed unreal and somewhat frightening to see this hollow stretch of plastic, looking more like a fragile canoe than a sea worthy vessel, cradled in its scaffolding. I was both stunned and in awe. A few days before there was nothing but space, and out of this nothing came something that gelled and cooled and took a shape that would eventually become my home and life support for who knew how many years. I'd gotten so used to waiting I had to adjust to the fact our dream would soon be a reality. I also had to adjust to how thin the skin was that separated my home from the sea.

Chapter 6

OUR NEW REALITY

⌒

To be one with life is to be like a drop of rain that flows
into the stream and goes with the flow.
—NATIVE AMERICAN

"You look ten years younger with your husband gone," shouted the *Tai Tai*, matriarch of the Shin Hsing clan, through the open office door. It was the first time the wife of the builder addressed me in all the time I had been visiting the Shin Hsing yard. Our main contact was with her eldest and favoured son, Kenwood, his Western name taken off a sewing machine label. Now I made sure to greet her with a smile and a wave each time I passed her doorway.

"Miss Rita," she called out a few days later, and beckoned me into her office. "You need Chinese name. Good luck. When you born?"

I gave her the information she asked for, and after some calculation she announced, "Shi Lin I."

"Shi Lin I?"

"Good name," she said. "Means wise lady."

She then asked about Bernard and calculated a name for him.

"Pong Pai Song," she declared. "Big Bear in the Pine Woods."

She handed me several scraps of paper with our new names and ordered me to "Get chop."

The chop, a small, rectangular stone or piece of wood with one's name carved into the bottom for stamping, was the glue that held the Taiwanese business world together. Contracts were signed with a chop. Artists signed their paintings with a chop. It was placed on cheques and all important documents. For Mother's Day, Jonah took a good part of his earnings to buy me a jade chop. Jade, highly valued in Taiwan, was meant to bring good fortune, and I was touched that he had thought to give me this gift. Much later, after the yacht was completed, I invited his friends aboard for lunch, and as a farewell celebration. After they left, I discovered the chop was missing.

The loss of the chop rattled me. It brought home that the yacht had marked us as privileged. Considering the years we had worked to acquire our boat, I hadn't thought of us as such. But I now understood that even to have been able to have this goal, both for the chance to pursue it, and the very act of opting out of the mainstream to enjoy it, singled us out that way.

I had asked Jonah how he felt about the theft. "Mom, it's not a big deal," he said. "It's just part of the experience." But for me it was a big deal. Even today when I think of the theft, I feel the loss.

In Bernard's absence, Jonah had developed a good eye for detail and took seriously the various facets of yacht construction. Still, I was anxious for Bernard's return. We were partners in this enterprise, and if a bad decision was made, I wanted us to share the responsibility. I hoped his visit to France would defuse some of the tension he'd been carrying since our arrival in Taiwan, but it was wishful thinking. He returned more wound up than before he'd left, and seemed to resent the pleasure Jonah and I had taken in the yacht's emergence. When Jonah tried to explain something that happened at the boatyard, Bernard snapped at him: "What's it your business? It's not your boat."

Jonah stopped going to the yard. "He has no interest in sailing," Bernard later said. Jonah was damned either way, and I fared no better. We had become target practice for the arrows he couldn't sling at the yard.

Out for a beer one evening with a small group of dreamers also building in Taiwan, one of them asked if I had ever sailed. "No," I replied. "And I wouldn't sail with just anyone. I feel safe with Bernard."

"What kind of bullshit is that?" Bernard spat out.

All conversation stopped. I cringed inside. I was too choked up to say anything and stared into space pretending I wasn't there. I wanted to kill him.

"What was that all about?" I hissed when we were finally alone. I could hardly contain my fury. "You humiliated me."

Bernard shrugged and looked away. "You always exaggerate."

"What do you mean I always exaggerate?" I was livid.

"Don't start a fight." He turned his back to me and headed towards the door. "I'm going for a walk," he said, and slammed the door as he walked out.

I couldn't figure out what was going on. What did I do? Why this sudden shift from trusted partner to adversary?

I brought up that conversation years later.

"I remember that evening," he said. "I didn't have the confidence in me that you had. I was starting to realize that I had dragged you and Jonah into this, not having a clue about what I was doing. I was scared shitless, and thought you were making fun of me." His reply shook me. So much misunderstanding left unresolved over so many years.

Why hadn't we talked more? Why couldn't he tell me? I had mistaken his silence for strength.

"But I wasn't dragged into it," I said. "It was a shared dream. Somewhere along the way you lost sight that I was as much responsible for that adventure as you were."

From the day he returned to Taiwan to the completion of the yacht, Bernard was at the yard from early morning to late evening watching every detail of the boat's construction. I told myself that his lashing out against Jonah and me was due to the strain of the building. I was sure his good will and acknowledgement of our partnership would return once the yacht was completed.

We worked together on the layout and finishing touches on the décor — a front and aft cabin, each with a bathroom (or head to be nautically correct), a user-friendly galley with the green marble counter top that we had decided on earlier; red, yellow, and orange striped curtains on the portholes to match the red microfiber upholstery on the berths, settees and pillows; a small table that pulled out from under the double berth in the aft cabin so I could write , and a chart table for Bernard in the salon. Our ideas for the finished product were completely in sync, and it brought us closer whenever we worked on them.

We, or I should say Bernard, decided on the name *Santa Rita*; that is, after he informed me the yacht would be registered in his name.

"What!" I blurted out. "How could you? We worked together on this."

I felt used, deceived. So many confused thoughts ran through my head. I wondered if he thought I might steal the yacht from him. Or that the boat was just his. Maybe it's an ego thing. Okay, I was bigger than that. Or was I?

"Why?" I asked.

"It doesn't matter. It's not important. We both know it's our boat."

He must have seen the bewildered look on my face.

"Look," he said, "you're so much a part of this journey that I want the boat to carry your name."

I didn't fight for equal ownership. Like so many women, who think they are independent until they're in a relationship, I felt stuck in a submissive role. I focused on the adventure and tried not to think about the legalities. I had to trust Bernard would never cheat me. Until that moment, I had no reason to think otherwise. I let myself be seduced by the name *Santa Rita*. I couldn't afford to nurse the feeling that I had been used. I had invested too much of myself in this adventure. I also found comfort in the fact I could relate to the attributes of this particular saint.

Santa Rita, the Spanish saint of all things impossible, is the one you went to when there were obstacles to overcome — your child is dying, your husband is abusive and/or philandering, you're widowed and penniless, or you have a wound that doesn't heal. You want something so badly that you sacrifice everything for it. That aspect of her power spoke to me. I had sacrificed everything to make this adventure happen. But she's more. She's the protective saint of women, who gives them the power to endure and become stronger. In time, that is who she was to become for me. But for now she was the saint of a seemingly impossible dream.

One of Jonah's friends owned a gallery in downtown Taipei and invited us to an opening by the Taiwanese painter, Earthstone Jo. He was sure we'd like the work, and he was right. I honed in on a large watercolour of an emaciated man seated before a plate with nothing on it but the skeleton of a fish. It was impossible to tell if the man was sated or hadn't had enough to eat. The ambiguity of the portrait held my attention. I felt an affinity for the man, and decided his gentle repose was what I needed for the journey. I bought the watercolour and had it framed to hang in the salon of the yacht. It greeted me every time I came down the galley stairs. I saw this man who looked beyond the fish bones as a fellow traveller on this temporary road we each pave for ourselves.

A week before we launched the *Santa Rita*, I invited my ex-student, calligraphy teacher and now good friend, Alice, to a restaurant to thank her for her friendship. So much of what I knew about Taiwanese life I had learned from her. She had taken me to a Taoist temple, where we burned incense, and then from a cylindrical box she asked me to select a stick that would hold my fortune. I drew a stick with the number one. A temple priest then read the meaning from a corresponding slip of paper. "Very auspicious," he said in Mandarin, or at least that's what Alice said he said, and I saw that as a positive sign for our journey. She also introduced me to traditional food I would never have eaten, and listened to me struggling through my limited Mandarin with a straight face. I wanted to do something special for her, and I knew she loved to eat.

"Let me order," I said. I had taken her to a western style restaurant, and she didn't understand the menu. My intent was to share with her a good memory from my culture.

"We'll have two steaks, medium rare," I said.

When the food came, I dug in. I looked over at Alice who was staring at her plate, pushing the peas around with her fork.

"What's the matter?" I asked.

"I can't eat this," she said. "It's too big and bloody."

I cut her meat into tiny pieces and mixed it with the peas and potatoes. She took a few bites and scattered the rest around her plate. I realized too late I should have taken her to a good Chinese restaurant where everything was cut in bite size portions to be eaten with chopsticks. I had never seen a knife at a setting in a local restaurant, and wondered if Alice had ever used a knife and fork at the table.

In spite of the disastrous farewell meal, Alice invited us to her wedding, our last social event before leaving Taipei. Alice's family had been converted to Catholicism by a French missionary several years before. Buried inside a billowing white wedding dress, her delicate face obscured by a multi-layered veil, she stood before the priest.

"We are five sisters, and we were all christened Mary," she confided to me during one of my calligraphy lessons. "I wanted my own name so I became Alice."

I knew that Alice was still a Buddhist at heart and felt that this was "dress-up" or maybe "just playing it safe." The evening before the fiasco of my surprise western dinner, she had taken me to a Buddhist temple to pray for my safety at sea. Over the months of our friendship, we had gone to many temples, but never to a church.

After the ceremony, Alice changed into a red cheongsam, slit up the sides to above her knees. It looked as though it had been sewn onto her, and was more flattering on her trim frame than the wedding dress. She showed us to one of the many tables that filled the reception hall, and ladled out the first course into our bowls — turtle soup with the shells floating in the tureen. We couldn't eat it. The next course was snake and sea cucumber. We also gave that dish a pass. There were a number of odd looking dishes that followed, but Bernard, Jonah and I didn't have an appetite for any of them.

Finally, when dessert came, we gorged. The eight treasures rice pudding consisted of sticky rice with bits of candied fruit, all ingredients we could more or less recognize. I remembered that Alice ate only the dessert in the fancy western restaurant I took her to. When I mentioned my observation to her, she laughed in recognition.

It's all a matter of conditioning. Some cultures eat monkey. The thought of it makes me want to cry. My Taiwanese students wanted to take me out for dog on my last day of teaching, a delicacy that made me want to wretch. I have rat recipes from Mallorca and Hong Kong that I will never try. And I know that grubs are a staple in parts of Africa, while dung beetle was offered to me in northern Mexico. I eat beef. That would be shocking in parts of India. The turtle and snake were not a part of my diet growing up, so I couldn't eat them at the wedding. While travelling, I never have a problem slipping into the habits and mores of the countries I visit, but food that's off the radar in my culture takes awhile — if ever.

Before leaving Taiwan, I wanted a statue of the goddess Matsu to take with us. She was the Taiwanese goddess that protected fishermen and sailors, and had over five hundred temples on the island dedicated to her, even though the Taiwanese were more inclined towards farming than fishing. But the island had been inundated many times during the typhoon season, and the people believed Matsu was the reason they were still there.

I already had a scrolled water brush painting of Matsu that I had originally hung in the bedroom in our apartment in Shilin, and a little painted carved statue of her on my bedside table. When our landlord, Mr. Feng, came for the rent, I proudly showed him my wall hanging of Matsu.

"No Matsu in the bedroom," he said. "People do bad things there that Matsu shouldn't see."

He wouldn't leave until I removed her from the bedroom wall and tacked her up in the living room. He didn't notice the small, beautifully carved, wooden one by the bed. That Matsu stayed with me in the bedroom. I found her solid, ample body mother-like and comforting, and didn't think she'd take offense.

From his small, insular world, Mr. Feng had strong views about everything. I had seen an interesting play performed on Taiwanese TV. I didn't understand the Mandarin, but it was so well acted I could follow the story. I mentioned to Mr. Feng how much I enjoyed the production.

"It's a classic," he said, "very old. We have a tradition of fine theatre. When your people evolve, you will also create great works."

I smiled politely. I didn't try to enlighten Mr. Feng on the history of western theatre. I knew from previous conversations that he wasn't open to any discussion that contradicted his view of the world. But it was interesting to note his perception of the West.

I mentioned to the *Tai Tai* at the Shin Hsing Boatyard that I wanted a Matsu for the *Santa Rita*. I thought it would please her.

"Good idea," she said. "We go together to find a Matsu. All Matsu not the same. Some good. Some bad."

She took Bernard and me to an antique store with a plethora of plaster statues. She held each Matsu for a moment and finally selected one.

"Very good," she said. "Very spiritual."

I found one that I liked better.

"No good," she snapped. "Commercial."

The *Tai Tai* paid for our purchase, an incredible act of generosity from a woman who counted every penny and didn't trust her fortune to anyone, not even banks. She marched out of the store, called a taxi and got into the front seat with the spiritual statue.

"Matsu rides in front," she said as she settled in and seated the statue on her lap. "This Matsu asleep a long time. We go temple to have her eyes opened. I bring you Matsu when she wakes."

Matsu stayed in the temple for a month and was returned to us the day the boatyard launched the *Santa Rita* into the Danshui River.

Chapter 7

PERILS OF THE FORMOSA STRAIT

Summer 1981: From Taiwan To Hong Kong

> *There is but a plank between man and eternity.*
> —THOMAS GIBBONS

The same day we launched the *Santa Rita* into the Danshui River, we moved aboard and started the preparations for our departure. Leaving Jonah in charge of the yacht, Bernard and I took a bus to Kaohsiung, a port city located in the southwest of the island, to buy equipment. Kaohsiung dismantled old cargo ships for their steel, and the boatyard told us we could find everything that we needed there for a good price.

We bought a life raft and an old fashioned bomb-shaped log to drag behind the yacht to measure distance — all from salvaged ships. We also found a good supply of second-hand sea charts at bargain prices. Bernard discovered a discarded dinghy along the shore of the Danshui while the *Santa Rita* was being built, so that was one less major purchase to think about. But it needed an outboard engine. Browsing among the second-hand stuff, Bernard unearthed an old Seagull, the type of engine you start by pulling a string.

"It looks like a piece of junk," I said.

"It's a good engine," Bernard replied. "British made. They used Seagulls all through the Second World War."

"Can't we get something that starts with a key? I don't like having to pull a string."

"You'll get used to it."

"Maybe," I mumbled. "I'm not so sure."

39

I spent most of my time working on provisions — covering eggs with Vaseline to extend their shelf life, burying bay leaves in dry goods to impede weevils — to little avail as I was to find out, and buying fresh produce to store in a net on deck. We had no fridge, so any small trick to keep our vegetables from wilting was crucial. As a personal luxury, I made my first foray into Tien Mou, the upscale sector of Taipei, and picked up several small jars of instant coffee, that cost triple what they did back home.

Bernard gimballed a two-burner Coleman camping stove, so that it would remain stable regardless of the inclination of the boat. His setting it on hinges to oscillate with the axis of the boat meant I wouldn't have to worry about pots falling off the burners when the *Santa Rita* heeled. Since the stove didn't lend itself to elaborate cooking, I didn't have to invest much in kitchen equipment. I did, however, invest a lot of time in figuring out nutritional one-dish meals that weren't boring or too time-consuming to prepare.

We spent the evenings getting a feel for our new space. I relished the fact that I was finally home after spending over a year moving from place to place and living in ramshackle flats. Everything here was suited to my needs and taste — the compact lockers with a place for everything, the efficient, user-friendly galley, the separate cabins with comfortable berths, and two bathrooms. It didn't matter that the bathrooms were the size of broom closets, where you had to sit on the toilet to use the tiny hand shower. Water was a limited resource, and we'd sponge bathe for the most part anyway. I kept stroking the teak interior. It felt like butter.

One evening we heard a dull, persistent thumping on the side of the hull.

"What's that?" I asked.

Jonah bolted up the steps before us and was leaning over the stanchion lines by the time we came on deck.

"Pigs," he shouted.

The three of us stared, transfixed. Dozens of bloated pigs bobbed by us, their backs half under water, their stiff legs stuck straight up in the air.

Bernard broke the silence. "Looks like the rainy season started early. It's flooding the banks, taking some of the livestock. We may have a wet crossing."

That night I lay in the berth and listened to the tap, tap, tapping of the pigs. Normally, what I'd seen would keep me up all night, but the movement of the water and the gentle tapping of the pigs lulled me to sleep.

Finally, in April 1981, with Guan Yin, the Chinese goddess of mercy, looking down on us from her mountain perch above the river and Matsu, the sea goddess of protection, secured on board, we were ready to motor down the Danshui to the Keelung harbour in southeastern Taiwan. Keelung faced the China Sea and was the departure point from where we would set sail to Hong Kong.

Escorting us to Keelung aboard the *Santa Rita* was a Taiwanese soldier. Our yacht, having been officially launched, was now considered a foreign vessel. It was a requirement by the government that a foreign vessel in transit through Taiwanese water needed a military presence. Our assigned soldier, terrified of being on water, clung to the mast. The movement of the yacht made him seasick, and he threw up on deck. We watched him closely to make sure he didn't do anything rash that could hurt him or the yacht. In his rush to leave us, he forgot his cap, a souvenir I still possess.

On our first morning, tied along the concrete walkway of the Keelung harbour, I stumbled almost naked and half-asleep into the galley to boil water for coffee. I was shocked awake by a dozen squatting men peering at me through the portholes with unblinking curiosity. Half-smiling my acknowledgement of their presence, I pounced on the small curtains that we had installed over the portholes and closed them. The curtains were a last minute decision. I was now grateful that we went for them.

In spite of my "monkey in a cage" introduction to the people of Keelung, I managed to overcome my initial embarrassment and befriend some of the locals. Our willingness to struggle with their language ingratiated us to them, and they responded with good-humoured appreciation.

A local artist asked us if he could explore aboard. "*Ke yi/ bu ke yi* (can/ can't)?" he asked.

"*Ke yi* (can)," Bernard responded.

In Mandarin there's no word for yes or no. The verb is repeated. If you add *bu*, it means no; if you don't add *bu*, it means yes.

I listened to Bernard's response, his delivery perfect, and wished he had tried to learn more of the language. The artist thanked us with a pen and ink drawing of Bernard that now hangs in my home.

The Japanese had invaded Taiwan in 1895, and held on to the country for the next 50 years. Although they left behind a lot of destruction and bad memories, they also left behind the secret of the best Japanese food ever. We took pleasure in our evening outings, gulping down freshly caught tuna sashimi and hand-rolled sushi specials with a splash of wasabi and soy sauce — all the while listening to Jonah test his impressive knowledge of Mandarin. I've eaten a lot of Japanese food since, but nothing as good as the fare we found in the in the local stalls along the Keelung harbour. Good memories amplify the pleasure of recalled sensations, especially when they're associated with happy times. For the three of us Keelung was a happy time.

Keelung opened the door to another memory, triggered when I spot a lone horse or cow in sunlit green pasture. I travel back in time to the bridge that connects the port city to the countryside. I'm standing on the bridge and watch two men and three women move through a wet rice field like actors in a slow motion film. The graceful, rhythmic flow of their movements reminds me of movies I've seen shot underwater.

In the midst of the field, a huge water buffalo stands motionless. Its dark brown coat looks painted against the brilliant green of the rice field. A tiny bird with toothpick-thin legs moves across its back pecking here and there. That scene of total integration of man, beast, and earth stopped time for me. I felt outside my body. Yet every cell in me was imprinted. For such moments, I don't need a photograph. A scene, an object, a touch will do.

When I came out of my reverie and looked toward the city, I could see the *Santa Rita* tied to the pier in the harbour. I wondered at how she had come into existence from nothing but a soup of chemicals. I felt an overwhelming pride of ownership — then tripped over my feet. Bruised as I was, I took it as a good lesson. There's a time for musing and a time for paying attention. We can't carry both at the same time. It was something to remember for our voyage.

I didn't have to remember long. Tied along the pier near us was a fat-bellied yacht, looking more like a chunky house than a sailboat. She was the pride of George and Marlene, a retired couple from London. They were about to make their maiden voyage to Hong Kong, but had never done long distance sailing before.

"Would you like to join us?" George asked. "We could use the help."

Of course, we'd join them. A flight back to Taipei wasn't that long, and it would be good to have a trial run with another couple before making our own crossing. The Formosa Strait had a reputation for being unpredictable, and I had never sailed except for those few hours on Lake Champlain. Jonah was happy to take charge of the *Santa Rita* while we were gone.

Towards nightfall on the first day out, the sea turned ugly. Below deck, water started to seep through the floorboards. It meant the bilge was already flooded. George ran to turn on the electric bilge pump, but it didn't work. The yard where they built their yacht had forgotten to clean the sawdust. It clogged the pump. We'd have to bail if we didn't want to sink.

"What do you want to do?" Bernard asked. "We can bail and try to make it to Hong Kong or we can go back to Keelung." Hong Kong was a five-day sail, but yachts were warned not to return to Taiwan because of its war with mainland China.

George looked bewildered. "I don't know. Let me go to the head and think."

Ten minutes later George was still in the head and water was creeping up.

Bernard asked Marlene if they had any buckets.

"Three," she said.

"Get them, and we'll start bailing."

I was stationed below deck. Marlene was at the top of the companionway ready to receive the buckets. Bernard was by the stanchion lines so that he could toss the water overboard. George eventually left the toilet and quietly joined the bucket brigade. He never said what he wanted to do.

Marlene panicked. Each time she passed me the empty bucket, she threw it, often hitting me in the head. Her aim became wilder as her hysteria grew.

She's going to kill me, I thought.

"Look, Marlene," I shouted from below. "We've got to eat. Didn't you buy string beans before we left? Why don't you start preparing them?" I sat her down at the galley table with the bag of string beans and put a knife in her hands. "Just concentrate on getting the ends off and the beans in the pot."

For the next half hour she sat at the table pulling strings from the beans. She looked like a mechanical doll as she methodically worked her way through the bag. Fear and focused activity can't take up space in the brain at the same time. I'd have to remember that. After an hour of bailing, it became clear that too much water was coming in for us to reach Hong Kong.

"We've got to turn around," Bernard told George.

"No, we're going to Hong Kong," George insisted. "They won't let us back into Taiwan."

"We'll take our chances," Bernard said.

"No, we're going on."

Bernard took the helm and turned us around. George was in a daze. I don't think he had any idea what Bernard had done. After a bit of squabbling with the harbour police, we entered Keelung as an emergency.

It was a brief sail, but I had learned two important things. I don't panic easily, and it wasn't going to be an easy passage to Hong Kong.

Bernard was now doubly cautious about checking to see that all our equipment worked. I was happy he had taken his time before picking the shipyard. Sometimes his thoroughness irritated me. But I was aware that it may also protect us.

A few days before we sailed for Hong Kong, two Frenchmen who had befriended Bernard in the shipyard came to Keelung to make the crossing with us. Each was building his own yacht and wanted to get a feel of the Formosa Strait. They had come to Taiwan with their wives and one had a young son. Neither of them had done much sailing, but we were pleased to have the extra hands. Crossing from Taiwan to Hong Kong was never an easy sail. Waves are short and choppy and the wind is erratic. Huge fishing trawlers and heavy junks clog the narrow passageway, and they're a serious threat in fog. Constant watch was mandatory.

We spent two weeks provisioning and preparing for the departure. Now we waited patiently for the coast guard to board and clear our papers. Matsu, goddess of the sea and protector of sailors, was in a visible spot behind the settee in the salon with an offering of incense and oranges. We were certain she would garner goodwill and expedite our exit from the country. We were wrong.

The man in charge of the Coast Guard delegation gave us a sour look. "No good," he said. He jabbed his finger at Matsu and shook his head. "*Bu hau*, no good," he repeated. He then turned to his assistant and spoke in Mandarin while we waited nervously to see what we'd done wrong.

He pointed to Matsu again. "Too low," he snapped. "No respect." He was visibly agitated. "Must be higher."

"Where do you think is a good place?" Bernard asked. He thought if he included the officer in the decision, he would show goodwill. In truth, to place Matsu in a proper position, we'd have had to raise the roof of the cabin.

Satisfied with our display of embarrassment, the outraged official softened his hard stance. With barely a look at our papers, he waved us on our way.

Within an hour of leaving the port, I already felt like a fly in a blender. The Strait, whipped by a strong northern wind, shook us in every direction. Jonah was instantly seasick and spent most of the voyage with his arms wrapped around the toilet. I was relieved that I didn't get seasick. I spent most of the time trying to prime the camping stove and boiling endless kettles of water for coffee, my butt braced against the galley's counter and my feet wedged against a narrow locker built beneath the stove. By the time the water boiled, the next meal had to be prepared. I hardly left the galley except for the occasional trip to the head, where I exchanged places with Jonah for the briefest moment.

On the third day, a dense fog rolled in. Our crew lay huddled in their berths, cold, tired, and scared. They refused to come on deck. Bernard pulled the younger of the two men out of his berth. "Listen," he shouted, "I need sleep or we won't make it." He half carried the guy up the companionway and stood him in front of the helm. The would-be sailor put his hands around the helm but stared, frozen, into the distance. Instead of holding the course, he turned the yacht in circles. His circling caused the cable from the log trailing behind the boat to get caught in the propeller. The *Santa Rita* stopped moving.

We were in the shipping lane and could hear the engines of trawlers and junks passing nearby, but we couldn't see them. Even worse, we knew they couldn't see us. We were in a fog so thick it was hard to say if it was day or night. We were waiting road kill for one of those monsters. Bernard turned on the VHF radio to contact the big ships to let them know we were out there. It was the first time we used it. It didn't work.

Bernard turned to me. "I've got to free that propeller." He grabbed a knife, tied a rope around his waist, and jumped into the sea.

I heard the splash, but couldn't see him at all. I went below deck and waited. I could feel my heart beating in my chest. My hands were trembling. I heard an engine close by and could make out the shadow of a fishing trawler passing within inches of the porthole I was looking through. I believe my heart stopped at that moment.

Bernard couldn't have been over the side more than ten minutes, but it felt longer than our entire journey so far. When he surfaced and climbed aboard, I wanted to hug him, but he was all business.

"I couldn't cut the cable." he said. "I had to unwrap it from around the prop. That log's no good anyway, too big for our boat. I'll pick up a smaller one in Hong Kong."

Most of our navigational equipment came off of scrapped cargo ships. I wondered how many other pieces of equipment we'd have to replace. "What about the other equipment we bought in Kaohsiung?"

"We'll see," he said.

He looked concerned. The stuff we picked up there was cheap and perhaps a big mistake. But now wasn't the time to talk about it.

Our crew slept a lot, but they were always up for meals and ate ravenously. I resented these two men who ate heartily, but contributed nothing. To keep the peace, I kept quiet. There was already enough tension aboard the yacht. Though Bernard had coaxed the older one into taking the helm for a while, I had more fear of what he might do than what the weather might have in store.

At sunrise on the fifth day, the fog lifted, and Hong Kong appeared before us like a mirage. The city rose straight out of the sea. Its towering skyscrapers looked as though they were suspended on water. I was awe-struck by what seemed like a magical kingdom rising from the seabed, and relieved that we had arrived safely.

As we sailed into Aberdeen Harbour, Bernard offered the two men berths until they flew back to Taipei. I said nothing, but I was fuming. I wanted them off the boat as soon as we moored. I was going to say something when we were alone, but it wasn't necessary. As soon as we tied up along the pier, they scrambled off the yacht and disappeared.

Meanwhile, I felt pretty good about myself on my maiden voyage. I didn't get seasick. I stayed cool and alert in a dangerous situation. And I could even handle a camping stove that had to be primed on a rolling sea. The crew never missed a meal. I waited for Bernard to tell me how well I'd done.

Instead of congratulating me, he pulled away. The romance of the dream was suffering the growing pains of day-to-day reality. We were locked in tension, exacerbated by our small container of a home in an unfamiliar culture, and the fickleness of the sea. I not only had to learn how to survive physically in my new lifestyle, a reality I had not seriously prepared for, but I was going to have to learn how to survive emotionally.

In the normal course of life, there are ways to diffuse tension in relationships. You can go to the movies, talk to a friend, take a walk, go to the gym, see a therapist. In short, a structured life on land offers opportunity to take distance and reflect, or just escape. Living aboard a yacht doesn't permit taking that personal space. You are in a small enclosed area, where you are always within sight of one another. There is nowhere to escape or take refuge or defuse. You have to deal with issues in the moment, and you have to deal with them in such a way that you can still keep your dignity, self-respect, and consideration of the other. Your survival depends on it. I had not yet learned how to do this. I was just starting to learn that I would have to.

Fortunately, Bernard's agitated and distant behaviour didn't affect Jonah. This was due to the arrival of his older brother soon after we docked. In Taiwan we had received a letter from the friend in whose house Stefan was boarding that told us he was depressed, wasn't going to his classes, and spent his time playing games in video parlours. We sent him a plane ticket so that he could join us in Hong Kong. Jonah was thrilled to have his older brother back, and accompanied me to the Kai Tak Airport to pick him up.

I was as excited as Jonah to see Stefan.. I had wanted him to come with us. It was his decision to continue with junior college. I left him in good hands, but I still worried. He was 19 with no family nearby, and he looked even younger with his slim frame and sparse facial hair. We waited at the arrival area until everyone left the plane. There was no Stefan.

"Do you think he missed the plane?" I was distraught and thinking about what to do next.

"I don't know, Mom," Jonah said. "Maybe he was hidden behind others getting off. Let's look around."

The area had thinned out and a stocky guy with long hair and a beard was walking about aimlessly, carrying a guitar.

"Do you think that's him?" Jonah asked. "Stef plays a guitar."

"My God, yes." I hadn't recognized my own son. In the year and a half that we hadn't seen him, he had filled out and grown a beard. I expected to find a kid. I found a man.

The two boys had always been close, and it was a relief to know that Jonah had someone near to his age to pal around with. They explored Hong Kong together, became friends with a group of French students living on a Chinese junk called the *Elf Chine* that was anchored in the harbour, and settled into a life apart from us.

There was another boat with young people aboard — a tall ship called the *Osprey*. The captain, an amiable young man named Doug, was an outgoing American who befriended us, and we occasionally visited the *Osprey* as a family.

"I think the boys should sail on the *Osprey*," Bernard said one morning over a cup of coffee. "They'll get proper training sailing aboard a big ship."

I was livid at the suggestion. I didn't trust his motive for sending them away. I felt he was trying to get rid of them. There was no way I would let them go.

"That's your job to train them," I said. "I have no intention of unloading them onto the *Osprey*. They're my kids. I want them here."

A year later, we heard the *Osprey* had sunk in a typhoon. There was one survivor, the cook. The captain and crew went down with the ship.

Chapter 8

HONG KONG: AN ISLAND LIKE NO OTHER

Summer 1981: Hong Kong

The mind is its own place, and in itself it can make a
Heaven of Hell, a Hell of Heaven.
— JOHN MILTON

In Taiwan, vitality is most evident in the inland city of Taipei, but in Hong Kong life begins in the harbour. Huge wooden junks crowd the waterways, and small sampans dart in and out hawking wares that range from fresh produce to clothing to household goods. Sampans motor deftly through anchored yachts leaving delectable scents that are impossible to resist. Almost daily we treated ourselves to roast pork, soy sauce chicken or pressed duck, placed over mounds of fragrant rice prepared aboard these small open boats. Off-shore seafood restaurants accessed by water taxis operated until midnight.

We met fishermen who had lived their whole lives in the water village and never came ashore, eking out a meagre living plying fish to passing boats. Looking towards the island of Lantau, boatloads of Vietnamese refugees sat silently in the water hoping to be admitted.

Sunday mornings, we abandoned the *Santa Rita* for Dim Sum establishments, where endless varieties of sweet and savoury dishes rolled past us on little carts. I looked forward to the flat rice noodles washed over with soy sauce and sesame oil. Bernard favoured the steamed baskets of pork and shrimp dumplings. Stefan and Jonah, being more adventurous than either of us, tested their palettes on duck feet and gloppy-looking tripe. If we had room left in our stomachs, we ordered the little packets of glutinous rice wrapped in lotus leaves and steamed to chewy perfection. Each meal ended with an order of delicious egg tarts washed down with our last cups of tea, an overindulgence that always put a stitch in my side, but I couldn't resist.

The dim sum houses were more than eateries for us. They were also cheap entertainment. Within cavernous walls devoid of decor, hordes of people descended, several generations together, to share in the ritual of communal eating. Babies cried. Toddlers practised with chopsticks pinned together like long clothespins. Mothers placed small delicacies into the bowls of their children. Everyone shouted across large tables, their voices rising above the sounds of clattering platters.

I enjoyed being enmeshed in this theatre of life, but was overwhelmed by the masses of people pressed together. I couldn't understand why they never got irritated with one another. The crowded waterways, densely populated streets, and shared restaurant tables seemed to bother no one but me. I remember waiting in line for a movie, keeping a proper distance from the person in front, when a woman wedged into the space. For her it was a gap in the line, a space to be filled. I wondered whether their tolerance for constant contact was conditioned behaviour from childhood or resignation because they had no choice. For me, living in tight quarters was difficult.

On the *Santa Rita*, Bernard and I weren't doing well in our cramped quarters. I knew adjustments and repairs had to be done on our newly-acquired yacht, but I wasn't responsible for the flaws, and bridled at his taking his frustration out on me. The final rupture came on a seemingly neutral day when a sampan motored up to the *Santa Rita* with an offering of barbecued pork.

Bernard, focused on a part of the shaft that had become loose during the crossing, didn't look up when I asked if he was interested. "Get what you want," he snapped. "I don't care."

"But will you eat it?"

"I told you I don't care."

"Why are you so edgy?"

"I'm not edgy."

"You raised your voice."

"I didn't raise my voice."

That evening we ate in silence. After the meal, I escaped to the fresh air on deck to get away from the gloomy atmosphere below.

I saw little of my boys during this period. They were old enough to be on their own, and did a lot of exploring without us. During the day they checked out the markets and antique shops where Stefan picked up an early American coin, an old Chinese lock, and a brass scale.

"What do you think, mom?"

He was thrilled with the scale. "It's really old, but I can still use it." He lined up the gradated weights for me to inspect.

"Great find," I said. I got a vicarious pleasure out of their explorations and discoveries, and felt hurt that Bernard had no interest in exploring the city with me.

Evenings, Stefan and Jonah visited the *Elf Chine* with its crew of French students. From time to time, they hung out with the crew from the *Osprey*. If they were aware of the atmosphere on the *Santa Rita*, they didn't let on. I was relieved they had one another and a circle of friends.

I felt invisible when I was with Bernard. I wanted to talk to him about it, but couldn't bridge his silence. To get away, I escaped to different parts of the city. A few times, I visited the aquarium and communed with the coral and sea life. I spent time wandering among sharks in an underwater glass tunnel because it put me into a timeless space with no thought.

One evening I took the tram to The Peak to see Hong Kong from 1300 feet up. I looked down on Victoria Harbour and up to the mountains behind the skyscrapers. I'd had no idea how varied the terrain of Hong Kong was. From The Peak, I saw the outlying islands and across to Kowloon and the new territories. The view was so sweeping and breathtaking it made me feel powerful and in control of my life. I imagined myself a god looking down from Mt. Olympus.

As the sky darkened, the city lit up and the buildings glowed like luminous stalactites. I felt euphoric, and I wished I could have shared the moment with Bernard. I knew he would have loved the view. On one of my escape days, I visited Madame Tussauds to check out the Beatles in wax. I felt guilty because I knew Stefan and Jonah would have enjoyed that visit, but I didn't ask them. I had wanted to see Hong Kong with Bernard.

"It's a fascinating island," I said over a morning cup of coffee. "Come with me. There's a lot to see."

"Can't you do anything on your own?"

He picked up his mug and went on deck without waiting for me to answer. I sat alone at the table, frustrated and seething at the unfairness of his comment.

I was in a foreign country with a husband who'd turned from Dr. Jekyll to Mr. Hyde. It never occurred to me that Bernard may have been afraid of taking on the responsibility of three unseasoned sailors, or that he was having second thoughts about sailing into treacherous waters. I just knew I was without a home to escape to and without any money to restart my life. Not that I wanted to restart my life. I loved Bernard, and I desperately wanted things to go back to the way they were before the *Santa Rita* came between us.

"Screw you!" I mumbled to myself. "I AM going to do things on my own."

I stopped caring about having Bernard join me and took pleasure in my daily outings. I wandered in and out of small shops, and took delight in discovering narrow alleyways where I walked in step to the click, click, clicking of mah jong tiles emanating from surrounding apartments. Gambling outside of designated parlours was against the law in Hong Kong, and mah jong was considered a gambling game. People were betting away their homes and children, and the government wanted to put a stop to it. But it was obvious that the law wasn't working. People were blatantly ignoring the government decree.

At first, the brusqueness of the people unnerved me, but I gradually acclimated. I learned that "thank you" was not part of the Cantonese culture, and stopped being offended. The language lent itself to blunt directness, so when I wanted something, I got right to the point and never said thank you. I discovered that a smile worked well in all cultures and over-rode any linguistic differences. A smile from Bernard would have gone a long way in bridging the distance between us. I could have forgiven his preoccupation with the *Santa Rita*.

During one of my downtown explorations, I stumbled across a second-hand bookstore that sold books and magazines in English at discount prices. I unearthed four dog-eared copies of the *Smithsonian Institute Magazine* and a scruffy hardcover book by a man named Joseph Murphy, who promised to show me how to bring joy into my life. I bought the magazines to lose myself and the Murphy book in an attempt to find myself.

I hoped the book would excise the litany of betrayal scenes from my childhood that buzzed inside my head like a swarm of trapped bees. Bernard's distance opened a Pandora's Box of wounds that had been long buried. Miss Powell, my grade one teacher, made me a cabbage in the Peter Rabbit play. Miss Cincinelli, my grade three teacher, didn't recognize my talent and claimed someone else did my drawing. Miss Dolan in grade six gave the poem I wrote to another child to read at graduation. Miss Rowland, the school principal, kept the red bag filled with money that I had found on the way to school. God didn't give me my sister's beauty. My mother never cuddled me. My dad told me my sister was a far better person than I was, after I had spent every college weekend home trying to "straighten her out" because he had asked me to.

I changed my name to Susan, my only association with the name being the bright yellow sunflowers that grew wild in the fields near my childhood home. I don't know what made me do it. I know I was angry with myself for having put so much trust in Bernard. Maybe with a different name I could reinvent myself. It also occurred to me that it may have been a way of taking distance from the yacht that had taken my name and my husband away.

"You were born with a horseshoe up your ... you know what," a friend had once said. I now remembered her words and hoped that Mr. Murphy's book would prove her right. His table of contents promised "nirvana," and I figured if I got only halfway there, I was ahead of the game. He offered visualization and relaxation techniques that bordered on meditation, and I felt a connection to something familiar.

Ten years earlier in Mexico I had meditated with Ejo Takada, a monk from Japan who had been sponsored by a group of Mexican psychiatrists to teach the technique to their patients. I met him at a house gathering in Mexico City, liked him immensely, and joined his weekly classes. The sessions with Ejo were enthralling but not practicing daily on my own. I gradually stopped doing the daily practice and then going to the weekly sessions. I now regretted I couldn't maintain the discipline. Maybe Bernard was right when he said I was not taking enough initiative to do things on my own. I was committed to changing that in myself.

I burrowed into the tiny settee Bernard had built for me in the aft cabin and memorized whole chunks of Murphy's book. I made a daily practice of using meditation and Murphy's subconscious training techniques to pull myself out of the dark hole I'd fallen into. It didn't do much to improve Bernard's disposition, but it did a lot for how I responded to him. I became less reactive when he'd suddenly snap or withdraw into himself. I smiled more and listened attentively to his complaining about the sloppy work the yard had done on the yacht.

"They're good craftsmen," he said, "but lousy mechanics. I have to test this yacht before we go further."

"That's okay," I said. "Take as long as you need here." I was sympathetic but not overly concerned. I believed Bernard could fix anything.

"The time spent here will be good for you and the boys," he said. "You'll get in a bit of sailing experience before we head for the Philippines."

In that moment I sensed the weight of the responsibility he was carrying — three people with no sailing experience aboard an unseasoned yacht heading into the China Sea. I felt an affection that I hadn't for a long time. I wasn't forcing anything. I just felt happier and less nervous — more positive in how I viewed our relationship. The atmosphere on the *Santa Rita* slowly changed from gloom to civility to an eventual re-kindling of friendship — and lovemaking.

Bernard and I had survived the harrowing crossing of the Formosa Strait by finding ways within ourselves to work through the fear, Bernard by focusing on the yacht's weaknesses and me by quieting my mind. Fortunately, we had the resiliency and determination to hold on to our dream. We saw yachties sail into the Aberdeen Harbour who didn't. They arrived tired and dejected, and lost the will to go on.

An American couple we'd met in Taiwan arrived after us in their bulky fifty-five-foot ketch that looked more like a small pirate ship missing some masts than a sailboat. "This is our dream," the man told Bernard when we were still in Taiwan, "our retirement home that we've been looking forward to for years." He invited Bernard aboard to show off the amenities he had installed for himself and his wife, Faith, whose name like mine graced their yacht.

"It's more like a houseboat than a yacht," Bernard later told me. "It has every piece of equipment possible — a satellite system, a ham radio, a full stove with oven and even a washer and dryer. It's so heavy from the washer and dryer that more ballast had to be added to keep it from listing to one side."

I watched them come into the Aberdeen Yacht Club, and saw Faith leap off the yacht the moment they were tied to the mooring. Faith's husband chased after her. Neither of them returned. *Faith* was put on the market. Their dream of an idyllic retirement in a cozy harbour was over.

A French aristocrat whom we had met earlier sailed his yacht into Aberdeen and abandoned it in the middle of the harbour. He flagged down a sampan to take him to shore, hired someone to dock his yacht, and moved into an apartment for several months. He eventually returned to his yacht and sailed to Manila, where the boat mysteriously sank in the bay.

The Australian couple that had built their yacht at the Shin Hsing Boatyard just before us was still in the Aberdeen Harbour when we arrived. This was the man with the hairdresser wife, who had taught me everything there was to know about provisioning; the woman who knew every nautical term and expression, and talked as though she had been at sea most of her life.

I remembered Bernard asking me why I couldn't be more like her. Between Taiwan and Hong Kong, Bronica had a nervous breakdown. I saw her sitting on the bow of their yacht in Aberdeen Harbour, mute, with a fishing line dangling in the water, but she caught no fish. Her husband went looking for crew to help him sail back to Australia. It was clear that the fully equipped beauty salon would never be used.

Chapter 9

SETTLING IN

There is no boredom with anything that varies in such a way as
always to tip one's thoughts just over the horizon: and the absence
of boredom must be one of the main attributes of happiness.
— FREYA STARK

I continued to meditate each morning before heading to the galley for my first coffee of the day. Bernard and Stefan were usually there with mugs in hand, discussing some aspect of the yacht in need of attention. Stefan shared Bernard's interest in solving technical problems. *Good*, I thought. He could be sailing with us for a long time.

"What are your plans?" I'd asked a few days after he arrived.

"I don't know, mom," he answered, "but I'm not going back. I have to figure out what I want to do with my life first."

Although I no longer tried to include Bernard in my daily excursions, I still wondered at his lack of interest in Hong Kong. I recalled our trips in Mexico and how he enjoyed trekking through unexplored places and talking to the local people in the small villages. He once built a hut of palms on a secluded beach in Playa Azul where the two of us lived for a week sustained by love and red snapper sold to us by local fishermen. I missed the Bernard who had once been so full of curiosity and adventure.

One evening he agreed to join the boys and me for a week of Chinese operas being performed near the harbour. Though I knew he had only agreed because the *Santa Rita* was within viewing distance, I was still pleased. We stood for hours with throngs of Hong Kongese in front of a makeshift outdoor stage to listen to the performances. The reverence the audience showed the singers was unlike anything I'd experienced in the West. From our vantage point we were able to observe the actors in the operas painting their faces — a white face for the villain, a red one for the hero, black for a bold or fierce character.

But while we observed, as the only westerners in the audience, we were also being observed. Jonah, with his large blue eyes, was a particular object of curiosity. People often stopped on the street, stared at him and then walked on. For the most part, he was used to it. But during a performance, an elderly man decided not to walk past. He stood directly in front of Jonah, his back to the stage, and stared unblinking into his eyes, absolutely transfixed. Jonah moved away in an effort to lose him. The man followed. He tried to look over the man's head. The man raised his head to match Jonah's movement.

"That guy gives me the creeps," Jonah whispered to me.

"He's in love with you," I said, teasing.

In exasperation, Jonah left the performance while the man, following behind for a few feet, stared after him. I thought of my American friend Katherine from Taipei telling me how strangers would touch her hairy arms, and I recalled seeing a man without legs getting on a bus in Taipei. Passengers ran to the bus door to watch. It took me a while to get used to this overt form of curiosity, but Jonah never got used to it.

When the theatre people took down the bamboo infrastructure and dismantled the stage, Bernard returned to his pattern of our once-a-week outing for dim sum with a quick return to the yacht. It was as though he were attached to the *Santa Rita* by an invisible elastic band — a short stretch out, snap and back.

He wasn't the only yachtie who didn't venture far from his boat. There was Captain Iredell, his brawny drinking buddy, who was moored beside us. Iredell, a seasoned sailor from the United States, had commanded cargo ships for American companies before retiring, and was now captain of his own small yacht. And though he sailed without crew, he still referred to himself as Captain Iredell and wouldn't reveal his given name to us.

Every night I sat on deck with my one bottle of beer while Bernard and Captain Iredell went through a 6-pack each. And every night I listened to them commiserating about how boring Hong Kong was.

"Of course you find it boring," I finally said to Bernard. "The two of you never go anywhere. You just sit around drinking and discussing boat hardware. What do you find so interesting about that guy?"

"He knows a lot about the sea," he answered. "I can learn from him."

Aside from Iredell's disdain for the world, I wasn't convinced there was much Bernard could learn. I also got the feeling Captain Iredell didn't like women, especially women on boats. He made a point of ignoring me except for one pointed comment that he threw at me when we first met.

"Jonah, you call him? Not a good name for a sailor. I don't like Stefan either. Why didn't you give your kids common names like Jim or John?"

"Maybe I didn't want them to be common."

"I'm going to call him John."

"His name is Jonah."

"Not good luck on a boat."

"I'll take my chances. I'm not superstitious."

Captain Iredell smirked and walked away. It was the last time he ever addressed me in a conversation.

During one of those nightly drinking fests, Bernard again brought up the theme of boredom.

"Know what we need?" Captain Iredell countered. "A television. Sailboats should come equipped with televisions."

Even I laughed at the idea. It seemed so farfetched. Besides, we planned to go for a sail the next day, and I felt that would alleviate some of Bernard's boredom. Cheung Chau, a small island about an hour away from Hong Kong, would be our first sailing venture since we had arrived, and it generated a lot of nervous excitement in all of us — especially Stefan, who was sailing for the first time.

"We'll be doing a number of test runs to the island," Bernard informed us. "We can't chance leaving Hong Kong without them." He worried, having already uncovered some glitches in the *Santa* Rita.

Halfway to Cheung Chau, Bernard spotted an object partially sunk under the waves.

"Can you make it out?" he asked no one in particular.

"Maybe it's a big fish," Stefan offered. Jonah and I shrugged. It kept appearing and disappearing, and even with binoculars it wasn't easy to see.

"I'm going for a better look," Bernard said. He handed the helm to Stefan, lowered the sails, and jumped into the dinghy. With grappling hook in hand, he fished a large Styrofoam-covered object out of the water.

"It's a TV!" he shouted. It was the first bit of enthusiasm Bernard had shown since our arrival in Hong Kong.

He extracted the bright red 12-inch television from its thick, buoyant wrapping. "A bit wet," he mumbled, mostly to himself, and carefully took it apart to dry on deck.

I looked with dismay at the scattered pieces. "You'll never get that thing to work, let along figure out how to get those bitty parts back into the right places," I said.

"Maybe," he mused, completely absorbed in the project at hand.

Once re-assembled, the TV worked on a 12-volt battery. Bernard couldn't wait for our return to Hong Kong to see the expression on Iredell's face. Coming into the harbour, he shouted over the put-putting of the engine. "You were right about us needing a TV. I've just fished one out of the sea." He held the set up for Iredell to see.

"Son of a bitch," Iredell exclaimed. "I don't believe it. You're pulling my leg, right? You bought the damn thing in Cheung Chau."

"Look, here's the case it was floating in. It was kind of wet, but I took it apart and dried it out on deck."

"You did what?"

I could tell that Iredell, who never liked to give credit to anyone, was impressed.

"Bernard has this uncanny knack." I said. "Whenever he puts out an intention for what he wants, it comes to him. And he can fix anything. It's a gift."

"Son of a bitch," Iredell repeated.

That evening, along with Captain Iredell and the boys, we settled back on the settees below deck, drinks in hand, and watched our first TV broadcast from Hong Kong—John Wayne in an old black and white western speaking in Cantonese. It didn't matter that his lips stopped moving before he finished speaking or that sometimes he started to speak with his mouth shut. It was hilarious to see this wooden actor spouting words in a language that didn't match the sets or his body movements. It was even funnier to listen to the other characters in the movie responding to him. The best part was that it brought some common ground of enjoyment into our lives.

We continued our regular sails to Cheung Chau, anchoring away from the port with its ferries, water taxis and fishing boats vying for space, its streets an extension of the frenetic life crowding the harbour. All activity was squeezed into the port area, streets so narrow, only miniature, toy-like emergency trucks and bicycles were allowed. I walked the streets much as I did in Hong Kong, strolling through the cramped back alleys, taking in the pungent food smells and familiar clicking of mah jong tiles. I wondered why all of Cheung Chau's life was packed into this small area while the rest of the island remained unblemished with golden sand beaches.

Bernard's testing and constant vigilance proved to be right. During one of our excursions, the salon flooded. Neither the electric bilge pump nor the hand pump worked. The boys and I bailed while Bernard searched for the leak, finally tracing it to a loose cap on the engine. Another time, as we motored into Aberdeen's narrow harbour, the engine died. Bearing down on us from behind was a huge tourist junk going too fast to stop. For one harrowing moment it looked as though we'd be rammed. Within seconds of that near crash, Bernard managed to restart the engine. A small air hole in the fuel feed had caused the problem. *Leave nothing to chance*, I thought.

Our last sail to Cheung Chau was for pleasure. Even Bernard wanted to witness the colourful Bun Festival. It was a time when the whole island went vegetarian, including the local McDonald's. We watched Pak Tai, the god of water and spirit of the north, lead a procession of children through the village. Young children, standing motionless in traditional clothing, are held high above the crowds on steel frames. Walking among the suspended children made me think of deceased children from another time floating upright through the air.

Arrhythmic drumming and clashing cymbals surrounded the children to protect them from evil spirits because the dead, who have no family to feed their souls, come on this day to eat. Three scaffoldings 60 feet high were completely covered with steamed buns to feed the orphan souls. Revellers waited for the dead to have their fill before they ate the leftovers. But those of us with less compassion for the hungry souls bought buns to eat as we watched the lion dancing through the narrow streets and cheered on dragon boat races in the harbour, accompanied by still more drumming and clashing cymbals. In the West we "let the dead rest in peace." In the East the dead are kept at bay by noise. I found it curious how our cultures differed in the way we thought the dead responded to sound.

While moored in the Aberdeen Harbour, I observed my fellow travellers. Some were as interesting as the culture I was experiencing. One was a quiet man from Scotland, who kept apart from the other yachties, and seemed pleasant enough, always polite and well-mannered, but I felt his presence and was alert to wherever he was around the harbour. As soon as he moored beside us, I was unable to sleep. His hull was pressed up against ours, with its aft cabin berth only a fibreglass skin away from ours. His head was inches from mine when we slept, and I could feel his energy through the hull. It felt as though he was sleeping in bed with me, and I couldn't bear it. I changed places with Bernard so that I wouldn't have to sleep so close to him.

"Do you mind?" I asked. "I know you'll be squeezed in." The *Santa Rita* was curved at the stern, and my side of the double berth was narrower than Bernard's. I slept on the inside part next to the hull because I was shorter.

"No problem," he answered. Bernard may have found my reasoning for the switch irrational, but he didn't question it. He trusted my intuition and never thought of my premonitions or "feelings" as anything but normal. His total acceptance of this aspect of my nature was part of what glued me to him in our relationship.

After the Scotsman sailed away, we learned that he'd been commissioned to supervise the building of the yacht he was on. Instead of delivering the boat to its rightful owner, he sailed off with it. Interpol was after him, but he always managed to be elsewhere when they came. In 1982, no country had legal jurisdiction over large bodies of water three miles off shore. It freed others as well as him to engage in cheating, theft, pirating, and murder. Before living at sea, I believed that police control was, for the most part, excessive. But I was wrong. Take away societal constraints and some of the most law-abiding citizens turn rogue. I witnessed the most arbitrary and petty crimes by "decent" people, because they could get away with it — from a retired jeweller from Toulon who sailed out of Aberdeen Harbour without paying the meagre fee for filling his water tank, to fellow travellers stealing equipment from neighbouring yachts.

Fortunately, most yachties tended to be more eccentric than criminal, like the New Zealander with his 30-foot yacht who sailed alone and lived solely on coconuts. He had hundreds of them aboard his boat, maybe thousands. They were stacked everywhere, above and below deck. With his long, messy hair and emaciated body, he looked like a zombie from *The Living Dead* TV series, but in truth he was a loner with a generous nature and gentle soul.

And then there was Charlie and Cat who lived together on a beat-up steel-hulled wreck anchored a short distance from the harbour. Charlie was an alcoholic who lived mostly on booze. Cat was rescued by Charlie from a cat farm somewhere in Hong Kong. Cat was destined for the meat market and Charlie changed the direction of his life. He also changed his appearance. Cat was smooth and pink from his neck down. According to Charlie, the big tom had fallen into a barrel of oil, lost his fur, and wasn't able to grow it back. As a result of being furless, Cat loved water, and the two used to scuba dive together.

Their life in Hong Kong was supposed to be temporary, but Charlie couldn't leave the country because he was at war with the Hong Kong government over the naming of his boat. He had applied to register it under the name of *Screw Driver*. The Government insisted *Screw Driver* was a dirty word. Charlie couldn't make them understand it was his favourite drink.

"And also a tool," I interjected into his story.

The officials kept rejecting his application. They were at loggerheads and neither would budge from their position.

Charlie told us that, once he got his boat properly registered, he was going to start a floating utopia of like-minded people. He had made drawings for a series of huge connected rafts that would float between Europe and the Americas on the trade winds. His people would grow their own food and have all their needs provided for within the community without ever having to go ashore. He had an engineer's mind and was totally focused on refining the blueprint for his vision. But he was in Hong Kong when we arrived, and still there when we left several months later.

Charlie and the coconut man from New Zealand were loners, men who were wounded or disillusioned in some way and could no longer live within a workaday environment. We met people like them all through our travels — solitary figures who didn't feel at home in a structured society. Many of these sailors didn't trust women and made total female transferences onto their yachts that were always referred to as "SHE," and where they, as captain, were always in control. I gleaned this information from women who paired up with these men at various ports. They were seduced by the romanticism of sailing and then disillusioned by the knowledge that the yacht was the captain's only love. They served as pillow mates, galley slaves, money providers, or charwomen until they got fed up and left.

I wondered about my own position. I didn't share ownership of the yacht, and worried that maybe something shifts in men at sea. Most of the time, the excitement of the adventure and practical considerations buried this needling thought.

Our sail from Taiwan to Hong Kong convinced us the Colman camping stove was too dangerous on a rough sea. Bernard threw it out and installed a gas two-burner with an oven. My beautiful, new stove stirred my interest in cooking. In one of the English bookstores I found a small paperback with simple Chinese recipes. This little gem of a book served me well through our adventure and has travelled with me through many countries since.

I had no problem trying most of the food products from China and was even willing to experiment with duck feet and bring aboard thousand-year-old eggs, but I was never able to overcome my revulsion to sea cucumber, a leathery tubular thing that crawls on tiny pods along the ocean floor perpetually eating and excreting. When attacked, it jettisons its organs from its anus and then regenerates them. Unless you're into science fiction, there's something unsettling about a vege-table-like animal that can almost disintegrate its entire body, and then put itself together again. And although it's one of the most disgusting looking animals on the planet, and looks even worse dried than alive (often compared to a glop of cement), it's a favoured delicacy of the Cantonese who spend days in its preparation to clean and cook it to slippery perfection. I could neither cook nor eat it.

Had I been less squeamish, there was another culinary possibility. One night at about two or three in the morning, I got up for a glass of water. As I entered the galley, I felt eyes on me. I looked around and could see nothing. I figured it was my imagination and turned on the faucet. Still, something creepy in the dark disturbed me; maybe a rob-ber was hiding aboard. I knew something was there. I was afraid to turn on a light because I didn't want whatever it was to know that I knew it was there. I calmly walked back to the aft cabin and poked Bernard.

"There's something or someone on board," I said.

He rolled over and faced me. "How do you know?"

"I just know." It wasn't much of an answer, but I refused to go away, and I wouldn't get back on the berth.

He finally got up, grabbed a flashlight, and headed for the galley with me trailing behind.

Right there, under the galley table, was a rat. Bernard picked up a woven stool with an open bottom and tried to catch it in the open end. The rat was a lot faster, gone before Bernard could pounce on it. Terrified of its coming towards me, I headed back to the aft cabin. The rat ran behind me. I jumped onto the berth and pulled the blanket over my head. The rat also jumped onto the berth. I could feel its little feet running across my back. I was running from it. It was run-ning from Bernard. For different reasons, the rat and I were both in a state of panic.

"Get it off me," I screamed.

Bernard laughed so hard at this absurd scene, he could hardly stand. He finally trapped the rat in a corner of the berth, took it on deck and dumped it into the harbour. I came out after him, and we watched to see where the rat would go. The little monster found the mooring line and started to climb back onto the boat. Bernard pushed it down with a broom, and we waited for a while to see if it would try again. For a moment, it looked as though it might, but thought better of it, and swam off. The next day we bought rat protectors (small shields that look like the cones vets use on animals after surgery) for the ropes.

Had I been native to the area, I might have seen the rat as a dish in the waiting that walked in and delivered itself. Shortly after the incident, the *Hong Kong China Post* published an article with a culinary tip on how to deal with rodent infestation. I cut out the recipe and tucked it into my new Chinese cookbook. Here is the recipe:

Rat Recipe for Gourmets

Catch one rat — plump and juicy after gorging on grain during
   the harvest season — scald with steam and plunge it into cold
   water to peel off the fur.

Carefully gut the bald rat and soak in brine, ginger and pepper
   before flattening it into a steak with weights.

After drying for a day, cook in a sealed pot with rice, bran and a
   soupçon of sesame oil until the aroma permeates the whole
   kitchen. Then eat it.

Chapter 10

MACAO AND BACK

~~~~~~

*The world is a book, and those who do not travel read
only one page.*
— St. Augustine

With a bit of cajoling, I managed to pry Bernard away from the
Santa Rita for a trip to Macao, an hour from Hong Kong by
hovercraft. The behemoth vessel that took us to the island skimmed
over waves on puffs of air inches above the sea, and gave the illusion
of sailing through space. So relaxing, I thought.

A well-dressed Chinese gentleman with a pocket mirror in one
hand and two coins in the other sat across from us. I watched him
deftly pluck his beard by placing a coin on each side of a lone hair and
giving a sharp yank. He had an extra long pinkie nail, an ancient
custom in China to show that one wasn't a labourer. But I knew that
long pinkie nails were also used as spoons for snorting cocaine. Was
this a foreshadowing of our visit to Macao, a city with a reputation for
drugs, prostitution, and gambling?

Stepping off the hovercraft was like stepping out of present time
onto a stage set in some exotic, tropical country. The streets were a
jumbled mix of 15th and 16th century Portuguese architecture, Chinese temples, baroque style churches with curved oriental roofs, and
slums. Brightly coloured buildings along some of the narrow streets
opened to wide plazas with stately colonial buildings in pastel colours.
Elegant doorways, arched windows, and balustrades vied for attention
with haphazardly placed signs in front of Chinese shops. Wooden
shutters in shades of green or burnt sienna with their patina of age
could be seen behind lacy wrought-iron balconies that shaded narrow
streets. I pictured myself in a 1940s film where at any moment I might

come across Peter Lorre nursing a gin and tonic while waiting for some local shady character.

Macao's history is filled with shady characters. In 1557, in exchange for eliminating deadly pirate raids by Chinese smugglers along the coast, the governor of Canton province agreed to let Portuguese traders use Macao for their lucrative silk trade. When silk stopped being profitable, the traders tried their hand at opium until the British quashed the business. They picked up the slack by indulging in human trafficking. Chinese men were captured and sold in Cuba, Peru, and Portugal, where they were in great demand, until 1761 when slavery was abolished in Portugal.

With its history of lax laws and a sliding scale of morality, it was no surprise that gambling became the next viable option for profit. By the time the island was returned to China in 1999 its reputation for illicit dealings was already well established, leaving the door open for prostitution and the notorious Chinese organized crime organizations known as Triads. They still exist but function more as successful businessmen in questionable activities than as thugs on the street.

Intrigued by its reputation as a Mecca for gamblers, we first made our way to the Lisboa Casino. It was just after breakfast when we arrived, but the place was already teeming with people from Hong Kong and the Chinese mainland. The dumpy building with its weird, tacky arcades was the main gambling house in the 1980s. Today's Lisboa Casino, built near its shabby sister, boasts being the tallest building on the island. Its lure is posh hotel rooms with mind-boggling luxury that comes with or without an in-house prostitute — legal in Macao. But I was glad to experience Macao in its more laid-back days, before the gambling strip took on the allure of a transplanted Las Vegas. I don't even begrudge the twenty dollars I lost within five minutes at the blackjack table — my cards swept away before I could count the numbers.

"How are you doing?" I asked Bernard when I finally managed to elbow my way through the pressed bodies that crowded the roulette table. He had chosen the roulette wheel over the blackjack table.

"This is where the high rollers are," he told me, amused to be among them.

He showed me his empty hands as he left the table, his spot taken instantly by another player. "You managed to last longer than me," I said, laughing at our limited gambling skills. All in all, we must have spent thirty minutes at the casino, five minutes for me and a half hour for Bernard.

Our early losses at the gambling house left us with the only other thing to do on the island — enjoy the Macao cuisine. Portugal's far-flung trading route had taken them as far as Africa and through countries bordering the China Sea including India. Along the way, they picked up people, spices, and cooking styles and brought them back to Macao. The Macanese are a seamless blend of these different cultures as is their food. To traditional Cantonese fare was added chicken dishes from Africa, spices from India, and the famous Portuguese *bacalhau,* a layered dish of salted cod, potatoes, and onions. Until we reached Singapore, I would never again see such a rich fusion of food. Bernard tried the African chicken in coconut milk, and I went for the *bacalhau,* both dishes washed down by good Portuguese wine. Food is so tied to emotions, we left Macao on a high.

Typhoon warnings greeted us on our return to Hong Kong, and brought our exuberant mood to an abrupt halt. We knew we had to move the yacht to a safe haven, but we were missing Jonah. He had left early that morning to meet Camelia Wong, a journalist, for tea in downtown Hong Kong. She was to interview him about our sailing adventure. After the interview, he planned to take the Star Ferry to Cheung Chau to spend time on the beach. We were going to sail there on our return from Macao to pick him up.

Stefan had been in charge of the yacht in our absence and was aware of the warning, but there was nothing he could do until we returned. It was imperative that we got to shelter as soon as possible, but we couldn't leave without Jonah. Stefan offered to take the ferry to get him. It would be quicker than sailing. We waited until nightfall but neither of the boys returned, and the storm was picking up.

Bernard and I sat below deck, each in our own world, drinking cup after cup of coffee. We were too tense to make small talk or even speculate where they might be. Bernard fiddled with little gadgets. I tried to read but couldn't. The wind howled, and the yacht jerked about violently.

I looked at Bernard. "What are we going to do?"

"We can't stay here," he said. "It's too dangerous. We've got to move."

I felt my stomach tighten. "How will they find us?"

"They'll figure it out. I'll give the watchman at the Aberdeen Yacht Club some money in case he sees them. That way they can find shelter."

The sea was rough but still manageable. Bernard threw on his slicker and took the dinghy to shore. I felt comforted that he thought to leave cash behind. It meant that the watchman knew they were gone and would be on the lookout for them.

On his return, we motored to Causeway Bay, where we hoped to find protection from the worst of the typhoon. From our safe haven, I prayed that the boys found shelter somewhere.

"Will they find us?" I asked in an effort to break through my anxiety.

"They'll be okay," Bernard said. "They're not babies. They'll use their common sense."

He was trying his best to comfort me, but his calmness fuelled my angst.

Later, Jonah told us he had heard the storm warnings and returned. By the time he got to the harbour, it was raining hard. He searched the waterfront but couldn't find us as we had already left, then spotted the *Elf Chine* anchored a distance off shore. He managed to find a sampan willing to take him to the junk, and spent a hairy night aboard. The *Elf Chine* heaved violently throughout the storm, rain pouring in through cracks on deck.

The next morning he left the *Elf Chine* to try to make it to Causeway Bay because Bernard had left word by radio with the *Elf Chine* crew that we'd be moored there. He got to the area by subway and bus. "It was like a ghost town," he said. "All the buildings were boarded up."

A lone person on the street told him he shouldn't be out, that the worst of the typhoon was yet to come. He climbed a hill to get a better perspective in his search for us.

"A pack of wild dogs attacked me," he said. "I tried to hold them off with a stick, when a stranger showed up out of nowhere and threw a rock at the leader making them scatter."

When he couldn't find us, he hitchhiked back to the subway where a Good Samaritan gave him money for a subway ticket.

"You didn't see the watchman at the yacht club?" I asked.

"No," he said.

Once back in Aberdeen Harbour, he slept on the pleasure junk of an English guy anchored there.

Meanwhile, Stefan hadn't been able to return because the Star Ferry had stopped running, due to the typhoon warnings. Stranded on Cheung Chau with no money and nowhere to shelter, he sat on a bench facing the water and wondered what to do next when two police officers approached him.

"What are you doing here?" they asked.

"I'm looking for my brother."

"You can't stay here."

"Can I spend the night in the police station?"

"No, you have to go to a hotel."

"I've no money," he told them.

They took him to a hotel anyway, and the manager let him sleep on a desk in the office.

The following morning, he rushed to the ferry terminus, but it was still closed. He met up with a dozen sailors from the Philippines who were also stranded. One had a girlfriend working as a maid on the island. She brought them food and bottles of San Miguel beer. They sat on benches outside a closed newspaper stand and filled up on canned sardines and beer. That night they covered themselves with newspapers and slept.

After two days the typhoon veered off towards mainland China. Stefan made it back to Aberdeen Harbour and found Jonah there. By the time we sailed back into the harbour, the boys had shared stories and were ready to tell us of their adventures.

I hadn't slept for two nights. I stayed awake on black coffee in order to nurse my angst and silently accused Bernard of leaving Aberdeen Harbour too soon. I couldn't say anything because rationally, I knew he'd done the right thing. Had we not left, our small yacht would have been badly damaged or worse.

As for the boys, they seemed no worse for wear. It had been an adventure for them. I wish I could say that was the last time I feared for their safety, but our journey had only begun.

Chapter 11

ANCHORS AWEIGH

Autumn 1981: Hong Kong

You can't cross a sea merely by standing and staring at the water.
—RABINDRANATH TAGORE

During our three months of sailing between Hong Kong and Cheung Chau Island, Stefan developed a good set of sea legs. Jonah still got seasick in rough weather but never complained, and I was now a whiz at preparing simple, nutritious meals on my new gas stove. Bernard, believing the *Santa Rita* to finally be seaworthy, installed an autopilot to take our place at the helm in good weather. Life would have been idyllic except for tension brewing between Jonah and Bernard. It started when Bernard discovered Jonah couldn't take heights after he'd ordered him up the mast. Bernard shouted at him that a teen the same age on a neighbouring yacht climbed the mast like a monkey.

"Look, I can't do it, that's all," Jonah said.

"You're too much of an intellectual," Bernard said. "You'll never learn to sail. I wish I had that other kid aboard."

"Why don't you leave him alone?" I said. "That other boy's a menace. Even his parents can't deal with him. Why do you find him so great?" I reminded him that Jonah was always willing to do his share of work. "When you were in France, Jonah went to the boatyard everyday to check out the progress on the yacht. You've never even acknowledged that." I waited for a response, but he said nothing. He looked past me, turned, and walked away. His reluctance to admit our journey was a team effort perplexed me, and I had no idea how to handle it.

An incident between Jonah and Bernard off Cheung Chau Island exacerbated the tension. Jonah was about to hoist the anchor over the side of the hull when it slipped from his hands making a loud thud on the deck. Bernard lashed out at him. "You clumsy idiot," he shouted. "You don't give a damn about this boat. You're a lazy write-off." The anger in his voice was so out of proportion to the "so-called" crime that I was stunned into silence. Stefan and I exchanged glances but said nothing.

"Do it yourself," Jonah said. "Why don't you get an automatic winch like other yachts? We do everything by hand, and that anchor is damned heavy." He walked away leaving the anchor where it fell.

Later, I couldn't find Jonah anywhere. He wasn't aboard, and it was more than a mile to shore. Panic crept into every joint of my body. I was sure he had jumped overboard and committed suicide. I couldn't think of anything else.

"He probably swam to the island," Stefan said.

"No, no. It's too far." I could barely see the shoreline, and couldn't believe he'd have swum that distance.

I turned on Bernard. "You killed my son," I cried.

Bernard didn't reply. He lowered the dingy and went to search for him.

I kept moving from one end of the yacht to the other, looking for Jonah, though I knew he wasn't there. "Why had I come on this adventure?" I kept asking myself.

Bernard returned half an hour later with Jonah beside him. "Found him sunbathing on the beach," he said. Jonah had swum to shore.

On the surface, everything looked resolved, but that evening Jonah said to me: "Screw sailing. I just want to be out of here. He can ask me anything. It's over. I'm not doing it."

The estrangement between Jonah and Bernard wounded me deeply. I wondered if Bernard was using Jonah to act out some angst or discontent he couldn't handle inside himself. I was having misgivings about having my sons with us, and grateful that Jonah, who had turned eighteen in April, would be flying out from the Philippines to start college at Middlebury in Vermont. I was also grateful he was a strong swimmer. I'm still impressed that he made that swim to shore without drowning.

As there were no more scenes between Jonah and Bernard, I tried to stay focused on the positive. I noticed that my coordination was better and my balance improved. In the beginning, I wobbled across the two-by-four beam that Bernard would place between a pier and the yacht for us to get ashore. Now I danced across it. I felt I could walk a tight rope and loved the sense of control it gave me. A yacht is never static, and I made constant body adjustments to compensate. It was a bit like sitting on an exercise ball but with no chance of getting off.

My body got stronger, and I felt healthier. I turned a nice shade of brown and kept my weight down without thinking about it. It felt empowering knowing that my body could function so well physically. Bernard and the boys were also in great shape — lean, tanned, and co-ordinated in their movements.

I learned how to reef the sails, but was stumped when it came to feeling the wind. I liked sailing, but I wasn't a natural. Bernard may have thought that Jonah lived in his head, but that was a lot truer of me. It gave him concern to see how inept I was. On the other hand, Bernard was right in his element. It was as though he, the *Santa Rita* and the wind were one. It gave me a great sense of security to see how effortlessly he handled the yacht.

"It's so easy, Rita. Why aren't you getting it?" He'd sigh and shake his head.

Fortunately, I could steer, a plus because manoeuvring into a crowded port was tricky, and someone had to do it while the other jumped ashore to secure the ropes. I thought I'd be a boon on windless days relieving Bernard at the helm, but we now had the autopilot, and in good weather the yacht stayed on course without anyone steering. Frustrated by my mediocre sailing skills, I compensated by finding the right provisions, cooking well-balanced meals, and keeping the boat physically tidy. I was the one who went ashore, struggled in various languages, tracked down the markets, learned to haggle, and searched for work in various ports. I was our lifeline to the outside world. Bernard handled the boat — the navigation, sailing, and repair.

I had no problem with this division of labour and felt the arrangement suited both our temperaments. He loved being aboard the *Santa Rita*, could spend hours doing maintenance, and enjoyed drinking with fellow yachties moored nearby. He could repair anything, and was in demand for his good-natured services. This was part of his adventure.

My adventure was exploring different cultures without a time frame, my home with me wherever I went. I loved the idea of not being bound by anything but the mutable sea. It was a time before borders were so closely monitored and before an internet profile of you could be sent anywhere tracking your movements. I thought of Columbus and Vasco de Gama and, like them, I wanted to venture to less trodden places.

A few yachties shared my interest in other cultures, but I discovered that the yachting world had its own culture and yachties, for the most part, had little interest in the countries they travelled through. Their interest was in exchanging stories about sailing — the mishaps, the technical problems, the expense of repairs, and the camaraderie that came from sharing those experiences. Shoptalk was their identity. The older Frenchman who had sailed with us from Taiwan invited us aboard his yacht one evening to have drinks with him and his silent, smiling wife. He and Bernard immediately fell into a conversation about plotting sea charts.

"Have you been to The Peak or Kowloon?" I asked.

"Yes, yes," he answered in an agitated tone and immediately shifted the conversation back to the sailing route he was planning to take to France. Like Captain Iredell, his only topic of conversation revolved around boat issues. In every port we entered, the pattern repeated itself, always accompanied by a generous supply of alcohol.

When we were ready to leave Hong Kong, Bernard, as usual, handled the boat duties while I took care of those on shore. I bought Jonah's plane ticket for the States having learned that the price would have jumped considerably had I bought it in Manila. Then I trolled the markets for whatever produce I thought would survive the trip, my main focus being the canned goods at the Chinese Emporium where I picked up tree fungus, grass jelly, canned meats and soups. I had to go by the pictures as the labels were all in Chinese.

My theory was that if the people in Hong Kong could eat it, we could too. Almost anything could be made palatable in a stir fry or as fried rice. Unfortunately, I couldn't bring the succulent pork and pressed duck dishes that had become part of our almost daily fare, but I did get some cans of tripe for Stefan, knowing he'd miss the tripe he'd buy off the carts in downtown Hong Kong — a pleasure I didn't share. Many years later, he still searches for canned tripe in Chinese grocery stores.

The evening before setting sail, we boarded the *Elf Chine*, with its coterie of young adults, to say good-bye. The junk was to leave a day after us, and we promised to keep in radio contact. Stefan and Jonah ran over to the boat club's watchman to tell him we were about to leave. He gave them a Chinese checkers set as a parting gift, but he wouldn't teach them how to play.

"The game is too complex for the western mind," he told them.

"What did you say?" I asked.

"We just thanked him," Stefan said. "I thought it would be rude to ask him why he gave it to us if he thought we couldn't learn how to play."

"Yeah, that was pretty funny," Jonah said. "But we'll probably figure it out on our own. It doesn't look that hard."

"Anyway, it's nice to look at," I said.

We left Hong Kong for the Philippines on August 9, 1982, hoping to make it to the island of Luzon before a typhoon developed in the China Sea. At seven in the morning on a bleak rainy day, we sat below deck and fortified ourselves with mugs of hot coffee before lifting anchor for Luzon, the largest island in the Philippine archipelago. By noon, the rain stopped and the sea turned dark blue, taking on the muted sheen and texture of rumpled taffeta.

Chapter 12

BRIBES AND ARMS

Autumn 1981: Luzon, Philippines

> *The sea has never been friendly to man. At most it has been an accomplice to human restlessness.*
>
> —JOSEPH CONRAD

Three days at sea since leaving Hong Kong, and we hadn't seen another craft. I couldn't shake a sense of foreboding. That night, heaving waves signalled a possible typhoon brewing in the China Sea. It explained why there had been no traffic in a shipping lane, and so few birds.

Meanwhile, a front was building near Luzon, where we were heading. We hoped to reach San Fernando, the nearest port on the island, before a full-fledged typhoon erupted. By late afternoon, it was clear we wouldn't make it before nightfall.

"I have to slow the yacht," Bernard said. "There's too much coral out there. I won't see it in the dark."

He turned the bow of the yacht into the wind, and the boys and I lowered the sails. We were now at a standstill except for some minor drift.

Throughout the night, the four of us took turns on deck keeping an eye out for freighters and flotsam. Intense bursts of light flashed repeatedly overhead. It terrified me. I sat on deck stiff as a statue, with my knees tucked under my chin and my arms wrapped around my shins. For hours, the electrically charged sky opened to illuminate the sea, first from one point and then another, but there was no sound of thunder, nor did the sea move. We were surrounded by an eerie stillness.

I waited anxiously for the onslaught of the storm, but nothing happened. The yacht seemed suspended in some alternate universe.

In the morning we discovered the *Santa Rita* had drifted away from the coast. After some calculations, Bernard brought the yacht back on course. An hour later San Fernando came into view with a welcoming palm tree at its northernmost tip, followed by an old battleship with half its hull, beached. San Fernando was home to Clark Air Base, the largest American military base outside the United States, established in 1848 when Spain lost the Philippines to the Americans. When the Japanese invaded during the Second World War, unspeakable massacres took place here. I wondered if the battleship was a leftover from that war. For the first time I felt a connection with the history I had studied in school.

As we neared the port, three men in a banana-shaped outrigger canoe known as a *bangka* motored out to meet us.

"Customs and Immigration," one of the men called out.

We shut down the engine and waited while three scrawny officials in filthy shorts with colourful rags tied around their heads scrambled aboard. I was taken aback by their outfits and a bit shocked that the government didn't have a dress code for its officials. Each man carried a machete. The most overbearing of the three showed us some official looking papers as proof of their authority and asked for our documents. After returning our passports and having us sign our names in a ledger, he ordered us to stay in the galley while his men searched the boat.

"What are you looking for?" I asked. One of the men smiled at me but didn't answer. I didn't insist.

Row after row of provisions I had bought in Hong Kong started to pile up on the galley table as each locker was opened and stripped of its contents. They even pinched the pickled ducks' feet that I wasn't too sure about. The "customs officials" studied each label carefully before setting the item on the table. One of them held up a good-sized can of what looked like Spam. He turned it in my direction so that I could participate in his pleasure of discovery.

"Very good," he said.

"It's yours," I replied.

"Thank you," he answered. He was effusively polite as he went about stealing our goods.

He then searched through our bag of weevil infested flour.

"For you," he said as he handed me the bag.

I found myself thanking him for his thoughtful generosity. I'd already forced myself to come to terms with the insect life that shared our food supply — all part of the food chain. I had by now started to view weevil as a much needed protein. They nourish themselves on our flour, and we on them. It helped that we couldn't see them in pancakes. The men stripped us of everything but an open bottle of cooking oil, a sack of rice, and the bag of flour crawling with life.

Bernard, Stefan and I were in the aft part of the galley while Jonah had stationed himself near the companionway leading to the hatch. As the so-called customs officers headed towards the stairs, the one in charge spied Bernard's pen lying on the chart table.

"Very nice," he said. He fingered its tortoise shell casing.

"That's enough," Jonah snapped as he grabbed the pen from under the thief's hand.

The man stared hard into Jonah's face. Jonah didn't flinch.

I felt a surge of fear through my body. "Give him the pen," I mumbled under my breath. *For God's sake, you don't need it. Give it to him, you idiot.* I hoped my subliminal message would reach his brain. But it became obvious that I had no telepathic control over my son.

Suddenly the head honcho's body relaxed. He smiled at Jonah and gave him a friendly punch on the arm. He nodded to the men, and they left with their haul, leaving Jonah with the pen.

Giddy with relief, I followed behind the debarking thugs, thanking them profusely for their visit as they boarded their *bangka* with bags of our provisions. I then raced below deck to where my family was cleaning up the mess the visitors had left behind.

"Why didn't you give it to him?" I shouted at Jonah. "It's only a pen. It wouldn't have mattered."

Jonah shrugged his shoulders. "It wasn't his."

It was a comfort to know that by the end of the summer he would be safely enrolled in Middlebury College. At the same time, I felt a mother's pride seeing his determination to hold his ground. Still, it could have ended badly, and I didn't know if or when we'd face the same situation again.

Once anchored in the harbour, we were again boarded by "government officials." The first to board looked about sixteen years old. "I represent the Health Department," he told us. We bought our rat clearance for a bribe of six dollars. Later we learned he was actually the doctor's son, impersonating his father or perhaps sent by his father, who was the official representative of the Health Department.

We sat and waited for other officials to come. It didn't take long. Two gentlemen, who also said they represented Customs and Immigration, showed up and asked for 5,000 pesos (about $134) for clearing our papers.

"We've already been boarded by Customs and Immigration," Bernard said.

They didn't seem surprised. It was obvious we weren't the first to be fleeced before entering the harbour. "Your documents from Hong Kong aren't in order," one of them said. They again asked for $134.

"No," Bernard said.

They quickly dropped their fee to twenty dollars, but Bernard still wasn't buying. "The health official only charged us six dollars," he countered.

The more ape-like of the two men claimed that Customs and Immigration was more important. He had an edge of violence about him, so we settled on twelve dollars. They insisted on having some spirits or cigarettes before leaving. When Bernard told them that the first party from Immigration and Customs had cleaned us out of everything, they became agitated. Bernard took out the one bottle of whisky he had managed to hide from our intruders. The men took turns drinking in gulps from the bottle until Bernard insisted on having a shot for himself. Once they had finished the whisky, they went through our lockers and drawers, and discovered for themselves that the cupboards were already bare. The men left with a can of mutton that had been left behind, and promised to bring our clearance papers the next day.

The last government official who said he was from Immigration and Customs was visibly annoyed that others fleeced us first. But he was polite and amiable and didn't open drawers and lockers. He asked for twenty dollars. We managed to negotiate the fee down to ten dollars. On leaving he asked us for cigarettes.

"For my driver," he said. "Or maybe some coffee." He didn't insist.

It was tricky navigating that fine line between not being completely taken while still giving enough to avoid repercussions. The government was trying to crack down on this type of thievery and wanted it reported, which we did — to the Port Authority. But I suspect not much was done. We were reporting to the very people who were involved in this activity.

Our next "welcome" came from the operator of a tricycle taxi. We needed pesos to restock our provisions. It was Sunday and the banks were closed.

"I'll take you to a market and get you a good exchange for your dollars," he said.

Bernard took out twenty dollars.

"One hundred would be better," he said.

Bernard smiled in reply. He took us to the market, parked his tricycle, asked for our umbrella as it was raining, and said he'd be back with our pesos. When he saw our hesitation, he told us he couldn't go far with our twenty dollars.

"You can trust me," he said. "My tricycle is with you."

He returned in tears and told us he had lost our twenty dollars down an open manhole while trying to close the umbrella.

"I'll take you to my home for the pesos." He cried all the way and kept repeating how poor he was. "I'll have to take the money from my mama's purse," he whimpered.

He entered a house that looked neither poor, nor rundown, and came out shortly after with less than half the value of the twenty dollars. "We'll go to the market to buy what you need, and then to my friend who'll lend me the rest."

Bernard asked him take us to the manhole where he claimed the money had fallen. He led us to the middle of a sheltered market where it was impossible for rain to fall.

"Why was the umbrella open in here?" Bernard asked.

The tricycle driver shrugged his shoulders, did a little more crying, and went in search of his friend who couldn't be found.

"I'm an honest man," he assured us. "I'll come seven-thirty, to-morrow morning, to give you the rest of your money." He asked for two dollars for gas as we'd taken every cent he had in the world.

Bernard gave him the two dollars. He felt the performance was worth the price. At least, this scoundrel provided some entertainment. As expected, at seven-thirty the next morning there was no tricycle taxi driver.

But we woke up to a beautiful sunrise and spotted another yacht anchored in the harbour carrying an American flag. Until now, we'd encountered only one other North American. We'd met a smattering of Europeans, an abundance of Australians, and one eccentric Kiwi; and although we were in the East, no Asians. Asians didn't do long range sailing. The sea is a fair-weather friend, and the Asians we met were a pragmatic bunch, not dreamers.

Captain Marshall and his girlfriend Dr. Payne, the couple on the other yacht, appeared to be somewhere in their forties and fit. They hadn't done much sailing, but Captain Marshall believed in technology. He trusted his satellite system and ham radio to fill in the gaps for his lack of knowledge.

"I don't know how to do the calculations," he told us. "I radio a friend who does them for me."

He was shocked to learn we had no satellite system and were sailing with only a sextant, depth sounder, log to measure speed, and a short wave radio. He was impressed that Bernard sailed by the stars, but didn't have faith in the infallibility of this system — man being liable to mistakes in judgement.

I, on the other hand, thought that, should any of Captain Marshall's equipment fail, he'd be dead in the water, the cliché seeming apt in this situation. I didn't understand why Dr. Payne would trust her life on the sea to a man who could read neither wind nor stars. But love makes us do funny things.

Bernard and I spent a day in San Fernando with Captain Marshall and Dr. Payne. Having been subject to so much corruption at the port, I expected to find a seedy, run-down hole. But aside from the beached battleship we saw on entering the harbour, there was no evidence of the scars of war or even that this was a military base. San Fernando, with its clean streets, middle class homes, and sprinkling of Victorian style mansions, was a pleasant, laid-back place.

Captain Marshall told us it had been raining for days, and the weather we had experienced on our sail from Hong Kong was the result of a typhoon to the north of us. We had managed to sail through before the low pressure system gathered enough energy to hit us directly.

Next morning, our yachts set sail for Manila Bay. We stayed close for radio contact, our VHF frequency limited to 40 miles. During the night a squall came up. We took down our sails and drifted, keeping an eye on the light from Captain Marshall's yacht in case he needed us. Soon after, Captain Marshall sent an SOS saying he was taking in water and didn't know what to do.

"There's water all over my floor below deck," he radioed.

"Where's it coming from?" Bernard asked.

"I don't know. I'll look."

After a short while he was back on the radio. "It's coming through the port hole in my head," he said.

"Shut it," Bernard said.

We waited for an up-date on the situation. It only took a minute or two. "Problem solved," he reported.

We weren't sure Captain Marshall would make it to Europe. But we knew that sometimes ignorance can work in your favour. In Hong Kong we'd been told of a woman sailing from Taiwan who got caught in a typhoon. She hadn't a clue what do, so she crawled under her salon table, rolled up into a ball, and didn't move. Two days later the sea was calm. She went on deck and beheld Hong Kong rising before her out of the sea. The yacht had taken itself into port.

Our sail from San Fernando to Manila Bay took two days. On the evening of the second day, we passed south of Corregidor, where so many American and Filipino soldiers lost their lives during the Second World War. Again I was reminded of a historical event that until that moment didn't mean much to me. I hadn't even known Corregidor was in the Philippines, and if I had, until I arrived I couldn't have placed the Philippines on the map.

Manila Bay was an appalling mess of disgusting pollution and general neglect. We ploughed our way through a cesspool of waste, oil slick, and discarded plastic bags before reaching the Manila Yacht Club. Had one of us fallen overboard, I'm sure we'd have dissolved in that toxic stew within minutes. I didn't know how the fish managed.

Marshall was full of surprises. He knew his way around the city far better than he knew his way around a sailboat. While serving in the army, he had been stationed in San Fernando and had spent off-duty time in Manila. We discovered he was quite good as a folk singer when he took us to a local bar and performed with a borrowed guitar from a musician he knew there. Before parting, he invited us to a fancy party in a hotel where a daughter of Fernando Marcos was a guest. It was his way of saying thank you to us for looking after him during our joint sail.

Soon after leaving Hong Kong, Bernard felt an unwelcome vibration coming from somewhere on the *Santa Rita*. Once moored at the yacht club, he set to work finding the problem and finally declared: "It's the shaft." He hired a Filipino fisherman to dive under the boat to remove the shaft while he stayed below deck to plug the hole as soon as the shaft came out. With shaft in hand, we hired a donkey and cart to take us to an area in Manila where we'd find a machine shop. The ride in the donkey cart was a visceral and unforgettable experience.

We passed gangs of street children abandoned by families who couldn't feed them. I was told older boys often acted as parent figures and looked after the younger ones. They wandered the city in small packs and slept huddled together in rubbish-strewn alleyways or along the polluted waterfront. These street kids formed makeshift families for survival. I wondered what happened to them when they grew up — if they grew up. We passed beefy, big-bellied middle-aged Western men with slim, under-aged girls, maybe as young as thirteen on their arms. I later saw them in bars and restaurants when we walked about the city. These young girls were either thrown into the street or sold by their families.

While in Manila, I took local buses known as jeepneys to explore the city. These eccentric-looking buses were originally constructed from surplus jeeps left behind by the U.S. military after the Second World War. Enterprising Filipinos stripped them, extended their length, and decorated them in brilliant colours, turning the discarded vehicles into works of art on wheels. One of my bus stops was Makati, the upmarket sector of the city with its clean streets and elegant shops. This area, crammed with towering skyscrapers, art museums, and luxurious houses in gated communities, was the business and financial district of the city. It was a shocking contrast to the scrap metal and rubbish shanties that housed the majority of the city's people. Every bank had a heavily armed guard at the door. The Philippines was not a relaxed place under the Marcos regime.

Back at the yacht club we had a visit from a yachtie we'd met in Taipei. He'd sailed out from Taiwan before us, was now anchored in Puerto Galera, and suggested we go there for our next port of call. "A protected bay and beautiful," he said. And then he asked: "Meet any pirates on the way down?"

Pirates! It never occurred to me that we would encounter pirates. Until that moment pirates for me were guys in filthy shorts with rags on their heads brandishing sabres. And suddenly I woke up. "Yes, we did encounter pirates. They boarded us just as we were about to enter San Fernando!"

"They're hard to catch," he said. "They keep crossing the line. When the fishing is good, they're fishermen. When it's bad, they look for other fish."

He went on to inform us that in the north they're Christian. They steal but they let you live. Once you reach Mindanao, you're in Muslim waters. There you're seen as infidels and have very little chance of surviving.

I wondered, as he talked, if we should go back the way we came, but I was determined to continue this journey.

"Lots of guerrilla fighting in Mindanao," he said. "The weapons come in from Indonesia, and the guerrillas are well armed. They've been fighting a religious war against the Philippine government for years."

It was a dangerous area, but if we wanted to continue on our route, we'd have to take the Palawan Passage, which meant sailing past Mindanao. He suggested we get some weapons to protect ourselves.

"See Father Brown," he said. "He deals in arms and gold." He went on to tell us that Father Brown was a church unto himself with a fairly large congregation. His parents had been missionaries and were killed in China during the Boxer Revolution. He was going to make sure this didn't happen to him or his flock. For years, he had been gathering weapons and hoarding food while he waited for the revolution he was sure would happen. On that day he would leave his bunker style accommodations and lead his people to a secret hideaway in the mountains where they would be out of harm's way.

Enlightened by our sailing buddy, we decided to pay a visit to Father Brown. We arrived at an unremarkable whitewashed cinderblock house, hidden behind dwarf, bushy-topped palm trees, situated in one of Manila's middle class neighbourhoods. Six Dobermans, salivating and pulling at their chains, lined a narrow pathway. Nearby was a bitch in heat that the males couldn't reach. To this day, I can't pass a Doberman without remembering that scene and feeling a slight chill.

At the front door a burly henchman led us inside. We were in an empty grey hallway composed of heavy steel and cement. Suddenly a huge slab of concrete slid to the side to reveal a large room with a man sitting at a desk at the far end. I assumed this was Father Brown.

"Enter," he said.

We walked through the opening in the wall.

"Stop and state your business."

We explained to him that we had sailed from Hong Kong, were travelling south, and needed weapons to fight off pirates.

He eyed us for a moment before getting up from his seat, and then strode over to greet us. He was a short, stocky man, strongly built. I was sure he'd had his hand in a drawer on a gun when he first saw us enter because he shut the drawer before he stood up to greet us. After asking us a few questions about our sail from Hong Kong, he offered to show us around his bunker. We were first taken to his store of food — endless containers of provisions preserved in a special gas. He told us that, because of the way it was stored, it could last for ten years and was enough to feed 10,000. He then showed us his arsenal of weapons and asked us to choose. We were at a loss as to what to pick.

"Why don't you start with Molotov cocktails?" he suggested, and spent some time showing us how they're made. I couldn't wait to get out of there and off his property.

After the demonstration, he showed us several models of sling shots from which the Molotov cocktails could be hurled. He recommended a stainless steel number that gripped tightly around the wrist. "Try it on and see how it feels," he said.

It felt like a prosthesis. I hated it. "Very nice," I said.

We exchanged some of our gold bullion for local currency and told Father Brown we'd have to think about what we might need.

Neither of us had ever used a weapon, nor had we a desire to. In any port we entered, Customs would confiscate our arms. They would be returned when we left, but we didn't want the bureaucratic hassle. Most of all, we felt that, should we be attacked, any attempt to fight off pirates would be an excuse for them to retaliate. They had bazookas and Kalashnikovs picked up in the Thai markets, originals and clones from the Viet Nam War. They also knew how to shoot. We didn't.

In the end we worked out a strategy. The yacht had both engine and sail. The pirate boats had small outboard engines. We were always on two-hour watches, so why couldn't we keep an eye out for a suspicious boat coming in our direction and turn the other way? We had a big engine and plenty of fuel. They'd have to eventually turn back for lack of fuel, and we could always come back by sail.

We now had to figure out what to do with Father Brown. We'd already used a good deal of his time, and he wasn't someone you wanted to annoy. We decided to tell him we'd settle for making Molotov Cocktails and would buy two slingshots. In spite of our nervousness, all went well. We explained about not wanting to declare weapons. We exchanged a bit more gold for dollars, and he seemed satisfied with the trade.

One last bit of business remained to be done before we left Manila. I couldn't control the sadness I felt about Jonah leaving for Middlebury College in Vermont. The four-mile cab ride with him to Manila's International Airport took less than ten minutes. I wanted the ride to last longer. I wasn't ready to let go of my son. He had wanted to go to Harvard, but I didn't let him apply. Knowing he'd be on his own, I wanted him in a smaller, more personal school. We'd had some words over this. I hoped he'd be happy at Middlebury.

After Jonah left, Bernard and I discussed sailing to Puerto Galera, on the nearby island of Mindoro, but I wasn't ready to leave. I wanted to see more of Luzon.

"Let's visit Baguio," I suggested. I had heard about the healers of Baguio, the psychic doctors who used faith to heal and did surgery without medication or physical invasion. Baguio was in the northern part of Luzon, and I thought it would be interesting to check it out.

"It's only seven hours by bus, and we're already on the island. We'll never pass this way again."

"Who'll watch the boat?" Bernard asked.

"Stefan," I said. "He'd like the responsibility, and it will give him some time on his own. It's only for the day. We'll leave early and take the night bus back."

Bernard appeared annoyed. "Why don't you go with Stefan? I have things to do here."

"This is supposed to be our adventure. Remember?"

His lack of interest in anything but the yacht frustrated me. I remembered a man who loved new experiences. Now his whole world had shrunk to our forty-five foot home.

"Would you like to see Baguio?" I asked Stefan.

"Sure," he said. "Not much happening here."

The two of us took an early bus to Baguio the next morning. I had already discovered that the Philippines was far richer in history and diversity than I could have ever imagined, but it hadn't prepared me for what I witnessed on our bus ride. I had done no reading about the country, and knew about the faith healers only because of a documentary I'd seen on TV. I thought the bus ride to Baguio would be nothing more than a necessary inconvenience to our destination. I'd never heard of the rice terraces of Banaue. And even if I had, I couldn't have imagined the awesome sight that opened before us as we climbed higher into the Cordillera Mountains.

For hours we travelled a mountainous road that took us through endless miles of carved steps flowing up the mountains in evenly spaced rows that climbed so high into the sky they felt like stairs to heaven. The Cordillera Mountains rose 8,000 feet, and each foot was manicured to a fine precision. Shadows on the terraces shifted the velvet green mountain ranges from emerald to hunter green giving the surface a luxurious texture.

I imagined this grand tableau to be the brain child of a brilliant sculptor who had conceived his masterpiece for the pleasure and spiritual enlightenment of the viewer. But in reality, this extraordinary feat of engineering was accomplished around 2,000 years ago by the Ifugao people who still tended the rice fields on these terraces with the same care as their ancestors had so many generations before. In recent years the terraces have started to deteriorate, but I'm grateful to have had the chance to see them intact.

Baguio, a pleasant city of flowers and evergreen trees, seemed flat after our spellbinding trip through the Cordillera Mountains. The sight of the rice terraces was so spiritually uplifting that I lost all interest in the healers of Baguio. I needed time and distance to process what I had just seen. Sometimes on our way somewhere we discover a totally different reason than imagined for the path taken. It's happened to me many times, and has led to unexpected epiphanies in my perception of the world.

Stefan and I wandered about the city, and passed a number of houses advertising faith healing, but I had no desire to visit them. I wasn't ill, so what would have been the purpose?

I felt at loose ends having lost my original intent and wondered what to do next.

"How about the marketplace," Stefan suggested. He was thinking food, but once we entered the downtown area, we found ourselves amidst cultures that neither of us could have imagined. Aside from the Ifugao, the Bontoc, Kalinga, Tinguian, and Ibaloi people also made their home in the Cordillera Mountains, and many of them were splendid craftsmen. They dyed and wove their own cloth for clothing, and their basketry was exquisite. Stefan enjoyed the hand carved utensils and small pieces of sculpture. I bought several hand dyed cloth woven by the Ifugao people as a keepsake of the rice terraces of Banuae.

One of them adorns the back of my couch. When anyone comments on the vibrant colours in the fabric, I relive that moment when I first saw the majestic terraces, now a UNESCO protected site, but crumbling from neglect. One day this eighth wonder of the world will be nothing but rubble, and even the memory of its existence will disappear. I treasure my cloth and think what a privilege it was to have been there.

A few of the older men milling around the market were heavily tattooed. When I asked about them, I was told that they were most likely Kalinga, a people who lived to the north of Baguio. Until early in the twentieth century, when the practice was outlawed, it was their custom, as well as that of several other northern tribes, to cut off the heads of their enemies. Every head cut was rewarded with a tattoo, and every man desired as many as possible. Tattoos represented status and courage, and an easier time finding a wife.

The ritual had a revival during the Second World War. The Kalinga were fierce warriors, who fought on the side of the Americans, and were valued both for their bravery and knowledge of their terrain. For every Japanese soldier killed by a Kalinga tribesman, a tattoo was etched into the warrior's skin. The Japanese knew about their wilderness skills and head hunting past, and feared them. The old men I saw in the marketplace were veterans from the Second World War.

For a long time, Filipino men were ashamed of this part of their history, but pride in heritage is growing. And in parts of North America some men of Filipino descent are asking to be tattooed in the multiple designs of their forefathers.

Another surprise the marketplace held was the abundance of fresh produce overflowing the stalls. It was in sharp contrast to the meagre selection of produce I had seen in Manila. Baguio's outdoor market was awash with every imaginable kind of fresh produce. It was hard to understand how there could be so little available only hours away in a country as fertile as the Philippines. I later learned that, under the corrupt government of Ferdinand Marcos, a proper infrastructure for moving goods from one part of the country to another had never been established. Walking in the cool mountain air of Baguio with its clean streets, stately pines, and well-tended flower gardens felt like I was in a different country.

Exhausted but content, Stefan and I took a late evening bus back to Manila, and a taxi to the yacht club. A day after we rested up, the three of us said goodbye to the island of Luzon and set sail for Puerto Galera, leaving behind Manila with its sordid sex trade, bands of street kids, and gated, fortified wealth.

Chapter 13

IN NATURE'S OWN CATHEDRAL

The Philippines

> *I long to embrace, to include in my short life, all that is accessible to man. I long to speak, to read, to wield a hammer in a great factory, to keep watch at sea, to plow. I want to be ... in open fields, or on the ocean ... wherever my imagination ranges.*
> — ANTON CHEKHOV

Sailing into Puerto Galera, the sea, unsullied and transparent blue, lapped against a pristine white beach that led to lush, dark green mountains behind. It was my first inkling that the Philippines was a diamond in the rough waiting to be polished for the world market. Years later, when Puerto Galera was singled out as one of the most beautiful bays in the world, I wasn't surprised. I felt lucky that I was there when the area still had its primordial glow unmarred by hotels, night clubs, and the creeping sex trade.

I had envisioned the Philippines as a few undeveloped islands, and thought our visit would be a stop-over en route to more interesting destinations. Instead, I found myself in a fascinating country made up of thousands of islands stretched-out along the China Sea. Many, like Mindoro, had wide beaches with fine, silky sand and rugged mountains dense with tropical vegetation. Others in the north had rocky shores and green rolling hills. Each island, different from its neighbour, reflected a wide diversity of cultures, languages, and religions. Some anthropologists believed there were even unexplored islands where people lived in the Stone Age.

Five or six Taiwanese-built yachts were already in the bay when we arrived. When not doing repairs on the *Santa Rita*, Bernard helped the less mechanical boat owners. He offered his services and stayed for drinks. The arrangement was all about good will and bonding sealed over bottles of local beer, but I resented that he never charged for his work. We had some gold and savings, but they would eventually run out, and his uncanny knack for fixing just about anything was a skill that could keep us afloat.

"Why don't you charge?" I asked repeatedly.

He'd shrug offhandedly as he always did when he didn't want to answer.

Finally, when I'd badgered him once too often he shouted: "You don't charge friends."

"Why are they friends?" I shouted back.

"It's too bad you don't like this kind of life," he replied.

I stopped asking. I saw no point in escalating tension, and he was partially right. I loved sailing, but not the social life. Hours of technical conversations buoyed by limitless booze bored me.

As I had done in Hong Kong, I wandered off on my own, and spent days exploring the bay, astonished by the variety of sea life. The coral reefs surrounding the island were like a gargantuan aquarium. Among its inhabitants were small fish shaped like boxes that must have carried curious scaffolding beneath their skins, schools of tiny squid that glowed florescent in the night and colourful angel and clown fish that I'd only seen in residential fish tanks. I witnessed fishermen making and eating brochettes of these little critters, their scintillating colours turning rust brown in the fire. It saddened me to see their beauty defiled, but for the locals, these fish were not exotic creatures but every day fare — and perhaps a treat. Their diet, and ours while we were there, consisted of rice, fish, coconuts and an occasional bit of tough chicken.

For anything more substantial, we'd have to go to Makati, the swanky, protected enclave in the centre of Manila, or be near farm land. As I had seen in Baguio, the country had fertile farm land, but no infra-structure to carry produce from one place to another. Without a developed tourism industry and no infrastructure in place for moving goods, the Filipino people had little opportunity for a more varied diet or a better life. The few outsiders I saw consisted of the middle-aged Western men I'd seen in Manila, their big bellies protruding over Bermuda shorts, strolling the beachfront with their young girlfriends, or the well-travelled recluse who'd found a small piece of paradise and had settled discreetly into the landscape.

Sometimes Bernard, Stefan and I explored the area together, and we always had a good time. The Filipinos were a friendly people with a gracious manner. Everywhere we went, the inhabitants made us feel welcome. I couldn't pass a person on the road without being greeted by a warm smile. "Hi Joe," they'd say. All westerners were "Joe," a holdover from the Second World War. On weekends, we looked forward to seeing the transvestite who motored to shore on her *bangka*, probably coming from the nearby island of Luzon, to visit family or a lover. We never knew. No one asked. But we agreed she was quite beautiful.

I fell in love with the Filipino people who were so welcoming, and dreamed of living among them in a bamboo house overlooking the sea. I saw myself picking mangoes in my back yard and setting them in a bowl on the terrace that faced out across the bay. A handful of westerners had built homes on the island. I could see one of those elegant homes from the deck of the *Santa Rita* and was told an Italian lived there by himself. I visualized visiting him and even thought about asking for the name of his workmen. Today, I don't understand why I didn't. He will never know how his house, just off the beach built into a hill of flowering trees and tropical brush, had enthralled me. Sometimes before I fall asleep, I imagine myself in one of his split bamboo rooms inhaling the sweet aroma of the freshly thatched roof while a night breeze plays about my face.

We did get to visit one ex-pat home. A Frenchman in the gas business had built a house near the beach in another bay, and invited Bernard and me for lunch. Our visit was cut short when Bernard noticed angry waves building in the bay and felt a squall was on the way. We made a dash to the *Santa Rita,* but not before the gentleman handed Bernard a pair of long pants since the temperature had suddenly dropped—a soft cotton pair that Bernard still has. Thinking back, it's hard to say if I wanted one of those homes because they were so aesthetically pleasing or because I was aware of how fraught with danger our adventure could become. I knew we would soon be leaving the island of Mindoro and sailing into more hostile territory.

When we lifted anchor in Puerto Galera for the next leg of our adventure, I wasn't ready to go. I wanted to explore more, but with a backpack by ferry, or in one of those *bangkas* that motored around the islands. You can't rush experience, and I hoped to come back one day.

Our plan was to make a brief stopover in Palawan, the last cluster of islands before leaving the Philippines, and then sail straight to Singapore. We didn't want to spend time in the China Sea knowing that the further south we went, the closer we'd be to Mindanao, an island plagued with civil unrest and endless guerrilla warfare, as well as pirates reputed to pillage and kill. We had our sling shots from Father Brown but knew we'd never lob Molotov cocktails, and we hadn't yet tested our strategy for pirate evasion. Bernard's idea was to stay away from the Sulu Sea, an area that would trap us should we be chased, and keep along the western edge of the islands that gave on to the China Sea.

A day and a half after leaving Puerto Galera a typhoon hit. It pummelled the bay and destroyed boats, driving them onto the shore where they broke apart or were badly damaged. We had by then sailed outside the typhoon zone. It was only when the threat no longer existed that I realised how tense I'd been. This penchant for denial in the throes of danger pulled me through many hair-raising experiences at sea. When we were sailing, I focused on what needed to be done, and didn't sense my fear until the danger had passed.

When we neared Busuanga, part of a small group of islands before Palawan, the sea flattened, and a disquieting stillness settled in. Night had fallen, so we decided to drop anchor among the islands and continue our sail at daybreak. About two o'clock in the morning, the wind picked up and carried with it what sounded like the earth moaning. The low, eerie wailing felt as if displaced souls were moving through the boat. I lay frozen in my berth, listening to the mournful cries.

In the morning, we were startled to find ourselves on a dark sea surrounded by towering rock shapes, some several stories high. The sun had just risen over the horizon and cast a red glow over black, karst formations that rose from the seabed. The monumental structures, eroded by eons of sea waves washing over and through them, looked like enormous sculptures carved by giants. A number of these sculptural forms had holes carved through them and looked like work done by the sculptor Henry Moore. A slight wind blew through the holes. It explained the wild moans and wailing we'd heard in the night, as these awesome figures sang their heartbreaking songs. The unexpected other-worldly appearance of the landscape shocked and seduced us. We felt dwarfed by the size of the formations and awed by the energy they emitted.

The *Santa Rita* drifted like a minuscule space ship among these majestic shapes, and I wondered if we had slipped through a portal to a parallel world. As the sun rose, the dark sea turned a brilliant emerald green, but the multitude of massive shapes rising up from the sea floor continued to convey a timeless dimension to the surroundings.

Later I learned these formations, made of quartz-rich sandstone and limestone, sat on marble schist at the bottom of the sea, and were formed during the Permian Age about 300 million years ago. That was long before the coming of the dinosaur, and perhaps when we were only one-celled life forms. It made me think how late we were as arrivals on this planet.

Bernard, Stefan and I motored through this mystical plane of other worldly delight until we came upon an azure-coloured, crystalline lagoon whose seabed must have been an underwater mountain. The sea surrounding the lagoon was so deep that our anchor had nowhere to grab, but the floor of the lagoon couldn't have been more than two or three feet deep. Within its borders, swam tiny tropical fish in every imaginable colour or combination of colours. Some were shaped like tiny triangles, others like empty tubes, and still others like the small square boxes I'd seen in Puerto Galera. Some sported dots, others were striped, making me think of tiny circus performers scurrying about before the start of the show.

The water was calm, so we were able to turn the yacht to stop her from moving, and then we scrambled over the side to walk among the fish.

"It feels like I'm walking inside a giant fish tank," Stefan said.

"I feel like I'm walking in space," I answered. Wherever I looked there was nothing but sea, and here I was standing in the middle of it, in the middle of nowhere, as though I were standing on the water, which gave the sensation I was floating a small distance above.

Bernard splashed around dispersing the fish and trying to see if he could catch a few in his hands — a futile task but fun for all of us.

Towards evening we set sail for El Nido, a small village on the northwestern coast of the main island of Palawan. We passed immense cliffs, the lower part etched out by the sea, which made it possible to sail beneath the stone overhangs. As we neared El Nido, we saw niches in the cliff walls, that told us some kind of bird must make its home here. When we entered the town, we were greeted by Fernando, a small businessman with bungalows for rent on the beach. He spoke English and took an interest in telling us about his village. We asked him about the niches.

He explained to us that a small swallow-like bird called a Swiftlet makes its nest there, and that it was because of the birds that the town got its name, which means The Nest in Spanish.

"We gather the nests," he said, "for export to Hong Kong. They're sold there for bird's nest soup. Collecting them is dangerous, but the high price that the Chinese pay makes it worth the risk. If you take me on your yacht, I will show you where and how the nests are gathered."

We knew he wanted to visit the *Santa Rita,* and we were just as anxious to see where the nest gatherers worked.

"It's a deal," Bernard said.

"Can I steer?"

Bernard handed Fernando the helm, and our small party, including one of Fernando's friends, set out for cliffs. We travelled a short distance, and then took the dinghy to shore where, during the gathering season, men scaled these sheer, limestone cliffs to gather the nests. Two hundred feet in the air, rope ladders hung limp with only thin bamboo scaffolding underneath. That was all there was to keep the workers from falling to their deaths. I was happy we were there out of season and didn't have to watch the process. Bird nests at the time brought $3,000 a kilo in Hong Kong, and in a poor country, I could understand the incentive — though it was hard for me to believe any-one would pay that much for a package of bird spit.

I was overwhelmed by the loftiness of the cliffs. Along with the karst formations we sailed through near Busuanga, the whole region called to mind graveyard stones scattered about a timeless cathedral — nature's own cathedral carved from the planet's bones and left be-hind before man ever arrived, a reminder of our ever-changing, never-changing universe, here long before we came and here long after we'll be gone.

We stumbled into this part of the world in 1982, and benefited from its lack of a tourist market. Today high-speed *bangkas* zip through prescribed routes to show off the region's unique landscape, followed by daily scuba diving, beach barbecues, socializing and shop-ping. There's no down time to take in the timelessness of the land-scape because that would take time.

Photos of the area fall flat. The camera can't capture the grandeur of the space; nor the feeling of being suspended in time because of the region's mating of stone and water in such a way that it evokes the sacred where life is ceaseless and death, an illusion. The area awakened in me the spiritual, and that has to be experienced, not viewed through a lens.

Our next port of call was Ulugan Bay situated about a third of the way down the west coast of Palawan Island. Within the bay was a narrow island about a mile and a half long called Rita. Bernard found it while studying one of the sea charts.

"What do think about visiting?" he asked Stefan and me.

"Sure," Stefan said because he was always open to a new adventure.

"Absolutely," I said because I was impressed that there was an island carrying my name.

Before we had even anchored, the inhabitants of Rita Island were lined up on shore to greet us. Rita was too small to be of interest to pass-ing yachts, and there was no tourism, so visitors were a rare occurrence and an occasion for celebration. The local people plied us with food from their meagre stores but refused payment. They felt honoured to have guests, and we felt as honoured to be treated like visiting dignitaries. We left the island in high spirits, and dropped anchor near a mangrove-dense inlet in the bay that opened into a river.

"Let's take the dinghy up that river in the morning," Bernard proposed.

"Great idea," I said. Stefan and I exchanged pleased looks.

Bernard was back.

I wondered at the return of Bernard's adventurous spirit. This was the man I used to know. He'd come alive when we were sailing. But if we anchored somewhere for more than a day or two, he'd lose interest in the outside world and focus all his energy on the yacht, or on new drinking buddies if another yacht happened to be nearby. He'd barely talk to Stefan or me, and seemed not to notice if we were even there. I hadn't yet associated alcohol with his shifts in behaviour. Every time he showed enthusiasm for our adventure, I believed he'd finally come out of his shell, and we'd be connected as we had once been.

The next morning, after we'd had our cups of coffee and some jam with a few slices of pan fried toast, I threw a box of shrimp crackers, a bunch of bananas and a big plastic bottle of water into a bag. I was ready to go. Bernard grabbed his camera, and the three of us jumped into the dinghy for our trip up the estuary and into the jungle.

The river was about twenty feet across, but so many mangrove trees crowded the banks that the massive tangle of roots snaked out into the water, leaving about six feet or less on each side of the dinghy. Behind the mangroves, the vegetation was dense, luminous green in places where the sun penetrated and dark, emerald green where the higher mountain area was exposed to the sun. Near us, the surrounding area was greyed by shadowed light filtering through trees.

Bamboo houses on stilts dotted the banks. Each house was anchored in water and had a small boat tied to it. The structures weren't close together. Mangrove and banyan trees separated one from the other. These were the homes of the Tagbanua people, indigenous to the area, and fishing families for the most part, who traded fish for produce or rice grown farther inland. The people smiled at us as we passed or watched us with mild curiosity. There was no feeling that we had invaded their private domain, though in fact, we had.

Strung along the banks, taking up whatever space the jungle left, were families of monkeys that had come to the river edge to feast. They sat stoically and stared at us as we passed, and we stared back just as intrigued. Some trees held hornbill families — white tailed black birds with large, bizarre-shaped beaks — that squawked raucously. There was a flock of blue and green coloured parrots that took flight overhead, also with unmelodious voices.

Stefan's eyes were everywhere, and I knew he was taking in the scene in his typical laid-back fashion. I wondered if he'd remember this trip in years to come, and how it would affect his perception of life. Bernard had his camera out and was taking photos. He was totally engaged. I had no interest in taking photos. I didn't want to separate myself from the experience. The magic of it and the accord between the three of us was something that I wanted to imprint in my brain and remember forever. I was looking for immersion. Bernard wanted a record. Today I appreciate his having taken the photos. Looking through them now gives a shape to the memories and triggers forgotten details that I thought I'd never forget. We followed the river until mangrove roots impeded our going farther and forced us to turn back.

We'd have spent more time in Palawan, but guerrilla fighting between religious factions on Mindanao Island to the East and pirate activity in the direction we were heading prompted us to want to pass through the area as quickly as possible. We had to sail through the Balabac Strait, once a part of the old spice and silk route, and pirating was a traditional way of life going back more than 1500 years. Fernando, the small business entrepreneur we had met in El Nido, warned us that pirates had knocked out the lights along the Balabac Strait. "The Coast Guard," he said, "are afraid to repair them. And even if they did, they'd be knocked out again."

It was hard to say if this was the real reason the lights had not been repaired or whether the reason was that part of the Coast Guard may have been working with the pirates since locals slipped easily from being fishermen one day to pirates the next. The fact that pirates often played other roles in society was one of the reasons it was difficult to eradicate them.

The Balabac Strait was an opening between islands that connected the China Sea to the Sulu Sea, so the pirates of Mindanao had easy passage from their island through the Balabac Strait into the China Sea. We were anxious to get past that area, naively thinking that, once we passed the Balabac Strait and made it to Borneo, our worry about pirates would be behind us.

Chapter 14

FROM BORNEO TO SINGAPORE

Winter 1982

> *If you reject food, ignore customs, fear the religion*
> *and avoid people, you might better stay at home.*
> —JAMES MICHENER

Relieved at having made it through the Balabac Strait in little more than two days without any pirate sightings, we relaxed into whatever adventures lay ahead. Our nearest landfall was Kota Kinabalu, the capital of Sabah in the Malaysian sector of Borneo. Before looking it up in an atlas, we had no idea the island was divided into three countries—Malaysia, Indonesia, and the Sultanate of Brunei, squeezed between the other two.

"I've heard of Kota Kinabalu," I told Bernard, "but I didn't know where it was. The name has a nice alliteration, and is probably why it got stuck in my mind."

Bernard, poring over a sea chart in search of some good anchorage, looked up. "It was called Jesselton when the British were there. Kota Kinabalu definitely sounds better."

"I'm going see if there's any poetry related to it." I looked through some tourist information on Southeast Asia, but found no reference to poetry. However, I did discover what the name might mean. "Revered place of the dead," I said. "There's something poetic in that."

"Or maybe it's a place we shouldn't hang around too long."

I laughed at his response, but in fact, we didn't stay long. Aside from some dense mangrove forests, many of which we'd already seen in Palawan, and jungle trekking that would mean leaving the *Santa Rita* unattended, there wasn't enough there to hold our interest. After a good night's sleep, we lifted anchor and sailed down to Labuan, a small island about eight miles off the Borneo coast. The idea was to have some quiet time before tackling a new country and a new culture. We pictured Borneo as an exotic mix of landscapes and people, and we wanted to relax a bit before taking it in.

About two o'clock in the morning, we awoke to Stefan's shouts. Bernard sprang off the berth and ran to the salon. In the split second that it took him to get there, Stefan was already out the hatch and on deck. Bernard darted up the steps after him.

"I was asleep," Stefan told him, "but left my cabin door open so I could get some fresh air. And then I heard some rustling. I came out as soon as I heard the noise and saw this guy take off through the hatch. I was right behind him. But when I got on deck, there was no one there."

Bernard turned on our searchlight to see if there was a boat nearby, but nothing was out there. The water was dead black and unruffled. I had a creepy feeling that the person might still be aboard. We searched everywhere, but the intruder had vanished like an act in a magic show. I questioned whether he might have swum under the yacht and would reappear when we were sleeping.

"What if he has a weapon?" I asked. "He could have a machete."

Bernard shook his head. "He's gone," he said.

"How?" I asked. "He's not a phantom."

We kept watch for the rest of the night — just in case he was somewhere near.

The next morning we discovered that Bernard's camera and all his lenses were gone, as well as a small bag that he kept on the chart table that contained odds and ends. The chart table was next to the companionway leading up to the hatch, so the thief didn't get far into the boat. He would certainly have taken more if Stefan hadn't called out. On deck, Bernard noticed that our oars were missing.

"He didn't use his engine," he said. "He rowed away. That's why we didn't hear anything."

"How could he go that fast?" I asked.

It was still a mystery to me that there was no sound of an engine and yet, within seconds, the thief disappeared.

102

Bernard and I took the dinghy to *Bandar* Labuan (Labuan Town) to report the theft, and were surprised to find ourselves in a spotless, modern city of high rise buildings that housed a multitude of banks, insurance companies and trust companies — all surrounded by well-manicured greenery. In contrast to the rural landscapes we had been experiencing until now, it was obvious a lot of money flowed through this town. I knew Brunei was rich because of oil, but Labuan was in Malaysia, and I wondered what brought so many financial institutions here. We stayed only long enough to talk to the police, who told us there was nothing they could do, or would do.

When we left the police station, Bernard told me that he had heard on our VHF radio, while we were still in the Philippines, that two weeks earlier another yacht had been robbed on the same spot where we were anchored. "It never occurred to me it could happen twice in the same place," he said. "I should have locked the hatch."

"Do you know what they took?"

"A camera and sextant."

"Maybe it was a pirate," I said. "It couldn't have been a regular fisherman. They don't go out far enough to need a sextant."

Bernard didn't answer. He never speculated. Either he knew something for sure or he didn't know.

In spite of the robbery, we didn't want to leave without visiting the Sultanate of Brunei. Slowly making our way through a herd of gigantic oil tankers berthed just outside the port, we entered Brunei's quiet harbour. Stefan placed fenders outside the yacht's hull while I threw a rope to Bernard who had jumped ashore to tie us to the port's cement pier. With parking done, we scrambled ashore to see what the region had to offer. The idea that we were about to enter a Sultanate conjured up images of arched windows, succulent bowls of fruit, and languid concubines reclining on brilliantly coloured brocaded pillows — romantic images I remembered from paintings I'd seen by Benjamin Constant.

The visit killed any romanticism I had about a Sultanate. Brunei was afloat in oil and timber money, but the Sultan invested his immense wealth in odd pieces of street sculpture and chubby high rise buildings — the squat look stemming from the fact that buildings were

RITA POMADE

not allowed higher than the mosque. Aside from its spacious, scrubbed
clean streets, Brunei looked like a vacant, western city. The exception
was the imposing and extravagant Sultan OmarAli Saifuddin Mosque
crowned by a gold dome that dominated the cityscape. A number of
multinational companies were housed in the low, high rise buildings,
but there was no pulse of life on the street.

Of more interest was a village near the mosque built on stilts over
the water. Wooden walkways connected a hodgepodge of buildings — some shabby, some upscale with modern appliances. But from
a distance, all of it looked look like a floating shantytown. Behind
Brunei was a dense jungle that seemed impenetrable. The city bore no
relation to the jungle behind, and gave the impression we were trapped
inside a life-size architect's model. It was hard not to think that at any
moment the present mock-up would be whisked away and replaced
with another. This was our first contact with a Muslim society, and I
would have liked to have experienced more of the culture. But the
people were distant and the setting didn't feel authentic.

That night we were awakened by loud scraping sounds against the
hull. It meant our fenders were no longer protecting the yacht. Once
again we flew out of the berths with our hearts racing. I was the last
one on deck.

"What happened?" I shouted.

"The tide's going down," Bernard answered. "There's a powerful
current coming from the river, and it's pulling the boat down. We're
starting to go under the pier. It's going to slice off the top of the yacht
like a can opener if I don't get us out fast."

He raced behind the helm and started the engine in order to man-
oeuvre the *Santa Rita* into a position from where we could move out.
Stefan grabbed the boat hook and was at the bow of the yacht using
it to push with all his strength against the pier. A small cargo ship
anchored perpendicular to us impeded our escape. It was a harrowing
race against time trying to move away from the pier before going
under without slamming into the other boat's steel hull. With deft
manoeuvring on Bernard's part, and Stefan's strength in holding the
pier at bay, we managed to slip past the cargo ship.

Earlier, we'd discussed visiting Kalimantan on the Indonesian

104

side of the island. We were told it was difficult to get clearance, but we were going to try anyway — maybe even sneak in. "It'd be interesting," I'd said. "The tourist book says that this rain forest is older than the Amazon, and we may even get to see some orangutans."

But after the low tide incident where we almost lost the yacht, coupled with the robbery, and our ongoing preoccupation with pirates, we'd had enough stress for a while. Dealing with local government officials was an unknown we didn't feel like tackling.

"Let's forget Kalimantan and head straight for Singapore," Bernard suggested.

Stefan and I agreed. We all wanted a safer haven for a while. The incidents of the last few days had dampened our spirits.

After five days of good sailing under a favourable wind, we passed through the Singapore Strait, dropped anchor in Changi on the eastern coast of the island, and headed over to Keppel Harbour to get our papers cleared. For months, our ports of call had been in relatively unknown, isolated places. Singapore was at the time the world's biggest port. The frenetic activity around us felt like we'd been tossed into a film that was revved to fast-forward. I wanted to get behind the movie projector so I could slow down the reel.

Tankers and cargo ships moved non-stop in and out of the harbour, while double-masted Bugis Phinisi ships with their graceful bodies and towering square-rigged sails glided between them. The Bugis were mesmerizing. I had never seen such beautifully handcrafted boats before. Many of these Indonesian vessels, built by the Bugis people of Sulawesi, constructed in the same manner they had been for centuries, still sailed without engines. I was later told by a fellow yachtie, anchored near us in Changi, that the Indonesians were superb sailors. Some sailed as far away as Australia without the backup of an engine. When they weren't plying their wares in distant places, they indulged in smuggling contraband closer at home.

The Bugis, always a sea-faring people, had a reputation for living outside the law. Fear of the "boogeyman" comes from when Bugis pirates plagued Dutch and English trading ships in the 18th century. Sailors returning to Europe told stories about the fierce Bugis that threatened their ships. It was amazing to see these ships with their swashbuckling history still being sailed. The tankers in the harbour looked like clumsy monsters next to these elegantly carved wooden vessels.

Another yachtie in Changi, after hearing where we'd come from, related a story that took away any misgivings I had about not staying longer in Borneo.

"There was this Norwegian fellow who's just sailed out," he said. "He came by way of Borneo, too. Told me his wife was coming out the hatch when a pirate shot her, blew her right off the boat into the water."

"Did she live?" I asked.

He looked at me as though I was crazy. "She was gone."

"Oh," I said.

"He had a small kid with him," he went on. "But I don't know the real story. Maybe he killed her and threw her overboard. He kept pressing his fingers into the kid's shoulder while he told me what happened. Maybe he wanted the kid not to say anything."

"Or maybe it was a nervous thing due to living through that trauma," I said.

The yachtie telling the story just stared at me. He wasn't buying my version of the shoulder kneading. I wondered if he knew what trauma was. He told the story in such a matter of fact way.

When a dragon boat paddle that Bernard had found in Hong Kong was stolen from the dinghy, we decided it was time to leave Changi. We motored to Jurong, a harbour further along Singapore's coast with easier access to the centre of the city. Jurong Harbour wasn't a commercial port back then, and exactly what we wanted.

"I can't believe it," I exclaimed as Jurong's shoreline came into view. "Isn't that the *Elf Chine*?"

"You're right," Bernard said. "They made it after all."

We couldn't wait to drop anchor and pay them a visit. This was the junk with the young French crew that we worried about when we left Hong Kong. They were supposed to follow behind us, but a typhoon hit just after we'd left, and we lost all communication with them. They never arrived in the Philippines, and no one we asked knew anything about them.

Making contact again after so many months felt like visiting friends that we'd known forever. The bonding that takes place at sea is accelerated by common experiences and shared dangers. On shore it would have taken much longer to create this feeling of intimacy, and in most cases, it wouldn't happen at all.

"Where's the dog?" Stefan asked. His question reminded me there had been one aboard when we were in Hong Kong.

"He fell overboard," one of the crew said. "Drowned before we could reach him."

It was the one sad note in a happy reunion. It reinforced for me that small children and animals do not belong aboard pleasure crafts on the high seas.

"What happened after we left you?" Bernard asked.

"We waited out the typhoon," the young captain said, "and then I decided to bypass the Philippines. We were already behind schedule for our return to France."

Bernard turned to the doctor aboard. "Take a look at this," he said. He showed him a small growth that had developed on his chest.

The doctor gave it a quick perusal. "Not malignant." he said. "When you have time, come over and I'll take care of it."

Next day Bernard took the dinghy and motored over to the *Elf Chine*. He was back in less than an hour with a wad of white gauze taped to his chest.

"Was it painful?" I asked.

"It was nothing. He burned it off with a soldering iron from the junk's toolbox."

"How could you let him do that?" I was grossed out and worried about infection.

"Nothing to worry about," he answered. "He sterilized the iron."

"Oh, great!"

Many years later, Bernard discovered the *Elf Chine* moored along the Seine River in Paris. It had become a floating bar in its retirement. He asked but no one knew about the young crew that had dispersed on their arrival in France. He did learn, though, that the doctor suffered a collapsed lung while scuba diving in the Maldives during the junk's return voyage.

After the *Elf Chine* sailed from Singapore, the harbour was almost empty except for the *Marley Coo* with its crew of four Australians a short distance away, a few small fishing boats scattered about, and a tugboat nearby. We were intrigued by the tug with its German captain and small crew of Filipino sailors. The captain told us that the owner of the tug hadn't paid them for delivery, and they had no money to live on. Every couple of days he sold another part of the boat in order to buy food. One day we watched as the crew removed the engine. Shortly after, a new owner arrived, and the crew left for home.

One morning Bernard asked the four young sailors on the *Marley Coo* about the name of their yacht.

"It's to honour Bob Marley," one of them said.

That cemented a friendship. From then on the crew from the *Marley Coo* never passed the *Santa Rita* without calling out a hearty "Hi Mite."

"Why do they keep calling me Mike?" Bernard asked in frustration. "They know it isn't my name."

"It's mate," I said. "You have to get used to their Australian accents."

The Australians told Bernard they were friends who decided to pool their money and come to Malaysia to have a boat built for them. They were now ready to sail home.

Before they lifted anchor, they came aboard with some of their homemade saki. It was very good.

"Easy to make," one of them said. "Rice, sugar, raisins, yeast and water — three days to fizz and then leave it for a month."

The next day Bernard bought the ingredients and set up a little still on deck. He found a large plastic container and punched holes in the screw-top cover to let the fumes out. "Now, we wait," he said.

Fully rested, we looked forward to exploring Singapore before we moved on. I especially wanted to visit Bugis Street, after having seen the stately sailing ships in Keppel Harbour. Bugis Street was a tourist attraction in the Malay section of the island, and well worth the visit. Transvestites owned the street, and strutted and flaunted their wares in gay array. Tourists came in droves to gawk and/or sample a bit of the flesh that the transvestites were hawking. I read that the most beautiful transvestites in the world congregated here.

I had seen them on city buses and at first thought they were incredibly beautiful women with too much make-up. They were like bright sparkles of light in the otherwise staid atmosphere of Singapore. The government has since demolished the old Bugis Street and re-birthed it with shopping malls. The name remains, but not the trade.

In spite of the government's aggressive efforts to homogenize Singapore, I still liked the city. Its tapestry of cultures — Chinese, Malay, Indian — lent an appealing charm that vibrated with life against the slick, no-nonsense architecture pervading the city. This intermixing of people intrigued me. Each group had its own quarters, alive with its own sounds, spice stalls, flowers, incense and food. Temples and mosques dotted the city.

But we had arrived at the end of an era. The government was labouring intensively to make the city as uniform as possible by building non-descript apartment blocks throughout the island where its three cultures were proportionally represented. Each block was to support its own health facilities, food markets, and schools, so that each part would be an isolated, integrated whole with no personal identity. Nice colonial buildings were rapidly coming down. Newfound prosperity was transforming Singapore from an exotic blend of cultures into a sterile state.

"What a boring place," Bernard remarked.

He didn't like any of it. He found the city too clean and the laws too restrictive. There was a fine for peeing in the street, for spitting, for littering, for smoking in public places, for J-walking, and for walking away from a toilet without flushing. Possession of a pound of marijuana was punishable by death. It made him feel oppressed, but the Singaporeans didn't seem to mind. They were a pragmatic, practical people, and less concerned with the idea of personal freedom than the West. So long as there was food and shelter, they liked the order. It probably helped that the country had the second highest standard of living in the East after Japan, and the people were proud of their progress. I felt no tension in the country. People were friendly, helpful, and good-natured.

Food seemed to be the only sensual pleasure tolerated by the government, and even Bernard was seduced by the rich flavours and exotic combination of spices in the dishes. Each morning, we ate *roti prata*, an Indian egg-filled type of pancake, at a hawker stand a short dinghy ride from where we were anchored. For lunch, we often had Indian *biryani*, a spiced rice and meat dish, at the same stand. I've yet to find a restaurant that makes a *roti prata* equal to what we ate at that makeshift place. Stefan became addicted to the *biryani* and still mentions it as his best memory of Singapore.

In the evening Bernard, Stefan and I went to the larger food malls and indulged in Hainese chicken rice, Hokkien noodles, or *nasi goring*, a delicious Malay noodle dish covered with peanut sauce. Stefan, with a more adventurous palate than Bernard and me, sopped up the raw egg and raw fish congees, usually breakfast dishes, but he'd eat them anytime.

The food malls were always crowded and noisy. People shuffled from stand to stand and sat wherever they could find a spot, while cooks worked at lightning speed keeping track of dozens of orders at a time. In spite of all the frenetic activity and bodies pressed against bodies, the kitchens were spotlessly clean with the cooks and servers all wearing hair nets. It was a miracle that the gradual sterilization of the city did not affect the cuisine. In contrast to the sterile, industrial look of the malls and hawker stalls, the food was richly coloured, highly spiced, and heavenly.

Meanwhile, in the quiet seclusion of Jurong Harbour, without the threat of foul weather or roving pirates, Bernard was able to think and figure out what to do about the yacht. He'd been complaining since we started the voyage that the *Santa Rita* didn't have enough speed under sail, and he wanted to solve that problem.

"A bowsprit will do it," he finally said.

"What's a bowsprit?"

"It's a wood pole I'll attach to the bow of the boat. It'll give us more sail, and we'll go faster with more stability."

"While you're looking around for material to make the bowsprit, can you think about a fridge?" I'd been asking for one since we left Hong Kong. "We'd eat a lot better."

To my surprise he did. The day he went out looking for stuff to construct the bowsprit, he returned with a compressor that's used in air-conditioners. "I can use this for making a fridge," he told me, "by attaching it to the front of the engine."

While Bernard was working on the two projects, I thought I'd look around for work. It was late autumn, nights were cool in spite of our being directly on the equator, and spending some time in Singapore didn't seem like a bad idea. The city felt safe, and it was easy to get around by bus. English was one of the four official languages, but many Singaporeans felt more comfortable in the languages of their ethnic roots whether Tamil, Malay, or Mandarin, so I thought it would be easy to find contract work as an English Second Language teacher. It didn't matter if we stayed a while. We weren't in a hurry to get anywhere, and keeping a yacht seaworthy was costlier than we had anticipated. The time worn saying among yachties that a boat is a hole in the water that you keep pouring money into wasn't a joke. Without money coming in, we were going to run out sooner than we'd expected.

It wasn't as easy as I thought it would be. The best schools hired from applications received outside the country. Those that would hire on the spot were seedy fly-by-night places that paid peanuts; that is, if you were lucky enough to be paid before they disappeared. We decided that, as soon as Bernard finished working on the fridge and bowsprit, we'd leave for countries where the dollar went further than in Singapore.

The first job he tackled was putting together the fridge. It had been an icebox that fit neatly into a space in the galley. Inside the box he put a coil of copper, a container with below freezing liquid, and a copper pipe that ran from the fridge to the compressor on the engine. If we ran the engine for an hour, it would keep the fridge cold for twenty-four hours. Bernard's uncanny ability to make anything from nothing endeared him to me. I thought that if the world ever came to an end and everything was destroyed, he'd be the one person I'd want to be with for my survival.

He solved the problem of the bowsprit by sawing six feet off a two-by-four beam and screwing it to the front of the yacht. He ran a cable from the end of the bowsprit, jutting out in front of the boat, to the top of the foremast so that he could attach a staysail between the two points. It did improve the yacht's stability and gave the *Santa Rita* the speed he was looking for. There were no stanchion lines around the bowsprit for protection, but there would be no reason to have to go out on it — or so we thought.

With the staysail in place, we were ready to lift anchor for the Malacca Strait — another stretch of water infested by pirates, this time coming from Thailand.

Chapter 15

HINDU MIRACLES, BUDDHIST SNAKES
AND A BROKEN MAST

Winter 1983: Malaysia

> *There is nothing more enticing, disenchanting,
> and enslaving than the life at sea.*
> —JOSEPH CONRAD

As we lifted anchor to leave Singapore, I already missed the *roti pratas* that had become a daily ritual in our lives. Our morning dinghy ride for breakfast at the *roti prata* stand had been the one moment in the day Bernard, Stefan and I were together as a family. It re-established our connection to each other and was a stabilizing interlude in our peripatetic lifestyle.

When we approached the Malacca Strait, I shifted my focus to what lay ahead—a planned pit stop or two in Malaysia, and some time in Phuket, Sri Lanka and the Maldives before the three-week stretch to the Red Sea. It was now late January and we had to get to the Red Sea by May to avoid facing the monsoons that tore through the Indian Ocean at that time of year.

The Malacca Strait was notorious for pirate activity. So once the *Santa Rita* entered the strait, we put our pirate evasion strategy into full operation. It meant constant vigilance to spot suspicious-looking boats before they got too close. That way, we'd have enough time to make our getaway in the opposite direction. A strategic part of our tactic was two-hour watches day and night.

There were other reasons to be vigilant. We were following the route of the big cargo ships. Huge containers were known to fall off these ships, leaving only a corner floating above water. We'd already heard stories about yachts smashing into these floating behemoths. I thought of them as stealth enemies lurking in the dark underbelly of the sea waiting to annihilate happy, little fibreglass sprites like our *Santa Rita* riding the surface.

There was also the issue of whales, who during mating season don't like smooth-bellied hulls crowding their territory. A Dutch couple we had met in the Philippines had their yacht rammed by a whale, and still had the dent in the side of their steel hull as proof of their story. Our fibreglass hull was too fragile to withstand the whack of a whale. We'd split in two and sink in no time.

Until now, we'd been lax about watches. The autopilot did much of the work, while we checked in from time to time to give a cursory look over the horizon or to tweak the sails. A whale attack or a floating container lying in wait seemed more remote than a bunch of fishermen, who could turn to piracy any moment. But we weren't chancing any of it.

I prepared myself for a bleary-eyed week of night watches when Stefan offered a way out. "I'll take the night watch," he told Bernard. "Give me from 10 at night to 6 in the morning. You and mom can take turns on the day watch."

He later told me he needed that time to think — that he always thought better at night and didn't sleep much anyway. He'd already told me in Hong Kong that he'd dropped out of junior college in Montreal to join us because he had no direction and didn't want to waste his time.

"I have to think about my future," he said, "and what I want to do."

"Fair enough," I said. I'd gone from high school to university without any notion of who I was or what I wanted — a decision I later regretted. I respected his courage for taking time out, for following his own voice, for searching for his own integrity.

Captain Elliot, a retired sea captain we met in the Philippines, told us the Malay coastline was the most beautiful in the world. The anticipation of seeing something unique helped quell some of the anxiety of a possible pirate encounter. I knew through my discipline in meditation, a practice I'd kept up since Hong Kong, that if I emptied my mind and focused on one point, it calmed me. This would become essential to my survival in the adventures that we were yet to encounter. For now it was the Malay coast, and I wasn't disappointed. Malaysia was lush and green with tropical rain forests tumbling down to the water's edge.

On the second day of our sail we entered Port Klang, a busy, uninspiring port town full of warehouses with a smattering of affable people who lived in houses built on stilts. Our destination was Kuala Lumpur, the nation's capital. Stefan took charge of the *Santa Rita* while Bernard and I took a taxi to the capital, about an hour and a half inland. We wanted to see how it compared with Singapore. We also thought we could get a nice variety of fresh produce there.

Unlike Singapore, Kuala Lumpur was in no hurry to rip away the old. In the heart of a verdant, tropical rain forest, the Malays had carved out a city of stately beauty and refinement. The city had once been part of an important trade route connecting China with India. In the 1800s it became a major tin mining centre. As a result many cultures passed through, leaving part of their architectural heritage behind. Each culture modified its building plans to accommodate the aesthetic of the Malay people and the tropical demands of the environment. It made the city not only beautiful, but refreshingly unique.

We strolled by Moghul-inspired buildings with arched stone windows, carved façades and Greek columns that sat side by side with Tudor and Victorian buildings. A gothic cathedral and a number of gothic-influenced churches shared space with domed mosques and ornate Indian temples. They all seemed to fit seamlessly into the city's backdrop of soaring high-rises. We eventually arrived at the Chinese sector where row upon row of shop-houses vied for space with hordes of people who crowded the narrow, winding streets. The area teemed with life. At one of the outdoor produce stands, I elbowed my way through the bulk of shoppers and bought three-inch eggplants, foot-long string beans and succulent mangosteens to replenish our dwindling stores of fresh food.

When our eyes grew tired and our feet started to flatten, we took refuge at a hawker stand to recharge our batteries. Like Singapore, Kuala Lumpur was a city that took pride in its food. It was hard to select from the wide array of Malay, Chinese and Indian dishes. We finally decided on a national favourite of rice and chopped chicken leg drenched in a chili and garlic sauce. Huge banana leaves were placed in front of us, and the chicken and rice dish dumped directly onto the leaves. The only utensil was our right hand. I took great pleasure in balling up the rice between my fingers and flicking the whole sloppy mess into my mouth with my thumb—a technique I learned by watching the diners at the neighbouring table.

I thought about how efficient it was to eat off a banana leaf, and wished I had been brought up where bananas grew in abundance so that I could indulge in this labour-saving way to eat. I did get a banana plant (not a tree, I discovered) when I moved to Mexico many years later, and I still love eating with my fingers. But I confine my illicit pleasure to the privacy of my home.

Bernard was less enthusiastic about eating with his hand. It surprised me as I'd thought of him as the earthier of the two of us. He was not in the least bothered by the infrequent bathing we could permit ourselves. Nor did he mind wearing the same clothes day after day, the problem being our small capacity for water storage. Seasoned yachties told me the best way to do laundry was to put the dirty clothes in a net and drag it behind the yacht. After one try, I settled for grit instead of sea salt in my clothing, but it wasn't a satisfying compromise. I concluded that being physical and being sensuous weren't the same. Bernard took pleasure in the nitty-gritty. I took pleasure in the senses.

After a day of walking the streets, engaging in small talk with strangers, and sampling a variety of rice and noodle snacks washed down with chilled coconut drinks, we headed back to the *Santa Rita* for the next leg of our journey to Penang.

As luck would have it, our arrival in Penang coincided with the full moon of the tenth month of the Hindu calendar, last week in January. The day marked the celestial time that Parathi, wife of Shiva, gave her warrior son, Lord Muruga, the necessary spear to fight and destroy evil in the world. We knew nothing about Lord Muruga, and still wouldn't know, if we hadn't arrived during Thaipusam, the yearly Hindu festival that honours Lord Muruga.

We walked off the *Santa Rita* and into an extraordinary scene on the streets of Penang. The Tamil, who are Hindu, but also some Chinese, who were probably Buddhist, and a few Sikhs living in this Muslim country were busily pounding coconuts onto the pavement, spilling their oozy contents on the cement and leaving sharp shells all over the street. In the middle of this activity, a huge silver chariot pulled by two decorated oxen passed by.

We later learned the crushing of the coconuts signified releasing the ego, and it was Lord Muruga in the chariot being taken from his home in one temple to be brought to another several miles away. A procession of people on their way to be blessed followed the chariot. They carried pots of milk on their heads or heavy semi-circular platforms that were decorated with ribbons, coloured paper, pictures of gods, and/or peacock feathers. I purchased several feathers to take back to the boat as they were known to bring good luck.

Makeshift stalls, decorated in flowers and coloured paper crowded the edges of the road. From these stalls volunteers handed out water, fruit and sweet buns to the followers of Lord Muruga and whoever else asked. It looked as though all of Penang showed up for this festival.

The next day was even more spectacular. Tamil men in loincloths stood stoically still while small groups of "trainers" or family members drove spears, skewers, and meat hooks through their tongues and cheeks, and into their backs, chests, and arms. Some of the hooks had chains that connected one hook to another. Others had fruit or heavy coconuts hanging from smaller hooks that were imbedded in their flesh. Still others had ropes attached to the hooks in their backs and shoulders from which ox carts were dragged, their skin stretching from the weight of the carts.

A number of men carried heavy platforms on their shoulders, similar to the ones I had seen the day before, but they were now attached to their bodies with strings tied to the hooks sunk into their flesh. Burdened in this way, the devotees climbed five hundred steps to a hilltop temple.

We saw no blood or any sign of pain. Later, when the hooks and skewers were removed, they left no marks on the skin. The holes filled up as though they never were. I asked a Chinese gentleman standing beside me about this ritual.

"Doing penance," he said. "At least some of them are. Others wish for their prayers to be answered or are giving thanks for having them fulfilled."

"How can they do that?" I asked. He shook his head and walked away. Bernard and I were stupefied and more than a little curious.

By asking around, we learned that the men had spent over a month in prayer and celibacy. Milk and fruit were their only nourishment. The heavy, semi-circular platforms they carried on their shoulders were called Kavadi and represented their burdens. These men were in some kind of trance, but I couldn't figure out how they got there.

Years later, I started to doubt what I had seen. I looked this festival up on the internet and found several articles by *National Geographic* verifying my experience. I remember being in awe of the profound commitment these supplicants had to their beliefs. I don't think I could ever believe that strongly about anything to give myself over to such an ordeal. The whole experience was mesmerizing and humbling. Even more so, given that the whole town, whatever their cultural or religious orientation, was involved in this rite. Spectators and participants were one and the same. We were among very few onlookers.

Perhaps I should have been more of a participant. A prayer or two might have saved us from an unpleasant surprise the following morning. Bernard discovered that during the night we had drifted too close to a neighbouring tramp boat. Our anchor got caught in the other boat's anchor chain, and when the crew lifted the anchors, our boom swung behind our stern and hit the tramp boat's massive steel hull, snapping our mizzenmast in two. When I came on deck, Bernard and Stefan were already there, inspecting the heaped sail and tangled ropes that looked to me like crushed wings and dangling tendons around the broken leg of a humongous stork.

"Oh my God," I mouthed. I had lost my voice.

Bernard gave me a quick glance but said nothing.

The broken mast cut my breath. I could feel my knees give, and

I had to sit down. The *Santa Rita* was more than an object of pleasure. She was our home, our shared dream of many years of hard work, and the investment of our total savings. Most important, this floating bubble of plastic was our survival. Now she was crippled, no longer whole.

"There's no boatyard in Penang," I said. "There's nothing."

I couldn't figure out how we'd be able to get another mast, and if we did, who'd have the expertise to install it. I had the panicky feeling we'd have to abandon the yacht. I was totally irrational.

Bernard appeared calm, but I knew he was hurting. Before leaving Taiwan, we decided to hang the painting by Earthstone Joe that we'd bought in Taipei in the salon. Bernard's tension when he had to put a nail into the cabin wall was palpable. It was a though he was mutilating his child. Now he had to deal with a real mutilation. I wanted to say something to comfort him, but I couldn't. He was too removed for me to reach him. He wouldn't even make eye contact. When Bernard felt a deep emotion, he disappeared within himself.

His total attention was on the snapped mast, and he spent quite a while in reflection, trying to figure out how to get the two halves to hold together. Stefan and I tiptoed around the deck trying to keep out of his way.

"That mast's hollow," he finally said. "I could jerry rig the severed halves by inserting something inside and screw the two halves to whatever I insert. But what?" He had to come up with a material strong enough to hold the mast together under a strong wind and in the worst possible weather. He settled on ironwood, a hardwood tree that grew in Penang and was said to be as strong as steel. He took the measurements of the interior of the mast and went to find someone who could carve out the proper dimensions in the wood for him to insert between the two halves of the mast.

While Bernard was involved with this project, I thought it would be a good idea if Stefan and I did some sightseeing. I knew from my Hong Kong experience the controlled nervous tension that was becoming more and more a part of Bernard's character could find its outlet in rejection and nasty innuendo. I wanted us to be out of the way until he worked through some of his pent-up frustration. I also noticed that he had started drinking his homemade saki even though it hadn't completely cured.

I learned the previous day there was a snake temple on the island. "Could be an interesting adventure," I told Stefan.

I read him an excerpt from the tourist brochure I'd picked up at the Thaipusan festival:

> The snake temple was built in 1845 to honour Chor Soo Kong, a Buddhist monk who lived in the ninth century. Chor Soo Kong was a famous healer but also known for giving shelter to snakes. In 1843 a British resident of Penang prayed to Chor Soo Kong and was healed. He donated the land for the temple. After the temple was built, snakes entered of their own accord and stayed on to pay homage to the monk. This temple dedicated to Chor Soo Kong is the only snake temple in the world inhabited by pit vipers.

"Let's go," he said.

Neither of us had an issue with snakes. I liked the fact they shed old skins as they grew — a nice metaphor for how we should all go through life. It also didn't bother me that they crawled on their bellies. I thought it showed strength and determination because it wasn't easy to move without legs.

Also, unlike cockroaches that sneak around in the dark and leave dots of excrement wherever they go, snakes enjoy nature and don't leave a trail of filth behind them. In Taiwan we had been inundated with roaches — flying ones, the size of small Mars bars. They flew through the windows and banged their heads against the walls before dropping to the floor. Their dried-out carcasses turned up in drawers, cabinets, and between the quilted blanket and wooden bed board we slept on. Even in death they couldn't seem to disappear.

Snakes, on the other hand, once commanded great respect. All cultures believed in the magical abilities, wisdom, and healing properties associated with the snake, an animal often thought to be mother earth herself. In short, I didn't believe they deserved their bad reputation, and I admired Chor Soo Kong who felt a need to protect them.

Unfortunately, our encounter with the pit vipers at the Chor Soo

Kong temple was a disappointment. As soon as Stefan and I entered the shabby, non-descript temple, a smoke screen of incense nearly drove us back into the street. After adjusting to the haze, we edged our way around the room looking for snakes. We finally encountered a few draped over umbrella-shaped bamboo ribs stuck into glazed pots near the altar. The snakes looked dead. On closer inspection they looked drugged — probably wiped out by the cloying incense. We found a few others scattered around, also in a trance. If I stepped on one, I doubt it would have moved. If we stayed any longer in the temple, we may have also ended up in a stupor.

When we returned to the yacht, Bernard was back with the prepared block of wood and ready to screw it into the interior of the mast. He and Stefan managed to finish the job in about an hour, but I was heartbroken. Every time I looked at the bolts, I felt the pain of the scarring. Our boat had been perfect. Now she was marked and crippled, no longer a flawless beauty.

Next morning, I watched with apprehension as Stefan helped Bernard lift anchor. Neither of them looked relaxed. Bernard's repair still had to be tested. Ironwood may be strong, but it was still a repair holding together two parts of what once had been a solid piece. There would always be a weakness. Maybe it would hold up in a squall, but what if we were caught in something stronger? If the mast cracked in a storm, what would that do to the balance of the boat? Would we still be stable on the water? Only time would tell.

Bernard and I didn't talk about it. I knew that, if I brought up my apprehension, he'd become agitated and answer curtly. I had learned to stick to the practical and stay away from the emotional, but I noticed he was drinking more and growing distant again. The evening before we set sail from Penang, he started to pick on Stefan.

"You're lazy," he said for no reason. "You'll never be a sailor."

Stefan kept reading his book and paid no attention. I couldn't figure what he expected Stefan to do since we were at anchor, and he hadn't asked him to do anything. I wondered why he'd be annoyed by Stefan's reading, and surprised that Stefan showed no reaction.

He then started on me. "You regret coming on this adventure, don't you? You miss being away from your friends."

Neither was true, and I resented his telling me what he thought I was feeling. I took my cue from Stefan and didn't respond, but I couldn't understand what was happening. When we sailed, there was no tension. I didn't question his authority, and followed orders without discussion. There could only be one captain on a ship, and I never took issue with that. We had met couples who were often locked in a power struggle. Both could sail and the female often felt smothered by "the captain" for not being given a big enough role in decision-making or the actual sailing. I wasn't confident enough to put myself in that position since I couldn't figure out wind direction or how to read a sea chart. But I had learned during our aborted crossing on the British couple's yacht from Taiwan to Hong Kong that I didn't panic in a crisis. Survival often depended on a clear mind, so I knew I was an asset. I had already witnessed seasoned sailors falling apart under dangerous situations.

Bernard's outburst soured the atmosphere aboard the *Santa Rita*, so I was glad we were sailing again, our next port of call being Phuket, an island off the west coast of Thailand. It had little tourism in the eighties, and seemed like a good pit stop on our way to Sri Lanka.

Within hours of our being at sea, a squall blew in. The intense rain-bearing 35-knot wind came with almost no warning, the only sign of its approach, a streak of black racing across the sky. When I saw that line moving towards us, my heart started to beat faster. This would be the first test of Bernard's jerry-rigged mast. I was at the helm when Bernard heard the wind, and raced on deck. The sails had to be reefed, and in order to do that, the yacht had to be turned towards the wind to slow it down. I joined Stefan in reefing the main sail, and then we lowered the sail on the mizzenmast, leaving the staysail off the bow for balance.

The Malacca Strait is narrow, which makes the waves erratic and choppy. Standing upright on deck was like trying to centre myself atop a basketball. I held tight to whatever I could grab, and kept my eye on the mizzenmast. Within a half hour the storm passed as though it had never happened. Our mizzenmast took the beating like a trooper. From then on, I relaxed. Still, seeing those ugly bolts screwed along the side of the mast never stopped bothering me. Everything changes with time. I had to learn to accept that.

Chapter 16

PIT STOPS IN SABANG AND PHUKET

Spring 1983: Indonesia and Thailand

> *Sticks and stones may break our bones,*
> *but words will break our hearts.*
> — ROBERT FULGHUM

The heavy squall we encountered off the coast of Penang, coupled with concern over how well our jerry-rigged mast would hold up under the gale force winds, left us depleted. We re-evaluated our plans and decided to drop anchor in Sabang, a tiny island in Indonesia off the northern tip of Sumatra. Since it didn't take us too far off course on our way to Phuket, it seemed worth the slight detour. We craved some light diversion, and providence delivered.

As we motored into Sabang's harbour, an enormous whale shark rose out of the water like a surfacing submarine. The fish, almost the length of the *Santa Rita,* must have been a good forty-five feet long. It was dark grey with white spots and stripes along its backside. Its cavernous mouth looked as though it ran the full width of the broad head. But the most remarkable thing about this enormous fish was how sublimely happy it appeared.

A dozen or so Indonesian kids from about five to twelve years old sat along the edge of the pier, feet dangling into space. They clapped and whooped as the whale shark performed one trick after another. It swooshed around, first lifting its massive head out of the water and then its tail. It glided back and forth in front of the kids in a graceful dance, basking in the appreciation of its enthralled audience. I could swear it was smiling.

123

The performance went on for about half an hour, and then the friendly whale shark acknowledged the last bit of applause with a tail flip and disappeared. We learned that it performed everyday for the children, never missing its noon matinee. I was amazed that it knew how to come at the same hour every day.

I asked a local fisherman, who had been watching the whale shark's antics, whether he thought the fish might damage our yacht. He said it was a gentle creature and would do no harm. "They don't even attack humans," he added. "They live on small fish and plankton." I couldn't believe there was enough plankton in the ocean to feed creatures that size.

We later learned these sharks suck in their food and expel the water through their gills. They have 36 rows of teeth, but don't seem to have much use for any of them. I was starting to see how little I knew about the natural world and how fascinating it was in its diversity and possibilities.

We learned from the island's movie man how whale sharks ate. He took charge of us soon after we disembarked and insisted we come to see a film in his lone movie house. I thought he wanted to practice his English. I was happy to oblige.

"No expense," he said. "You're my guests."

He led us through streets heaped with cloves warming in the sun while waiting to be ground for cigarettes. The entire island smelled of cloves, and the aroma was intoxicating. Clove cigarettes, packaged under the name Garick and sold throughout the East, were Sabang's main source of income. Bernard bought several packets to smoke on the boat. I liked the sweet scent that wafted through the air as we walked the streets. But later, inside our small salon on the *Santa Rita*, the invasive, heady aroma was overwhelming and gave me a headache.

The movie theatre was a square room in a square wooden building housing several rows of threadbare seats. We took seats in the middle — first Bernard, then me, followed by Stefan and our host. We were the only audience. As soon as the lights went off, Stefan jumped up and raced out the theatre. Bernard and I followed to see what had happened. My first thought was that he had been stung by an insect. The movie man stayed behind.

"That guy started to feel me up," Stefan shouted. "He put his hand on my crotch."

So, I thought, it wasn't English practice he wanted. My first impulse was to confront the "nice man," but I kept my peace. This wasn't our country. Who knew what the fallout might be.

"We'd better go straight to the boat," Bernard said.

I agreed. Bernard had a sixth sense about situations that could turn bad. I'd already experienced that when we lived in Mexico. We had gone with friends to a remote village in the Sierra Madre Mountains to witness an unusual Day of the Dead ceremony. The following day, some of our group wanted to stop in the nearest town for drinks. Bernard felt the local people were hostile to outsiders, and it would be dangerous. The others dismissed his feeling as paranoia; that is, until we were all ushered into jail at gunpoint on a trumped-up charge of drug possession. Had some of our party not had connections in Mexico City, we would have been transferred to the main jail in Oaxaca, notorious for the way it treated inmates. Since then, I've trusted Bernard's instinctive capacity to smell danger.

Our only other local contact was another English-speaking islander named Dodent, who kept a scrapbook of foreign boats docking off Sabang's shores. Dodent was a fisherman with a love and thirst for adventure. He motored to the *Santa Rita* and asked us for stories and a drawing to put into his book. We leafed through its pages and found the names of several yachties we'd met along the way, and enjoyed reading about their experiences at sea. We then added our own to Dodent's collection.

"As a poor fisherman," he'd told us, "I'll never be able to leave my island. I travel through the adventures of others."

We weren't the only foreign boat anchored off the island. A small distance from us was a seventy-foot schooner that had been illegally boarded by an Australian named Captain Jim. We first met the Captain in Borneo and then met up with him again in Singapore as he was about to lift anchor for Thailand.

"I'm delivering the boat for an Italian consortium," he had told us when we met him in Botneo. "They're taking delivery in Phuket."

"We might see you there if we make it before you leave," I'd said.

Now it appeared the Italian owners had failed to pay him for delivering the schooner. They hired a crew behind his back to board the boat and sail her to South Africa. When Captain Jim learned that the crew had made a stopover in Sebang, he flew in to repossess the schooner until he received the money owed him. The day after we arrived, he went to Medan in Sumatra to find a lawyer. That evening he was back on board and announced over his short wave radio that he was armed. He warned that he'd shoot at any boat that came near and turned on every light on the schooner to look out for anyone approaching. From what we could tell, he was alone. We had no idea what happened to the newly hired crew, weren't about to ask, and thought it would be a good idea to lift anchor and sail on to Phuket.

Leaving Sebang took us out of the Malacca Strait and into the Andaman Sea. At the point where the currents meet one another, the waves are short and create a zone of strong vertical waves. I was below deck making lunch when Bernard shouted down for me to come up to take a look. As far as I could see for miles around, it looked as though we were travelling over rapidly boiling water. It brought to mind my boys sailing their toy boat over soap bubbles in the bath, except the *Santa Rita* wasn't a toy and we were living creatures inside. Excellent sailing conditions permitted us the luxury of enjoying the phenomenon without having to focus on the boat. I took in the unique scene and was thrilled that I had opted for this journey.

"It's incredible!" I shouted over to Bernard who was at the bow with Stefan leaning into the water. "How many people will ever get to see a scene like this?"

Bernard turned and came over to the cockpit where I had braced myself, partially on the top stairs and partially out the hatch. He was smiling and obviously excited by the unusual event.

"You know what causes this?" he said. He then gave me a technical explanation for what created this odd condition, but all I could surmise was something about the current from the Indian Ocean fighting an opposing current coming from the Malacca Strait.

I didn't totally understand the scientific part, but it impressed me. Bernard had a wealth of information stored in his head. His understanding of natural phenomena grounded me. It made me feel safe.

We arrived in Phuket in less than two days, but hours before seeing land the scent of frangipani crossed on the wind. It was the first time since we had set out on this adventure that I was aware of scent coming off the land before entering a port. The fragrant aroma of the flowers put me in a euphoric state. I felt its essence enter and spread throughout my body, and I gave myself over to the sensation. The sea was a scintillating, cerulean blue turning to aqua, and crystalline clear right to the bottom. We dropped anchor, lowered the dinghy, and headed towards the white sandy beach. It was silent except for the lapping of water.

A distance away we saw some thatch-roofed shacks selling fish. And within view there were a few odd-shaped islands, or rather large karst formations that rose gently from the sea and broke the line of the horizon. Everything was clean and bright and sparkling.

The *Santa Rita* had functioned beautifully under the southeasterly wind that brought us here. The repaired mast proved itself worthy of heavy storms. Since we had all performed well together under sail, I thought the worst was over. I was totally unprepared for what happened next.

Bernard was looking out towards the horizon, and I walked over to join him. "It's so peaceful here," I said. I slipped my arm through his and pressed close. It had been a great sail, and I'd hoped for an affectionate acknowledgement of a job well done. Instead, he pulled away and walked further down the beach. He remained apart from Stefan and me for the rest of the afternoon. I tried to shrug it off, and spent my time collecting shells while Stefan read.

I didn't want to acknowledge that these odd moments of distance were happening more often, and I could never predict them or say why. There was never anything overt leading up to them, and they often happened when we were in a relaxed situation. It started shortly after we arrived in Taiwan when he snapped at me for using the word "bathroom" instead of "head" when referring to the toilet. He let me know that I didn't think like a real sailor, and he was worried that I might be a liability on the boat. And then suddenly between Borneo and Singapore he announced that he would no longer be sleeping in the aft-cabin where we shared a double berth.

"I'll be sleeping in the salon from now on," he had said. "That way I'm ready for anything unexpected." His moods never lasted. And when those moments passed, it was as though they had never happened.

Towards evening I approached him and said I'd like to go back to the yacht.

"Take the dinghy," he said.

"You know I can't start that engine." The engine was a salvaged relic from World War Two. It needed to be primed with a string to get started, and I didn't have the physical strength to pull hard enough to ignite the charge. Even he had to make several attempts to get the thing running.

"I can't do everything for you," he said. He turned back towards the horizon. "I should have never taken you on this adventure."

I was stunned. Worse, I felt betrayed. His words were like a knife in my chest.

"You bastard," I shouted. I couldn't think of anything else to say. I stood there with my hands in fists, absolutely tongue-tied, and wished I could crush him with the weight of my rage. I was aware that Stefan was observing the scene, and I didn't want to do anything that would make me look out of control. So I did nothing more. I just stood there with my mind racing. At that moment, I knew that I could no longer pretend that his growing distance was a momentary intrusion.

I had invested seven years of my life working hard and living frugally to make this dream a reality. And I had spent years prior to that dreaming about it. I wondered what happened to the man with whom I'd gone to New York to buy the yacht's VHF radio — the one who, over a bag of shared peanuts while sitting on a bench in Central Park, told me how grateful he was that I supported him on this adventure that had been his dream since childhood.

"I know you're doing this for me," he had said. "And I won't forget."

But it was becoming obvious that he had. I wanted him to acknowledge that this was a shared adventure, and I wasn't extra baggage he'd picked up on the way, even though he was making me feel that way.

Bernard didn't respond to my outburst. He turned and strode towards the dinghy in long deliberate steps. Stefan came up beside me and the two of us followed behind silently.

It embarrassed me that Stefan heard me shout. Throughout the trip he'd been mainly an observer, helping when asked, and keeping his thoughts to himself. I knew when he left us for university, we'd never live together again as a family. I wanted him to leave with happy memories, but I was no longer sure that would happen.

The magic of Phuket was ruined. When I came into the galley the next morning to make myself a cup of coffee, I found Stefan at the table hunched over his book. He looked up when he heard me.

"Are you okay, mom?" he asked.

"Yeah, I'm fine," I said. He nodded and went back to his reading. It's what he expected me to say. There was a tacit agreement between us that we stay away from any discussion of Bernard's growing mood swings. Our lives were in his hands, and neither of us wanted to escalate tensions by forming some kind of "him against us" pact.

I picked up a yachting magazine but had a hard time concentrating. I went into the aft-cabin and tried to journal, but I couldn't write anything. And meditation was out of the question.

Bernard busied himself replenishing his saki supply. He had almost finished his first brew, and was in the process of starting a second batch before he ran out. In the beginning, I liked the idea of our homemade saki, but his constant imbibing had turned me off to the pleasure of that evening drink. I resented his obsession with the little still he had created, but I hadn't yet connected his drinking to his mood swings.

Towards mid-day, I came on deck and spoke to Bernard for the first time since the incident. "We have to provision," I said. It wasn't essential, but I needed something to distract me.

Bernard was in a good mood. It was as though the day before had never happened. "Sure," he said. "Just tell me when you're ready to go."

I didn't understand the sudden change in behaviour, but I let it go. If I poked, I knew I'd rekindle the tension.

That evening, Stefan took charge of the *Santa Rita* while Bernard and I set off for the night market at the edge of Phuket Town. The liveliness of the market was totally unexpected after the solitude of the beach. A wall of people milled about make-shift stands that sold everything from plastic shoes to puppies. Fruit and vegetable stands, looking like still-life paintings under their incandescent light bulbs, shared space with food stalls that dished-up local treats.

The movement of the people among the array of goods and food stuff gave a festive air to the market. I got caught up on the energy of the place — as did Bernard. We stuffed ourselves on fish cakes and pork *satays*, and poked around the new and used crappy stuff for sale. Before returning to the *Santa Rita*, I filled our basket with mangoes, bananas, red peppers, and some greens. I also picked up a fair quantity of rice now that our rice supply had been sacrificed to the saki god.

Once Bernard had secured his new batch of home brew on deck, we lifted anchor and set sail for Sri Lanka. The island had been one of my fantasies, having read the writer Arthur C. Clarke's glowing description. I imagined us luxuriating in the flowering paradise, and wondered if we'd make it our home. Clarke did. Why not us? We had no commitments — one of the perks of our lifestyle. Maybe Bernard would be happy there.

Chapter 17

EN ROUTE TO SRI LANKA

Spring 1983

> *For whatever we lose (like a you or me).*
> *It's always the self we find in the sea.*
> —E.E. CUMMINGS

As soon as we sailed out of Thailand, Bernard turned playful, taking pleasure in studying the sea charts, checking the depth sounder and working the sails. The wind was in our favour, and we cruised effortlessly at seven or eight knots under a cloudless sky. We let the autopilot do the work while we munched on fruit we'd picked up in Phuket, sipped coffee, and watched a pod of dolphins that had been following us since the Philippines.

"Great, isn't it?" Bernard shouted over the whoosh of the boat cutting through the waves.

"Fabulous," I shouted back.

He gave me a friendly pat on the backside, and I felt that all was right with the world. I did not let on that my exhilaration at the speed and angle of the yacht was tinged with fear. The *Santa Rita* had never sailed this fast. She heeled at such a sharp angle that to walk along the deck felt like walking cross-wise on a hill. The ocean came almost even with the leeward side of the deck, and sea spray washed over us.

I hadn't known how far a yacht could lean in a strong wind. And even though it unnerved me, I could see Bernard and Stefan were enjoying it. I calmed myself by focusing on the dolphins. There were about ten of them, and they were enjoying the waves as much as the guys. They swam in and out of the wake, dove under the hull, came up the other side, and took giant leaps in front of the bow while giving us amused looks. They love us, I thought. I knew for sure that I loved them.

Next morning, I sat on deck with a mug of coffee and idly watched Bernard as he focused the sextant to calculate our position. Most yachts we'd come across had satellite systems for navigation, but Bernard preferred to set our course with a sextant.

"Electronics can fail," he'd said. "It's better not to rely on them and to know what you're doing."

I agreed with that. I didn't like the idea of drifting in circles in the middle of an ocean with a dead satellite.

"Here, let me show you how to use it."

I looked at the device he was holding and panicked. It involved geometry, a subject that had always confused me.

"Why don't you show Stefan first?" I said.

Stefan had a feel for sailing, and I couldn't understand why Bernard didn't want to share more knowledge with him. Aside from barking at him to clean the deck, or lift the anchor, or scrub the hull, Bernard hardly spoke to him.

Bernard ignored my suggestion. "It's easy," he said.

He handed me the sextant, and I went blank. "I can't," I said. I felt it was beyond me.

"What if something happens to me?"

"Teach Stef."

He snatched the instrument from my hands. "Can't you make an effort?" he mumbled.

Not waiting for a response, he turned towards the sun and went back to his calculations.

It irritated me that he wouldn't acknowledge my contribution to our adventure, and was always ready to point out my shortcomings. But I also felt he had a point. A boat is a technical piece of equipment, and because I shied away from that aspect, I was only partially there. Had anything happened to him and Stefan, I would be floundering at sea without a clue as to how to save myself. Today, I look back and know I should have made the effort. If I sailed today, I would. But everything back then was new. I fluctuated between apprehension and anxiety, and that kept me stuck in familiar patterns of behaviour.

Years later, long after we had sold the boat, long after our marriage had dissolved, Bernard told me that he couldn't forgive me for not learning how to use the sextant. He felt I deliberately refused to learn anything he could teach me as part of a power struggle between us. With distance and time, he recognized I had a fear about learning technical things that had nothing to do with him.

This wasn't the only time we misread each other's intent. Each time our desires were thwarted, we took it personally. It required more maturity than we had at the time to understand that we were two independent people who were together by choice, joined at the heart, but not at the hip.

The sail into Galle, the port of entry into Sri Lanka, had none of the relaxed, bucolic charm of Phuket. The harbour, encircled by fortress-like stonewalls, was filled with a hodgepodge of boats — some for fishing, some trampers, and a handful of sailboats. Dozens of bare-chested brown-skinned men in sarongs and flip flops ran about the wharf bringing in fish or taking goods off trampers. Galle had been an important port for spices travelling from the East to Europe, and the Dutch had built this fort-like older section of the city in the seventeenth century to protect their shipping interests. The exotic paradise I had anticipated looked more like a small European port city.

In Sabang and Phuket, we casually dropped anchor and went ashore without notifying authorities. But Galle was a thriving city with an established bureaucracy, and we knew we'd have to enter through official channels. As luck would have it, we spotted a number of yachts that belonged to the small group of fellow yacht builders we had met in Taiwan.

Among them was Heiko, a young German adventurer who befriended us when we first arrived in Taipei. At the rooming house on Chung Shan Road, the three of us became drinking buddies, sharing tales of woe and frustration at the great cultural divide in communication between us and the Taiwanese builders. He sailed out before us, and I never expected to see him again.

"Hey, Heiko," we shouted.

He waved to us with a beer can in one hand and the other around the waist of a slim young woman.

"Where do we go to get clearance?" Bernard asked.

"Windsor, Don Windsor," he shouted back. "He's the man to see. He handles all the paperwork. He'll take care of everything. Look for the giant Buddha. His house is across the street. Then come aboard for drinks. I want you to meet my girlfriend."

The huge golden Buddha, erected by Don Windsor in honour of his parents, was a beacon that led to the Windsor house. In less than five minutes we walked onto the spacious veranda of a Dutch-style tropical manse that served as agent's office, gem shop, restaurant, art gallery, boarding house, and home to the Windsor family.

Windsor was an affable, shrewd, entertaining Singhalese gentleman who showed us around his sprawling premises. He then led us back to the shady veranda with its caned chairs and whitewashed wall, crammed with photographs of skippers and crews who had passed through before us.

He offered us cold drinks. "Everything in my home is at your disposal — for a small fee, of course."

My focus was on the shower and washer and dryer. I hadn't seen such luxury since we'd left Taiwan, and I knew I'd be a permanent fixture at the Windsor house. While he nodded his head left to right and left again, and talked on and on about his charitable contributions to the local community, I visualized dirty underwear spinning round and round in hot soapy water.

We spent the evening at a restaurant with Heiko and his girlfriend who had flown in from Germany to join him. We drank endless bottles of Lion stout, a Singhalese brew first introduced to the island by Scottish tea planters in the 1800s. And over a meal of curried rice and chicken served with *sambal* — a coconut, tamarind, chilli condiment — and shrimp chips, we recounted our adventures and misadventures since we had last seen each other. Bernard imparted the saki recipe to Heiko in return for his generous hospitality.

"Can't wait for your brew to ferment," Heiko called after us as we climbed into our dinghy for the ride back to the *Santa Rita*.

That night Bernard was in good spirits.

"Do you mind if I sleep in the aft cabin?" he asked.

It had been his decision to sleep in the salon. His asking permission to return to the aft cabin seemed odd as I had never pushed him out. I scooted to my side of the berth, and lifted the cover for him to get under. He hopped in and stroked my face. I was elated he had returned.

The next day he and I went ashore to explore the old section of Galle. We walked about the granite ramparts, examined the stone walls, took in the hybrid Dutch influenced houses with their large verandas, red tile roofs, and flowering courtyards, and did a quick tour of the defunct Dutch Reformed Church.

The Dutch, at the behest of the king of Ceylon as Sri Lanka was then known, liberated the island from the Portuguese in the seventeenth century. A number of Dutch remained behind or immigrated to Ceylon to work mainly as civil servants, and married Sinhalese women. Their descendants, known as Burghers, had once lived in this section. The quarter, with its houses of gracefully decaying gentility, felt to me as though I were walking through a parallel universe. The only intrusion into this time warp was the endless stream of ragged children and touts tugging at us to visit some shop or site for the price of a coin.

New Galle was a jumbled mess of dilapidated, concrete houses and one-room storefronts strewn together every which way. But life was here, and where we preferred to be. Women in saris and workers in sarongs shopped, ate, and haggled along the narrow streets.

Saffron-robed Buddhist monks with begging bowls edged their way through the mass of humanity walking like a line of ants to the better homes near the old port to ask for their ration of rice. I wondered if the street beggars hadn't been influenced by their more pious brothers. We'd passed through many places as poor as Galle, but I had never seen so many people squatting on the street with their hands out. Nor had I ever seen so many deformed people and wondered about that. One day I took a local bus and sat beside a well-dressed woman in a silk sari with gold bangles circling her wrists, holding a pudgy little girl about a year old on her lap. The child stared at me with an infectious smile that lit up her large, dark eyes.

"Your daughter is beautiful," I said.

The woman turned to face me, took hold of the child's hand and held it out towards me palm up. "Bon bon," she said. She repeated this request for candy over and over in an effort to have the child repeat her words while holding the little girl's hand out to me. She finally stopped when I turned away to look out the window in an effort to distance myself.

It was impossible to relate to anyone on the street. To ask directions meant paying for the response in advance. To look lost meant that someone would approach to try to drag you to his father's or his uncle's or his brother's shop. To look at a building meant someone would accost you, mumble something, and then ask for payment as a guide. The one time we had a local aboard in a friendly gesture of camaraderie, we discovered we were missing our radio when he left.

One afternoon, after a meagre lunch of curried fish and rice at Windsor's, Bernard and I went in search of a gem merchant. We had passed a number of storefronts on our earlier walks and decided to check out some of the places. We had heard that Sri Lanka was famous for its blue sapphires and moonstones. The sapphires were a bit pricy but incredibly cheap compared to the west, and the moonstones were almost given away.

Bernard, in an expansive mood, bought me a moonstone necklace, then a bracelet, then a number of rings, and after that more rings and necklaces for gifts. When we had exhausted the possibilities in handcrafted ware, he bought a box of loose moonstones, many of which I still have in an old plastic film container. I love moonstones, but too much of anything starts to lessen its value. Still, I loved the unexpected extravagance that was in keeping with the light mood and affection Bernard showered on me that day. We held hands, walked with our bodies in synchronized step, and laughed at each other's comments and observations of the local scene. It was as though we were a young couple who had just discovered love.

In the local post office we asked if any mail had come for the *Santa Rita* via Poste Restante, which is how mail arrives at sea. The clerk handed Bernard a letter from his mother with some unexpected news. Dedé was on her way to Sri Lanka, bringing with her the young mistress of a wealthy gangster neighbour she had admired for years and who had recently died. She would arrive from France in a week.

Not good, I thought. This stocky, bull-necked woman, built like a tank and with as much sensitivity, had never forgiven me for marrying her prized possession and favourite son. She had once asked if I was happy with Bernard and when I said yes, she broke down and cried. "Life isn't fair," she sniffed. "I was never happy with *le docteur*." It was the way she always referred to Bernard's father. "And you have taken away my son."

That was the only conversation she and I had had when we visited her in France. She spent hours in animated conversation with Bernard, but as soon as I approached, she became silent. When the two were looking at family photos and I entered the room, she quickly put them away. Now, in the cramped quarters of the *Santa Rita*, I was going to spend several weeks with her and a woman I'd never met.

"This isn't going to work," I said. "The yacht's going to be claustrophobic with the two of them aboard. Your mother takes up a lot of space, and she'll want Stefan's cabin. That means this woman whom we don't even know and Stefan will be sharing the salon."

"I know," he said. "I thought about it. There's a nice hotel near the harbour. I'll reserve a room for the two of them there."

Next morning, I awoke to find Bernard sitting up beside me with his back against the bulkhead staring into space. This surprised me as his habit was to grab a cup of coffee upon waking and sit in the cockpit to watch the sunrise.

"What's up?" I asked.

"I had the weirdest dream," he said. "I dreamt I was having sex with my mother."

I gave a nervous laugh, as I knew Bernard had a lot of reservations about his mother — one of the reasons he had moved so far from his country of birth.

His dream rattled him, and I had a twinge of foreshadowing.

The day before Bernard's mother arrived, Heiko offered to throw a welcoming party for her and her friend at an apartment he'd rented near the harbour. "I'll pick up some wine and a couple of things to eat," he said. "What do you think?"

"Good idea," Bernard said.

That was the last day the two men ever spoke to each other again.

Kenwood and family

Workers at the Shin Hsing boatyard

The Santa Rita under construction

Salon of the Santa Rita

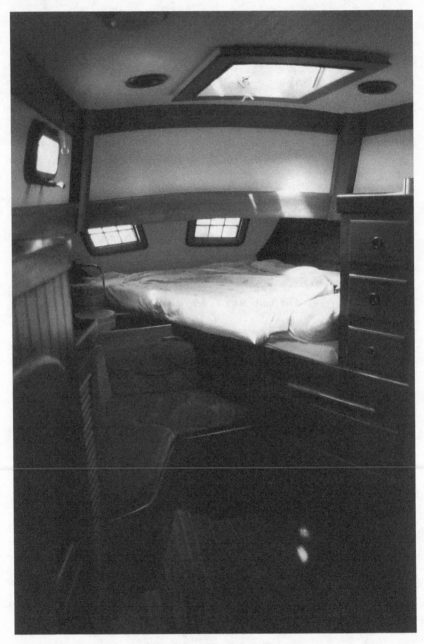

Aft cabin of the Santa Rita

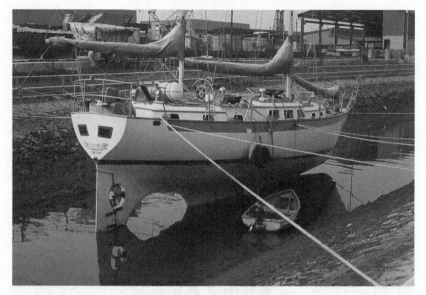

The Santa Rita being launched in the Danshui River

Santa Rita under sail

Me at the helm in Hong Kong

The Santa Rita anchored among Chinese junks

Chinese opera on outdoor stage in Hong Kong

Floating child during Bun Festival in Cheung Chau

Stefan and Jonah tying the Santa Rita to a mooring

Journey into the Palawan interior, Philippines

Bernard and Stefan in the Philippines

Anchored along the coast of Malaysia

Swimming with the whale shark in Sabang, Indonesia

Dede examining her new ring

Elephant orphanage in Sri Lanka

Santa Rita in Dry Dock in Galle

An Indonesian Bugi at sea, Jurong harbour

With Colleagues from the British Council

Bernard skimming the waves in Singapore

Me on the bosun chair skimming the waves

Stefan in Singapore bringing provisions

Bernard and me with Dr. Pomade in Singapore apartment

Bernard, Lola and me

The Santa Rita on the way to India

Street scene in Cochin

Visiting Sudan

Heading towards the island of Lipari, Italy

Me afloat in the Dead Sea, Israel

Bernard and I below deck in Palma de Mallorca

Chapter 18

VISITORS FROM HELL

Spring 1983: Sri Lanka

> *Time past and time future*
> *What might have been and*
> *What had been*
> *Point to one end, which is*
> *always present.*
> —T.S. ELIOT

Until the day Bernard's mother arrived, our life had an easy rhythm. Bernard spent his time fiddling with the converted tractor engine that seemed to need constant attention. Stefan read, or helped Bernard with repairs when needed, and then spent the rest of his time with a young guy he'd met at Windsor's who was crew on another yacht. I cooked up my usual stir fried whatever and luxuriated in showers and the smell of clean laundry.

Restaurants were so cheap it cost almost more to prepare a meal, so we often ate out. Unfortunately, Singhalese cuisine lacked imagination. Tiny platters of curried fish, curried chicken, or curried vegetable served with mounds of rice and a small side of *sambal,* were the daily fare. The *sambal* was actually an interesting condiment if you could tolerate its heat. But the dishes tasted like a textured base for curry and hot chili.

The only creative bit of culinary art was the *string hoppers* made from rice noodles and shaped into a kind of pancake. Bernard, Stefan and I tried them one morning, but the bland taste wasn't enticing enough for us to want them daily. A Tamil gentleman, who worked on the docks, told us he'd been a cook on one of the big ocean liners.

He tried to open a restaurant in Galle, but got vandalized by the Hindu community for not being the appropriate caste for that enterprise. It was a loss for us, though a much greater loss for him.

After dinner we usually sat on Windsor's veranda with a handful of other yachties and shared sea stories while chugging down Sri Lanka's fine stout. Heiko and his girlfriend were always there, as well as the two French skippers and their wives whom we'd met in Taiwan. They were the two men who'd sailed with us aboard the *Santa Rita* during our difficult crossing from Taiwan to Hong Kong. Obviously, they had overcome their terror of the sea though I suspected they would still be a nightmare to have as crew. Eventually another yacht arrived in the harbour, and her crew joined us on the veranda. They were a clean-cut, handsome young couple who said they had sailed from the Mediterranean.

Another foreigner who was anchored in the harbour, but didn't join us at the Windsor's, was Helene, a strapping, young woman we had first encountered defecating off the stern of her yacht in Singapore. She was still practicing her questionable hygiene, and had now taken to going topless while working on her yacht. It delighted Bernard. He never missed a chance to grab his binoculars when he spotted her on deck. He found it hysterically funny, but I wasn't amused.

One day, after he'd spent hours on the engine with hardly a break except to pick up the binoculars, I'd had enough. "I guess I'll get more attention from you if I walk around like that," I spat out. I ripped off my t-shirt and started up the companionway. Bernard grabbed hold of me and carried me back down. He wasn't as amused to see me topless on deck, but I was frustrated with the bloody engine taking up every spare moment of his time; that is, when he wasn't ogling Helene, who was forever doing repairs, her pendulous breasts flapping in the breeze as she bent over one project after another.

As I write this story, I'm back there in every detail — the t-shirt I was wearing, its feel on my skin, the tug of tearing it off, the heat of the morning sun and the light spilling down the companionway — memory and sensation so closely intertwined. From early childhood, many memories, both good and bad, come to me fully experienced once conjured up, complete with sound, smell, and tactile sensation.

Memory must live in every cell of our body, not merely stored as dusty files in some hidden chamber of the brain.

Revisiting the past opens the possibility of reinterpreting it with the wisdom of the present. Today, I'm aware Bernard's fixation on the engine was a form of meditation. It shut out the voices in his head that told him he was ill-prepared for the journey, that I couldn't survive if anything happened to him, and that danger is always a hair's breadth away. I didn't focus on these issues. I believed blindly in Bernard's strengths and capabilities. The only anxiety I felt was the imminent arrival of Dedé.

Bernard's mother, Dedé, arrived with her usual flourish and saccharine niceties. I greeted her with as much civility as I could muster. Geneviève, an attractive dark-haired woman in her late thirties, came as her travel companion. The unlikely alliance of the older and younger woman was cemented by their passion for Monsieur B, an old gangster who had made a lot of money in questionable dealings and finally died to the relief of many. Geneviève was the last of his mistresses. Dedé was a kind of groupie, enthralled with the rich and powerful regardless of their morals. She had adored Monsieur B.

Throughout his childhood, Dedé had bombarded Bernard with stories of Monsieur B. *"Monsieur B has beautiful gardens and greenhouses that he tends himself. Monsieur B flies his own small plane. Monsieur B sent us to the Canary Islands on vacation at his own expense. Monsieur B always has beautiful women."*

Bernard's father was a country doctor. Monsieur B had been his patient. In place of payment for medical treatment, Monsieur B sent the family on paid vacations. *"Le docteur,"* Dedé would say about her husband, "is an idiot." It irritated me that she refused to call her husband by his given name. So arrogant, I thought, and so snide. "He treats patients for a chicken and a handful of eggs."

She couldn't forget that he tended the poor during and after the Second World War for next to nothing. Or that he gave up a chateau that they had rented during the war to build his own home. Or that he had put the fireplace where she had asked him not to. Dedé had a long memory, and I was subjected to these stories whenever I visited France. Now she was here with Monsieur B's last mistress. It didn't augur well, but the *Santa Rita* was my home, my turf, and I felt I could weather whatever was to come.

Bernard settled the two women into the hotel he had found near the harbour. While he was there, Heiko dropped by to say that he was preparing a spread for us late afternoon. When Bernard returned from the hotel, I conveyed the invitation from Heiko. He nodded to acknowledge he'd heard me, and then set to work dissembling and greasing some of the winches. He stayed at it for hours. Around 4 in the afternoon, I reminded him of Heiko's offer and suggested he pick up his mother and Geneviève.

"Go on ahead," he said. "I'll just finish up and we'll meet you there."

Heiko and his girlfriend had outdone themselves in preparing a smorgasbord of delectable treats — enough to constitute an evening meal. They had decorated the living room with crepe paper and had bottles and wine glasses set out on a buffet. "They'll be by shortly," I said. "Bernard has to finish putting some winches together, and then he'll pick up his mother and Geneviève."

We waited for over an hour, and finally had some wine and then some of the goodies to temper the wine. The rest of our time was spent clock-gazing. My embarrassment grew with each passing minute. Finally, I couldn't bear waiting any longer.

"Something must have come up. I'll look for them," I said. I raced out of Heiko's apartment and towards the port. On the way I heard voices speaking in French on Windsor's veranda. I shifted direction towards the Windsor house and found Bernard and the two women seated at a small table sipping beer and chatting.

"You were supposed to be at Heiko's two hours ago," I blurted out.

Dedé looked in my direction. "Bernard told us Heiko's an alcoholic. I don't like that sort of company." I was taken aback at her remark. Bernard was far closer to being an alcoholic than Heiko.

The three went on chatting in French. I looked on, shaking from anger, my skin burning from humiliation. I knew that if I expressed my outrage, Dedé would use it against me. This is what she was hoping would happen, so that she could show Bernard how unstable I was. Dedé was a manipulative woman, and I wasn't going to fall into her trap. I took my anger with me and returned to the yacht. This visit was going to be a nightmare, and I had to figure out how to deal with it. I had one thought that saved me. There's not enough room on the yacht for them to stay with us.

The following morning Dedé showed up at the pier, suitcases in hand and Geneviève at her side. "I'm not comfortable in the hotel," she said. "We've decided to stay with you."

Stefan gave his berth with its private head in the fore cabin to Dedé. He camped on deck for the duration of their stay. Geneviève's berth was the long settee in the salon opposite the table where we ate. The rest of the salon was taken up with their suitcases.

It's only two weeks I told myself. I'll manage.

The next morning I found Dedé going through our laundry. "What are you doing?" I asked.

In one hand she held a pair of Bernard's skivvies. The other hand was buried somewhere in the dirty clothes. She continued rummaging while chastising me for being an inadequate sailor. "People, who live on boats, do their own laundry. They don't use washing machines." She snatched a few more pairs of Bernard's underpants, and a couple of his sleeveless undershirts.

"Windsor has a wash basin," she continued. "I'll be washing Bernard's things there."

"Suit yourself," I said.

When Dedé returned from Windsor's with her precious cargo of wrung-out undies, she told me she had met the lovely young couple who had sailed in from the Med. "They're such a charming pair. And that young girl, that's a real sailor. Someone like her is more suited for this adventure."

Screw you, I thought.

"Think so?" I said, smiling. I was determined to make it through their visit with no show of agitation.

That afternoon we went for lunch in one of Galle's dreary hole-in-the-wall restaurants. Serving portions in Singhalese restaurants are minute, and the clients bulk up on rice. After everyone had ordered, I asked for a large bowl of fried rice for a few extra cents so that there would be sufficient food to abate hunger.

"Wouldn't you know it," Bernard commented, looking straight at his mother. "She would order the most expensive dish."

The two women nodded as though they knew I was a horrible spend thrift. My determination to hold my tongue for the two weeks was starting to weaken, but I was still resisting. It was clear that Bernard was picking up on his mother's hostile energy. I couldn't stand that she had such a strong hold on him, and that he was so unaware. He slipped into another skin when he was around her.

After lunch Bernard was feeling good. He led the group of us through the old section pointing out to the women the various historical sites. We stopped in front of the shop where he had bought me the moonstone jewellery.

A short while later we emerged from the store with Dedé sporting a sapphire and moonstone ring that Bernard had generously purchased for her with our dwindling funds. Moonstones were cheap, but sapphires were a whole other story. I was livid. I separated from the group and stomped furiously ahead though no one appeared to notice. Shortly after, while preparing dinner, I slammed the cabinet doors as I pulled out various ingredients for the meal, and banged the pan hard on the stove before throwing in a shot of cooking oil.

That evening, after waxing ecstatically over my stir fried dish, Dedé turned to Bernard and inquired in that falsetto voice she uses when she comes in for a kill: "Rita seems unhappy. Is there a problem?"

"There's nothing wrong with her. She's just jealous because I bought you the ring."

I wanted to curl up and die. I couldn't understand why Bernard wasn't able to see what his mother was doing. It seemed as though this visit had propelled him back to some earlier relationship they had together. I totally disappeared from his radar. If this wasn't happening in my life, I would have found it an interesting pathological study.

The next morning Bernard decided we would take a bus to Unawatuna, a well-known beach not far from Galle. I was thrilled that Bernard was willing to leave the yacht for a few hours. Stefan, as usual, would stay behind to watch the *Santa Rita*.

Through the window of the bus I spied the stilt fishermen sitting motionless on poles six feet above the water, each with one hand on a fishing rod and the other on the pole to stay balanced. From a distance the scene looked ethereal, and the men made me think of flamingos scattered randomly along the edge of a great body of water. But the reality was very different. These men sat for hours with nothing but rags on their heads and sarongs around their waists to protect them from the brutal sun, hoping for a meagre catch to bring home or to the market. I couldn't think of a more uncomfortable way to eke out a living.

Unawatuna was a visual delight. Coral reefs protected this portion of the bay from the greater ocean so only gentle waves in shallow water lapped the beach. The emerald sea glistened in the sun. Thick groves of coconut and palm trees rimmed the edge of the beach that curved around the ocean in a long arch. A dozen or so kids splashed about in the water while their parents, in bathing suits, lay on thin blankets oblivious to the elephants strolling about. Here and there mounds of elephant dung shared the otherwise pristine beach with the sunbathers. The thought of lying almost naked while those giant hooves walked about me was terrifying. Geneviève and Dedé must have felt the same since they also showed no enthusiasm for sunbathing.

In lieu of sitting on the beach, we decided to walk its length and explore the area. Bernard and Dède walked in front holding hands, while Geneviève and I followed behind like a pair of chaperones. Every once in a while Bernard stopped and picked up a shell to show his mother.

When I first envisioned Bernard and I together on this journey, I pictured an idyllic scene like this for us — not the mishaps, tension and periods of silent withdrawal. I put in the work. Now, I felt Dedé was getting the dream. My only thought was to get back to the *Santa Rita*. The day had been ruined for me.

"How about our sailing to Colombo tomorrow?" Bernard suggested when we returned to the yacht that evening.

That cheered me up. I never said no to a new experience, and I wasn't going to let my unpleasant guests spoil my love of discovery.

On the sail to Colombo, the ocean was rough and the yacht bounced around erratically, but Dedé took it well. I had to admit that impressed me. I saw where Bernard got his grit. As for Geneviève, it was hard to tell how she felt about anything. She was like Dedé's shadow. When I spoke to her, she'd look at Dedé before answering, and then with as few words as possible. Before we'd sit down to one of my meals, she'd look at Dède and wait for her to approve the dish before she ate. Dedé always expressed nice but surprised comments about my cooking. The implication was what a surprise that an American could actually turn out something edible. Dède was an extraordinary cook.

Geneviève, with her knock-out body, had taken to running about our cramped quarters in tiny bikini bottoms. She also started offering bits of food from her plate to Bernard, as she had seen me do. She made no eye contact with me, but went out of her way to serve him. I wondered if Dedé had brought Geneviève as a possible replacement. As the days went on, I became sure of it. Dedé was the ultimate mother-in-law from hell.

Colombo was a huge unattractive industrial port with gigantic freighters and cargo ships. We dropped anchor in the harbour instead of tying up at the pier in order to avoid any possibility of collision. Shortly after, the harbour master came aboard to inspect. Bernard mentioned in friendly conversation that I read palms.

"I'd like a reading," he said.

I was terrified. I read palms, but only for western clients, not for a person where palm reading was part of the culture. What I knew, I had learned from books purchased at second-hand book stores. I was worried he'd think I was a fraud. I explained it was only character that I did, not predictions. He seemed happy with that and I proceeded to tell him what I believed the lines, texture of his skin, and shape of his hands revealed.

"You are very good," he said. "I will send you clients."

I felt good that I had impressed this man with my skill, but more than that, we had made an ally with a government official, which was always good when sailing in a foreign country.

Among the big freighters in the harbour was an old wreck carrying a Polish flag. It was in the hands of a captain by the name of Kujinsky. I think the harbour master must have spoken to him about my palm reading skills because we were soon visited by Captain Kujinsky, who invited us to come aboard his ship.

The ship was falling apart. There was very little equipment and what existed was dated and would never have passed inspection in the West. He explained that they had little money and were never sure when they'd be paid. There was unrest in Poland, he told us, and they never knew whether the government would hold or not until they returned. The crew and Captain Kujinsky hoped to stay afloat long enough to see the fall of the communist regime.

We were invited aboard the ship for drinks. The captain fussed over Dedé as an older woman, and she basked in the limelight. I hoped she'd remember this day as she always claimed to have had a miserable time after any vacation she'd been on. Things were always better in France.

A while after we had settled in, the first mate arrived with a rolled-up chart under his arm. When Captain Kujinsky unrolled the paper, I saw that it was a diagram of the engine. He looked at it for a moment and then took a pendulum out of his pocket and started moving it around the diagram.

"There," he said. "There's the problem." The first mate nodded and left.

"We have so little in the way of financial resources, I have to use my divining gift to keep the freighter afloat," he explained. He added that he was sometimes called in by the Belgium police to find missing bodies.

"What can you tell us that might be useful?" I asked.

"Never live near weeping willows or your life will only know sorrow, and see that there are evergreen trees wherever you are. They give health, happiness, and a good life."

"Thank you, Captain Kujinsky."

Every time I see a weeping willow or an evergreen, I think of the captain. I will never live near a weeping willow as beautiful as I find them, and I love the energy of evergreens. Fortunately, I live in a country where they grow in abundance.

About six the next morning, the *Santa Rita* started to rock violently. A sudden squall with winds gusting about 80 miles an hour loosened the anchor of a huge freighter near us. It got caught in our mooring and was dragging us. Bernard scrambled on deck and saw we were only twenty feet from the pier. The wind was so strong he couldn't remain on deck. The only thing we could do was sit below deck and wait out the storm. We were in luck. The mooring held.

Not willing to give in to the erratic weather we were experiencing, Bernard and I hailed a cab to take us to the American Embassy where I had a distant relative who was an attaché. The next day was Saturday, so we thought we'd invite him and his wife for a sail if they were free. The invitation was accepted and Bernard met them at the pier with the dinghy and brought them aboard the *Santa Rita*. We were not out very long when the swells on the open ocean were more than they could take. We had no choice but to take them back to shore. The two ladies were not perturbed. Again, I was impressed by Dedé's resilience, as well as Geneviève's stoicism. It was frustrating that they behaved in such a hostile manner towards me.

Anchoring in Colombo wasn't safe for our small, fibreglass yacht, so we decided to return to the more protected harbour in Galle. All we had seen of Colombo was the uninteresting downtown section with its fair share of cars and the occasional elephant vying for road space.

The return was not easy. We again found ourselves in the middle of a violent squall. Bernard and I put on our rain slickers and went on deck to steady the boat. The weather was miserably cold. Bernard took the helm and turned the bow into the wind so that we could reef the sail and lower the jib. Once he turned the yacht back on course and gave the helm over to the autopilot, we returned below deck. Our guests were quite relaxed. Either they trusted us completely or were totally oblivious to the situation.

Back in Galle with the *Santa Rita* safely moored in the harbour, we decided to take a train to Kandy, the famous tea country that spawned the Lipton Tea Company. Spending a few days in a small hotel out of our cramped living conditions would be heaven. Stefan as usual was left aboard the *Santa Rita*. He never complained, and I suspect he was happy to get some alone time when we left him behind. He had already told me he needed time to think, to figure out his future. A boat crowded with people and constant maintenance responsibilities wasn't very conducive for that.

Our plan was to take a bus to Colombo, and then the train from there through Kandy to Ella. We had read in several tourist brochures that the train from Kandy to Ella travelled along some of the most beautiful landscape in the world. I was a bit sceptical, having already passed through so many beautiful places. But during that stretch of railway, I realised that this part of Sri Lanka really could be called a paradise, and I wasn't disappointed that we made the journey. Sri Lanka didn't live up to our fantasies, but the passage through the tea country made our stopover worth it.

The railway had been built by the British over a hundred years ago to carry tea from the plantations to Colombo for export. Our train passed through tunnels that opened up to undulating green hills and broad valleys that spread out to majestic purple mountain peaks half-hidden in mist. Bridges passed over rivers with cascading waterfalls tumbling down mountainsides. Small villages sprouted up and disappeared along the train route. They appeared etched into the landscape as though an artist had painted the tableau for the pleasure of the travellers. If I had to conjure up a biblical image of the Garden of Eden, it would be the tea country of Sri Lanka.

We travelled without reservations, but had no difficulty on our arrival finding a hotel in the small town of Ella. Geneviève and Dedé shared one room and Bernard and I had another. Within seconds of settling in, Dedé banged on our door to complain they had no towels or toilet paper. Bernard rushed into our bathroom, snatched the towels and went for the toilet paper. I got to the toilet paper first and pressed the roll to my breast.

"Hold on," I said. "I also bathe and use paper."

I tore off a wad of toilet paper and thrust it into Dedé's hand. I was annoyed that I hadn't been fast enough on the towels. Bernard's mouth dropped open at my outburst. He just stood there looking stunned. I tracked down the manager and came back with two sets of towels and three rolls of toilet paper. I threw the toilet paper on the bed.

"This should hold her for a while."

Ella was serene with lush green rolling hills, stately trees, and elegant homes. The tea plantations, spread out for miles over the hills, were worked by the Tamil. Several generations earlier they had been brought to Sri Lanka by the British, who had colonized the country, to do administrative work because they didn't believe the local population was sufficiently efficient. It was during those years when Sri Lanka was known as Ceylon, and stories of the island's serenity filled listeners back home with romantic longing for a gentler way of life.

But the reality was that once the British left the island, the Tamil lost their protection. Few jobs were available to them. One was working in the fields of the tea plantations. The work was backbreaking and their living conditions appalling. The Singhalese prejudice against these people along with the limiting of their rights made me think of the American south during the years of slavery. I wasn't surprised that civil war broke out a few years after we departed. The wounds of discrimination had been festering for generations, and it was obvious that it was only a matter of time.

In Kandy there was an elephant orphanage, one of the few in the world, and the elephants are treated with respect. They're well fed and cared for. I love animals and was happy to hear about the orphanage, but found it an irony that citizens of the country couldn't be given the same consideration. Many Singhalese suffered from poverty. The gap between the rich and poor was enormous, and nothing was being done to change the situation. Families lived by begging or bilking the unwary tourist. It made my stomach clench every time I was accosted, which was often. Though I understood the desperation, I hated it, and was frustrated by the fact that I could do nothing about it.

Before leaving the hill country, we decided to visit the temple caves in Dambulla, a town a few hours by bus from Kandy. We got there early morning before the doors opened and had to wait. As usual Geneviève and I were together, and Bernard and his mother shared another sitting area. While Geneviève and I watched the antics of a group of hyperactive monkeys, Dedé spent the time combing ringlets into Bernard's hair. Though I tried to focus on the frisky monkeys, intent on entertaining us, I kept being drawn to this bizarre scene of an adult man having his hair played with by his mother.

By the time the doors opened to the temple, I had lost all interest in seeing the incredible groupings of stone-carved statues, most of them depicting Buddha's life, and the exquisite murals covering the ceilings and walls. I just wanted to get out of there and back home. I had a hard time playing second fiddle to my mate's mother, and I was angry at Bernard for being oblivious to how he was pushing me out of his life. Today I regret not having paid more attention to these sacred caves.

My sole consolation at knowing that our guests would soon leave us was short-lived by the horrible outpouring of venom Stefan received on our return. While we were gone, he had invited a friend for a visit. When Dedé found out, she was furious. She felt he had no right to have anyone aboard while we were gone. Since this was his home and not hers, I thought she was way out of line to chastise him. She stormed off and left Bernard to finish what she started. Bernard berated Stefan for several minutes, and when Stefan didn't respond, he started calling him names. He finally ran out of steam and left to join his mother. I held myself back from interfering because I wanted Stefan to speak up. He was almost twenty-one and perfectly capable of defending himself.

"Why didn't you say anything?" I asked. "You didn't have to take that from Bernard." I felt so much pain for what I thought he must be feeling.

But Stefan didn't feel what I was feeling. He answered me with no hint of agitation.

"Mom," he said. "Bernard is a very angry man who is trying to hold it all together. He was pushing me to respond so that he could feel justified in releasing that anger. I wasn't going to give him the satisfaction. Let him carry it and deal with it."

It occurred to me at that moment that my son was a lot more mature than I was. But it didn't stop me from feeling that we were both being bullied. My first thought was to jump ship. I wanted to offer myself as crew on another yacht and just get away. But I wasn't going to leave my son behind. And I didn't want to lose the time and investment I had put into making this adventure happen. I also had no money and no place to go.

More than anything, I wanted to sell the *Santa Rita*. Being treated as an uninvited guest on my own boat was not what I bargained for when I envisioned this adventure. I was going to enjoy what I could of our journey, but I no longer had any illusions about a perfect life in some beautiful paradise or two happy soul mates on the same path. Wherever I was, was where I was as a single adventurous soul on a personal journey. There was no idyllic place where one lived happily ever after. I'd always be taking me with me, and it didn't matter so much what was going on outside or who I was with, as what was happening inside. The yacht was now a roof over my head from which I planned to take control of my life. It was no longer a magic carpet.

Next morning I saw Dedé sitting alone by the pier. She looked spaced out and dejected.

"Is something the matter?" I asked.

"I had a dream," she said. "My cat had a wounded ear, but I couldn't heal it."

"That's not so bad. It's just one of those frustrating dreams where we try to get something finished, but it never happens."

"The wounded cat was Bernard," she replied.

Whose fault is that? I thought.

"Maybe," I said, taken aback by her desire to analyse the dream. I never would have guessed she had such an inclination.

Later that day, Dedé decided to go for a swim. A slight breeze came up and Bernard panicked. He called for Stefan to throw her one of the rubber tires we used to buffer the yacht from other yachts or for protection against a concrete pier. As Stefan went towards the tire, Bernard started to shout at him for moving too slowly. In truth, his Dedé wasn't in danger, and Stefan wasn't moving slowly. At that moment I would have been happy if Dedé drowned, or at least panicked and flailed about in the water.

Since Dedé didn't drown, she and Geneviève decided to spend their last day buying gifts for friends and family back home.

"What would you like, Rita?" she asked. "We want to give you with something for having us."

"Maybe a skirt," I said. The market had cheap, cotton wrap-around skirts that would be ideal for getting in and out of the dinghy.

That afternoon they returned with a stash of gifts to take home, including a batik sarong for Bernard.

"I'm sorry," Dedé said. "We didn't get you anything. The skirts were too expensive."

I couldn't have cared less. The best gift for me was to see their backsides as they left for the airport.

"Thank God they're gone," I said to Bernard as we headed back to the *Santa Rita*. I was so relieved to have my space back.

Bernard was offended. I explained to him how much he made me feel like an outsider when they were with us. "You only included me in a conversation the day they were leaving, and then made me appear like an ingrate when I couldn't respond." I went on to explain how I went out of my way for them, but the good will was never reciprocated.

I lashed out about Geneviève. "She slept in what still is my home, ate the meals I prepared, used my hospitality for two weeks and thanked me with devious behaviour and a ten cent plastic hair clip. That she has a big personal income doesn't change the fact she sucks off others."

"Stop the soap opera," he responded.

His response to my obvious hurt was cruel. I sat down and wrote him a letter in the hope that I would get through: "Soaps are successful," I wrote, "because they take their material from recognizable human experience. It's not the other way around. By calling all emotional expression soap, you degrade humans to the level of objects and elevate the sociopath to the level of socially evolved."

I also mentioned my concern with his drinking, and how it affected his behaviour. I know I wrote this as well as much more, because I have the letter. When I told Bernard I was writing the memoir, he handed me the yellowed, crumpled letter that I had written more than thirty years ago.

"You saved it," I said, "Why?"

He looked puzzled. "I don't know."

I was touched. From everything that had been aboard the *Santa Rita*, this was the one thing he kept all these years. Had he been aware of the pull of his mother and its destructive effect on me and just couldn't deal with it? He still couldn't talk about it.

Several days after our guests left, Interpol came looking for that lovely, young couple that Dède liked so much. Apparently, they had thrown an elderly couple overboard near the coast of Columbia and took possession of the yacht. Now the international police were trying to track them down, but with no luck. They had left over a week before and no one knew where they were heading. I thought about Dedé's ability to judge character. Perhaps I should feel grateful she didn't like me.

Chapter 19

TERROR ON THE HIGH SEAS

Summer 1983: Sri Lanka To Singapore

> *We are the sea's and as such we are at its beck.*
> *We are the water within the wave and the wave's form.*
> — P.K. PAGE

With Dède gone, Bernard slipped back into the easy relationship he'd had with Stefan and me before her arrival. I was caught off balance by his sudden shift from blind devotion to Dède to bringing us back into his life. I hoped he'd be receptive to talking about it.

"What happened?" I asked. "Why did you turn against us when your mother was here?"

Bernard looked puzzled. "What are you talking about?"

"You know, yelling at Stefan and putting me down in front of her whenever you could. You hardly talked to us and behaved as though we were strangers."

"What have you got against my mother?"

I remembered him telling me years before that his mother was a controlling and manipulative woman, and that I should be careful of her. Now he was defending her. I wondered what had changed. But then he smiled and gave me a hug, and my anger and suspicion disappeared.

Sri Lanka wasn't the paradise Clarke wrote about, so we weren't planning to stay long. However, the visit of Bernard's mother delayed our leaving by several weeks. We now had a shorter window of time to cross the Arabian Sea before the start of India's southeast monsoon season. A tropical storm over such an enormous body of water made sailing through one too dangerous to attempt. We had to leave soon, but needed to work on the *Santa Rita* before our departure.

With the yacht raised onto its cradle on dry dock, Bernard and Stefan took turns climbing a ladder to the underside of the hull to scrape the hard crustaceans that held fast. Barnacles that clung below the waterline created a drag that slowed our speed under sail and burned too much fuel under engine. The antifouling applied in Taipei should have protected the hull for a longer period of time, but the boatyard skimped on the application. Now we had no choice but to repaint the hull's bottom before we sailed.

On one of Bernard's trips down the ladder, he slipped and fell, cutting his shin. I had the first aid kit ready the minute he scrambled into the boat. As I was about to clean out the wound, I asked him what he thought the white stuff was in his leg.

"Bone," he said.

"Oh," I muttered.

I handed him the paraphernalia for dealing with the problem, backed myself into the settee on the other side of the salon, and went into a slight swoon.

Bernard quickly cleaned and dressed his wound, pulling the two edges of his cut shin together with a butterfly bandage. In less than a half hour he was back outside working with Stefan to lower the *Santa Rita* into the waterway leading to the ocean.

"We've no time to lose," he said. "I can't wait for this leg to heal."

He showed no irritation or impatience with me for my inability to help him dress his wound, but I felt ashamed. I knew that, if I had been hurt, he would have looked after me with the same calm efficiency he had shown while working on himself. I admired his clarity of mind, resourcefulness, and control in times of danger. I relied on him totally for any crisis.

By the time the *Santa Rita* was ready to sail, the winds had shifted, and we could no longer make it across the Arabian Sea.

"We're not protected in Galle Harbour," Bernard announced. "We should try to make it back to Singapore before the bad weather hits full force."

I agreed.

"We can wait out the season in Jurong Harbour," I said. "We already know the place, and it's out of monsoon range."

Within two days of our leaving Sri Lanka the winds picked up, followed by relentless rain. The storm turned fierce and the waves so violent that we wouldn't have been able to turn the yacht around even if we tried. We had no choice but to move ahead. We took down the mainsail and mizzen to slow down the yacht, leaving only the small staysail in front of the bow. But even that was too much. The yacht shook violently as we approached hull speed. A little faster and the *Santa Rita* could break apart.

Humungous waves, reaching thirty or forty feet, welled up behind us and threatened to overwhelm the boat. The autopilot went berserk. Bernard held tight to the helm carefully manoeuvring each wave so that we wouldn't capsize.

"We're going to break apart if we go any faster," he shouted to Stefan. Over the noise of the thrashing waves and rumbling hull, his voice was barely audible. "You've got to take down that staysail."

Stefan, in rain slicker, inched across the deck clipping and unclipping his harness every foot or so to the wooden railing on top of the cabin to keep himself from being washed overboard. I had been ordered to go below deck and watched him through the portholes. They didn't want me on deck.

"Your mother doesn't have the weight to withstand the wind," Bernard had said. "She'll be swept overboard in no time." Stefan nodded in agreement.

I hadn't argued. I knew they were right. I was spent trying to brace against the unforgiving wind. It sapped every bit of my strength. But it was just as bad doing nothing, watching my son through the portholes crawl towards the bow sprit — a four-foot long narrow beam jutting out into nothingness from the end of the bow, with no stanchion lines around it for safety. Foaming ocean surrounded him. A thin, wire cable that attached the fore sail to the mizzen mast was all he had to grab onto. With one leg wrapped around the stanchion line that ended at the foot of the bow, the other on that narrow piece of wood jutting out into the ocean, and a hand on the cable, he slowly unhooked the stay sail, one ring at a time, with his remaining hand.

With Stefan balanced on that narrow finger of wood, the waves drove the bow ten feet into the air. The next second, the waves buried him under water. Each time a wave took him down, I didn't know if he'd still be there when the bow came up. I couldn't believe I had done this to my child. I had offered him an adventure with no idea of what it would entail. I was consumed with guilt. I knew that if he didn't come up on the next wave, I'd jump in after him. I wouldn't be able to live knowing that I'd been responsible for his death.

I tried to find some busy work to keep my mind off the scene outside, but there was nothing for me to do. The interior of the *Santa Rita* was designed to take rough seas. Every item had its place. Well-fitted teak lockers lined the fore and aft cabins and the salon, giving ample storage space for all our possessions, including charts and instruments. Whatever rattled around was locked tight behind well-secured doors. The portholes that I forced myself to look through were airtight.

However, I was left unsecured, with no way to brace myself if I continued to stand by the portholes. The yacht pitched and heaved and threw me in every direction. It was impossible to get a footing. I bruised myself by first bumping my hip hard into the chart table and then scraping my arm against the galley counter. To ground myself, I leapt to the salon table and held on tight while slowly inching my way around to the inside settee. I wedged myself between the settee and the table and braced my legs against the table's base.

I tried not to think about Stefan out in the storm by focusing on the water seeping through the hatch and down the galley stairs each time a wave washed over the top of the yacht. I took in the Zen-like beauty of the interior of the *Santa Rita* and thought about the elegant coffin I would be buried in at sea, but felt no emotion attached to the thought.

Finally, the sail was down. Like watching a stop-frame film in slow motion, I saw Stefan inch his way through the rain towards the cockpit. He'd pass one porthole and then disappear before appearing again in front of the next. Each disappearance tore at my heart. Each re-appearance elated me.

Once below deck, Stefan dropped to the floor without removing his rain gear. Exhausted, he lay in a puddle made by his soaking oil-skins and didn't move. I felt seasick and wondered whether it was because of the turbulent waves or the angst of having witnessed my son in so much danger. I managed to open one of the lockers behind the settee I had wedged myself into, and reached in for earphones and a tape of the Beatles that I had stored there along with my Walkman. I discovered that if I buried myself in the music, I could hold back the nausea.

With Stefan safely back, I drifted into a reverie buoyed by the music. I watched Stefan breathe, and remembered doing that when he was born, afraid that if I took my eyes off him, he'd stop breathing. After a while, he rolled over on his side, looked up at me and smiled. I smiled back.

"What you did was incredible," I said, removing the earphones.

He didn't answer, but I sensed a change in him. He had crossed the threshold from adolescence into manhood, and I could see that he was pleased with himself.

"Do you want to listen to the Beatles?" I asked.

"Sure," he answered. I handed him the earphones. With the stay-sail down, the boat dropped enough speed for the trembling of the hull to stop. We weren't out of danger, but at least, for the moment, we weren't going to break apart. My relief, however, was short lived.

"Stefan," Bernard called from the deck, his voice distorted in the howling wind. "I need you up here. I've got to take a break."

On deck, Bernard coached Stefan on how to adjust the helm in relation to the waves. It was a hairy moment. Stefan had never done this before, but Bernard needed sleep. He'd been at the wheel for almost a day with no rest, his body in constant tension bracing against the storm. If he were to fall asleep at the wheel, we'd be consumed by the ocean's fury. He had no choice but to trust Stefan at the helm.

Below deck, Bernard took a brief nap on the spot where Stefan had lain. In less than two hours, he was back on deck relieving him. His fortitude in front of our harrowing situation was super human. How does he do it? What will happen to us if he can't? I was plagued by these thoughts until my mind thankfully went numb.

Hour after hour we tossed about in a savage ocean, the *Santa Rita* no more than flotsam on a vast body of water. There was no horizon, no sign of anything sentient, nothing but wave after wave of black, roiling water with its deafening roar, and loud cracks of thunder and sheet lightning coming from all directions. I dared not think about how long our thin fibreglass hull could hold its own against the furious wind and pounding waves.

And then it all stopped. The rain tapered off. The wind died away. The ocean flattened. The *Santa Rita* drifted like a soap bubble on water. Bernard tumbled into the cabin, collapsed on the floor next to Stefan and fell into a deep sleep. Almost two days had passed since this nightmare began, and then it abated as abruptly as it came. We were alive. We had survived the storm from hell and were nearing Indonesia where we would no longer have to face the threat from India's monsoons.

When Bernard awoke, I brought him a coffee and sat on the floor beside him. I loved this man so much. I stroked his back, his arm, his hair. Bernard never trusted words, but he understood touch. He put his free arm around me and held me against his still damp slicker. We drank in the warmth of each other's bodies until he was ready to get out of his wet clothes and re-chart our course.

I went on deck and surveyed the ocean spread out before me like a flat sheet of shimmering foil. I wondered at the tempest we had endured. It seemed as though the entire ocean was out of control. But it wasn't. Only the surface was in turmoil. The ocean by its very depth could not have moved. I felt the presence of a vast stillness beneath the surface. There is a constant in the universe. The playbill is all that changes. The stage set remains. Hidden from view is something subtle and profound and eternal.

Chapter 20

SINGAPORE REDUX

Summer 1983 — Winter 1984

> *The really important kind of freedom involves attention,*
> *and awareness, and discipline, and effort, and being able*
> *to truly care about other people and to sacrifice for them,*
> *over and over, in myriad petty little unsexy ways.*
> — DAVID FOSTER WALLACE

In June of 1983, we sailed into the Malacca Strait and once again had to worry about tiny fishing boats, huge cargo ships, and freelance pirates. We now had the added stress of summer electrical storms that flashed intense lightning every thirty seconds. We were constantly reefing sails because of endless squalls. Still, it was nothing compared to our life-threatening ordeal on the Indian Ocean.

I whiled away the time between cloudbursts, dreaming of the dishes I would eat once we anchored in Singapore. Sri Lanka was blessed with a great variety of every imaginable fruit and vegetable, but the local cuisine lacked imagination and was saturated with lethal doses of chili that practically decimated my taste buds.

Stefan had the same problem. "You know, mom, I can't taste food anymore," he said during one of our nights out at a local eatery. "Do you think my taste buds will ever revive?"

"It's just temporary," I said. But I wasn't sure.

My concern was short-lived. Within days of our return to Singapore, Stefan was hunting down the hawkers for their specialties and savouring every bite. It felt good to be back in Singapore after our stay in Sri Lanka. The widespread poverty and racial tensions in a country that had so much beauty unnerved me. Singapore was less exotic but, with its humane social structure, people thrived. I relished its clean streets and clear rules, where handicapped beggars didn't harass me for money. Dropping anchor in Jorong Harbour felt like coming home. Little did I know we'd be anchored there for the next year and a half.

The refurbishing of the *Santa Rita* in Sri Lanka had been more expensive than expected, and our savings were slipping away. Before our journey, we had talked about finding work as we travelled. If that didn't work out, we agreed to sell the yacht. Now plans were less clear. Drinking more heavily, Bernard's clarity of thought diminished. He wasn't dealing with the reality that we had to earn a living. Unless we found a way of sustaining ourselves, I couldn't see how we'd be able to keep the boat.

"We could charter," he finally proposed as a way of reassuring me. "Or buy objects in one port and sell them in another."

"That's fine," I answered. "But we have to start soon or we won't be able to continue living on the boat."

The conversation ended with Bernard finding a chore that took his attention. When I insisted on pursuing the subject further, he became defensive.

"You never wanted to be here, did you? You'll use any excuse to sell the yacht."

I dropped the subject and waited for another opportunity to bring up the necessity of work.

Several yachts were anchored near us in the harbour. One belonged to a young French couple committed to this lifestyle. They planned to put their yacht in dry dock while he worked on an oil rig. When they had accumulated an appreciable amount of money, they hoped to sail to South America and charter there. They were very close to realising their dream.

I suggested to Bernard that he do the same.

"You're a geologist," I said. "You probably have a better chance than anyone to find work on a rig."

"Can't do it," he said.

"Why?"

"How do I know someone won't steal or damage the yacht?"

"I'll keep an eye on it."

"No, something can happen."

"What are you going to do?"

"I'm thinking of putting in an electric winch for the anchor. Anyway, I'm not happy with this boat. I see a lot of things I could have designed better. We'll get another yacht that's better."

I didn't acknowledge that he'd just changed the subject. I'd wanted an electric winch ever since Hong Kong, ever since the dreadful day Jonah dropped the anchor on the deck of the *Santa Rita*. There was no way I could lift that leaden hunk of steel, and Stefan would soon be leaving us.

"Good idea," I said. But now I had to think about how we'd survive financially from Singapore to the Mediterranean Sea, and how to get money to send Stefan back to Canada. He was ready to return to school, but without working papers, his chances of finding work in Singapore to earn his way were slim. He did manage to get hired as a cook on a motor yacht belonging to a burned-out American captain and his British girlfriend, but that brought him little more than pocket money.

Before we started on this adventure, I had my horoscope done to chart my planetary positions in different parts of the world. I dug out the map from the back of a locker to study what my planetary positions said about Singapore, and discovered I had a sun/Jupiter conjunction on the mid-heaven. According to the little booklet that came with the map, I'd be able find excellent work opportunities without much effort. Armed with this knowledge, I aimed for the best and highest paid position I could find teaching English, which in this case was the British Council in downtown Singapore.

I dressed as well as I could, squeezed my feet into street shoes for the first time in years, put together a hasty CV and marched off in search of work.

"Who do I see to apply for a position?" I asked the first person I encountered inside the building.

A young man shrugged his shoulders. "Ian Anderson, I guess." He pointed to a door down the hallway.

I opened the door on a neatly dressed, attractive man behind a cluttered desk. He didn't seem very busy.

"May I come in?"

After a brief moment of awkwardness, we discovered how much we had in common. Ian had lived in Mexico City at the same time that I had. He had taught English at the American School. I knew all about the school. I had taught English at a girl's high school, and he had heard of it. We knew the same places and felt the same way about teaching English in foreign countries. We compared stories and laughed a lot. He hired me to teach two hours of beginners' English two evenings a week. I left his office with several books under my arm, feeling elated.

The day I was to start class, I was accosted near the classroom by an angry, red-faced madman.

"Hand over those books," he shouted. "How dare you think you can teach in this institution?"

I had no idea who this man was. I held the books close to my chest.

When I remained clutching the books, he went on to tell me he was Dave Willis, the director of the school, and I had no right to be there.

"Ian Anderson hired me," I said.

"He had no right. He's my assistant. I do the hiring. I was on vacation. He overstepped his authority."

He took the books, turned on his heels, and left.

I was furious, not so much because I had lost the position, but because of his curt and aggressive behaviour towards me.

I raced back to the yacht fuming and wrote the nastiest letter I could to the British Council about this Dave Willis saying he was not up to the role of good-will ambassador. The British Council was an organization spreading Britain's good name across the world. Mr. Willis, I wrote, should be removed from his position. I made two copies, one for Mr. Munby, the head of the British Council in Singapore, and another to shove into the hands of Mr. Willis.

Early the next morning, I stormed into the building armed with my letters of indignation. As I entered, Mr. Willis rushed out of his office, and startled me with his enthusiasm at seeing me again. He was gushing.

"Rita, glad you're here so early. Come into my office. I have your materials for you."

He handed me a couple of books and shoved me into a classroom.

It was 8:55. My class was to begin at 9. The students were all sitting and waiting. I had no idea what they were to learn but improvised as best I could for the next three hours. Before I left for the day, a contract was brought for me to sign. I had lost the twice a week position but was hired as a full-time teacher.

I learned a few days later through teacher room gossip that the woman who was supposed to teach had gone on vacation to Bangkok, met a French diplomat in her hotel, and quit her job to follow him to France. It was the first day of class and the school hadn't been notified until minutes before I entered the building. I also learned that as an American I wasn't supposed to be hired because the school was obliged to hire only teachers from the Commonwealth. There was also a long waiting list because the school paid so well. Over time I met ex-pats who had been waiting for years for a teaching position at the British Council.

As an extra bonus, The Council offered me a paid one-year course that would certify me as a foreign language teacher in English, making it easier to find work wherever we went. It meant we'd be in Singapore longer than we had anticipated. Bernard was fine with extending our stay.

Sun conjunct Jupiter over my mid-heaven. I thanked my lucky stars.

On school days Bernard took me by dinghy as far as he could, but I had to wade through water to get to shore. The daily drudge of carrying my shoes and all the school paraphernalia through muddy water with my skirt hiked-up got to me. I decided to rent a place and return to the *Santa Rita* on weekends. It wasn't going to be easy. Most Singaporeans, with government help, owned their condos. Apartments were scarce and expensive.

I managed to find a room with a Hokkian Chinese family in their sparsely furnished, tiny wooden house. My rent included delicious curry dishes every evening, cooked on an open fire set between stones on a dirt floor in the kitchen area. I learned that curry was the best preservative for meat when you don't have refrigeration, something I planned to remember when the refrigerator unit on the yacht broke down — as all technical things do at one time or another on a boat. The room was temporary because the house was to be torn down at the end of the year to make space for more family-owned apartments. Still, it gave me time to network for sharing possibilities with my fellow teachers.

As luck would have it, an opening came up in an apartment within weeks of my having to leave the Hokkian family—a room in a three-bedroom apartment, vacated by a teacher returning to England. I now found myself sharing with Penny, a delightfully engaging free spirit, whose grandfather Clement Attlee had been Prime Minister of Great Britain, and Gill, a dour born-again Christian who insisted I was going to hell for dabbling in palm reading.

"The devil will get you," she admonished each time a colleague came over and asked for a reading.

I suspect she already felt the devil had gotten Bernard, who came over regularly to visit. His physicality and strong sexual presence disconcerted her. "Don't leave me alone with him," she whispered to me one day. "He scares me."

Penny, on the other hand, enjoyed Bernard's wicked humour and flirtatious posturing. "I like visiting you girls," he'd say, teasing, "because I don't get to see many beautiful and sexy women in the harbour." Penny would laugh in appreciation. She loved theatre and saw Bernard as an actor on his own stage. Years later she told me how touched she was when she had cut her hand badly with a kitchen knife, and he cleaned and dressed the wound with tender concern. She saw an inherent kindness behind his brazen façade.

I now lived a triple life—in the classroom, with my young roommates, and on the *Santa Rita* where I managed to do the housekeeping and some sailing with Bernard and Stefan on weekends. Elspeth, one of the women I worked with, but didn't know well, saw Bernard and Stefan pick me up at the Council one afternoon. "You have it made," she said, "living on a luxury yacht with an older man and a younger lover."

I smiled. It would have been too complicated to explain, and this story was so much better than the real one.

I felt good in Singapore, unshackled for the first time since the start of the adventure. It's an illusion to think of a sailboat as a symbol of freedom, though easy to do when a yacht in full sail enters a harbour. In truth, it's the wind that's free. A yacht needs constant funds to stay afloat, as well as constant vigilance for fear of robbery or accident. Yachties walk on eggshells as tension builds when people are crammed into a small space for long periods of time. I loved the *Santa Rita*, but I loved her more now that I came to her by choice and not because I had nowhere else to go.

Away from the *Santa Rita* made me think about that luxury. Poverty, religious views, social mores and lack of education trap people in situations that limit their choices. In my case, I trapped myself. I let Bernard make most of the major decisions, including the ownership of the yacht. I had vowed I'd be an independent woman and not be like my mother. I remember as a teenager watching television with her when my father called her to the kitchen to peel him an apple. Why couldn't he peel his own? Why did she acquiesce all the time? It made me angry, but now I found myself doing the same.

In Singapore, women were allowed access to the same higher education as men, and many were taking advantage of that possibility. Not wanting to live the lives of their mothers, a good number had decided not to marry because the men hadn't moved in step with them. The birth rate for the Chinese population fell and the government worried that the delicate balance of its many ethnic groups would be upset.

The country initiated a program called "Love Boat," that offered cruises to Hong Kong. Women didn't pay, but men did. It was hoped the young adults would connect with one another and marry. The women took advantage of the free holidays, but they still didn't marry. They could now make choices, and they did. It brought home to me that I was in some respects less liberated than these women, and that my culture still had challenges to overcome.

At the British Council I earned a good salary. I could put money aside to send Stefan back to Montreal and still have enough for our adventure. I told Stefan he could quit his job on the neighbouring motorboat, his small salary not worth the depressing atmosphere of two drunken people squabbling all the time. I felt empowered having this control over my life, and it energized me.

At first, Stefan and Bernard did well without me. Every morning they'd take the dinghy for their daily *roti prata* at the little stand near shore. They shared an appreciation for Singaporean cuisine. But the idleness of port-side living, combined with the endless rounds of alcohol consumed by yachties on their social visits, started to break down their alliance. Bernard complained endlessly about Stefan's laziness and inability to understand anything about sailing. Stefan in his usual stoic manner didn't respond, but his body language was clear. He stopped listening to Bernard's commands, wouldn't face him when he spoke, and spent more time in his cabin reading.

Every Friday afternoon after work, Bernard met me at the British Council, and we'd return to the yacht together. On one of those Fridays, he told me he had moved the *Santa Rita* to another harbour to the north of the island for a change of scenery. When we arrived at the new destination, we found the yacht missing. At first, we couldn't comprehend how something that large disappeared without a trace. And then panic set in.

Was the yacht stolen? Was Stefan kidnapped?

A week earlier, we had heard over our VHF radio that an American war ship was attacked by pirates not far off the coast of Singapore. The pirates came aboard using grappling hooks and the ship was calling for help. We didn't hear the end of the story, just the SOS. Was there a connection?

Stefan's disappearance took my breath away. I was trembling inside. For a moment, I couldn't move. Bernard looked drained of colour. We grabbed a taxi and urged the driver to go full speed to our old anchoring spot in Jurong. We hoped that by some miracle the yacht with Stefan aboard would mysteriously appear there. I couldn't think beyond that, nor could I really believe it.

As we entered the harbour, we saw the *Santa Rita* arrive with Stefan at the helm. He had single-handedly taken the yacht into Malaysian water and brought her back to Jurong Harbour. Bernard was stunned. It was the last time he goaded Stefan about his lack of seamanship. For Stefan, it was another milestone in self-sufficiency. There was a change in his walk after that incident. He seemed more confident and self-assured.

Aboard the dinghy on the way to the yacht, Stefan related the story of his adventure.

"The Coast Guard came by," he said. "They told me the *Santa Rita* was illegal where she was and that she would have to be moved. I told them the captain wasn't on board, but they insisted I take her out of the harbour. So I brought her out to sea and back to Jurong Harbour."

I marvelled at how matter-of-fact he was in telling us the story. He had taken charge — no panic, no grandiosity — just common sense and a sure hand at the helm. I had been concerned about sending him back to Montreal. I worried about how he would re-adjust after living a lifestyle so different from his peers. And I worried about how he'd feel registering as a mature student at university when the other students were now all younger than him. His handling of this unexpected event reassured me that he had the inner resources and strength of character to do just fine.

I felt both relief and sadness when I said goodbye to Stefan at Singapore's Changi airport. He had joined us on this voyage as a somewhat confused adolescent, not too sure of himself. He left as a man focused on moving ahead with his life. For me he would always be my child, and I was happy that he was going to a safer place. That summer he picked grapes in the south of France to earn some cash. And before leaving Europe, he visited Jonah in England, who was about to start his junior year at Oxford.

He made it back to Montreal in time to enter Concordia University for the fall semester. In his senior year at Concordia, he received a scholarship to U.C.L.A. to pursue a master's degree and doctorate in biomedical physics. His grit and determination, enhanced by the years aboard the *Santa Rita*, served him well.

After Stefan left, Bernard withdrew further into himself. His drink of choice was now Mao Tai, a strong alcoholic beverage favoured by the yachties anchored round us. Each weekend that I returned to the yacht, he was more difficult to reach. I cooked and cleaned up the mess he had made during the week. He worked on repairs. There was silence. He livened up only when his drinking buddies came aboard.

One evening, a colleague from the British Council and her husband visited us. They were so drunk by the time they left that they destabilized our dinghy, and it capsized. The woman swam to shore losing her skirt in the process and had to go home bare-assed. Her husband couldn't swim. Bernard saved him from drowning by swimming with him in tow to a rubber dinghy tied to a neighbouring yacht. I watched from a porthole horrified by the scene and impressed by Bernard's lightning response. I wondered how he could be so competent and present to the moment, but couldn't take better control of his life. It was a long while before I understood the influence of alcohol on the brain.

Yachties could buy cartons of duty-free Johnny Walker at a local warehouse because they were all in the process of sailing out. Bernard had his stash and had sold the couple a carton to take home with them. The box of alcohol sank to the bottom of the sea along with the dinghy. In the mornings, Bernard went out with scuba diving equipment and tried to find our dinghy and maybe salvage some of the alcohol. He also hoped to find the pipe that the man lost when he went overboard. A group of fishermen came daily to watch Bernard's efforts from the shore. They finally saw him pull on something.

"Did you find the body?" one of the men shouted. They were sure the focused intensity of his search had to be for something more serious than a dinghy and a few bottles of Johnny Walker.

We now had the dinghy, sodden but none the worse for having been submerged for several days. The alcohol and pipe remained at the bottom of the China Sea.

I was frustrated with Bernard's indifference to our financial situation. It was as though the boat was some kind of hole he'd crawled into and shut himself off from the world. In the evening he'd come out to drink and joke with fellow travellers and then crawl back in with no awareness of the passing of time.

"You spoke about chartering. Why don't you do it?" I was relentless in my effort to mobilize him to earn some money for our adventure.

He was equally relentless in his refusal to hear me. He wouldn't answer, but the resentment on his face said it all. My presence irritated him. I had become an annoyance and suspect in my motives to suggest ways for him to earn cash.

One morning, at the *roti prata* stand, two men approached us and asked to charter the yacht for the weekend. Bernard agreed. I was ecstatic. I thought if he did it once, it would break his resistance.

The two men had an agenda. They didn't want to go anywhere in particular, other than to sail around the island. Instead, they spent the weekend trying to persuade us to work for the CIA.

"It's easy money," the older one said. "Yachties always need cash. We'll give you a postal box to leave information and send your cheques there. You don't have to do much — just a few lines about the feel of the place in the countries you sail to."

The older man was persistent. We were just as persistent in our refusal. The younger man never said anything. I was relieved to see them go.

After they left, Bernard discovered some damage on a cushion and was furious. "One of those bastards burned a cigarette hole in the settee, the son of a bitch."

"It's not a big deal," I said. "It can be fixed. You've got to expect some wear if you charter."

Bernard couldn't be consoled. His identity with the yacht was so extreme that any mark to its body was a wound to him. It was our first and last attempt at chartering.

But he loved taking out my teaching colleagues for day sails. These were party days with food and alcohol and lively conversation and laughter. It was on one of these trips that Lola came into our lives.

One Sunday afternoon, a bunch of us were out on the China Sea, sprawled on the deck of the *Santa Rita* chugging down Ching Tao beer and gorging on shrimp chips. It was a typical scorcher of a day. A slight breeze offered some relief, but not enough to offset the numbing humidity that glued our limbs. Bernard rigged a bosom chair under the boom that he extended out from the yacht. We took turns sitting out on the slab of wood with the wind on our backs, letting our toes be sprayed by the seawater as we skimmed over the waves. The ride refreshed us just enough to keep from falling asleep.

We'd settled into a comfortable stupor when Bernard called out that he'd spotted an octopus about ten yards off the stern on the leeward side. Scepticism and the weight of our perspiration kept us glued to our seats. We were more interested in our next turn to swing over the cool sea on the bosom chair than his discovery.

Bernard jumped into the dingy, primed its engine, and set off for a closer look at his discovery. He was back in less than five minutes with a repulsive thing slung over the crook of his arm. My first impression was that I was looking at a huge rat; a water-logged creature a step away from death.

Ahmad, a Malay fisherman that Bernard had invited to sail with us was on board. "It's a monkey," he said, "maybe drowned."

He walked over to Bernard, took the limp creature from him, and laid it on the deck seat. He breathed into its mouth and pumped its little arms. The matted ball of fur gurgled deep in its throat, spit up some water like a little fountain, and stared with unfocused eyes at the cheering crowd gathered round it.

Ahmad looked up. "It's a baby, a female," he said, "about six months old."

We moved away to give it space. "I didn't know monkeys swam," I said.

"She's a Crab Eating Macaque," he said. "They swim." He took a penknife from his pocket and cut through the cord tied around her neck. "Contraband," he said. "Monkeys aren't allowed in Singapore without papers. Rich people pay a lot to eat their brains. It's not legal, but people still want them. They get smuggled in from Indonesia. The smugglers must have seen a customs boat and threw her overboard." He turned to Bernard. "She's been swimming a long time. Probably wouldn't have made it if you hadn't seen her."

The monkey appeared to be listening to every word the fisherman said. She didn't take her eyes off him, and as he talked, you could feel her growing stronger. To our surprise, she jumped off the seat where he had laid her and onto the deck, still looking fragile, but determined. She seemed desperate to tell us her story. As she moved from person to person, she chattered non-stop. It was clear she had no fear of us and felt compelled to reach out.

It was love at first sight between Bernard and the macaque. He scooped her up and sat her on his palm. "I'm going to name her Lola," he told us. He looked Lola straight in the eyes. "Welcome aboard, mate."

The saviour and agitated fur ball stared each other down. Neither one blinked. Bernard grinned idiotically. It was evident that he was a proud father. It was hard to know what Lola was thinking.

She cried the first night we had her, so Bernard wrapped her in a blanket and put her in the berth with us. I understood in the morning that toilet training would be an issue. We couldn't walk her like a dog, and she didn't have the fastidious habits of a cat.

We discussed what to do about it. I told Bernard that Lola was his monkey, and he'd have to find a solution. He went out that morning in search of a box of Pampers. On his return, he carefully cut a hole for her tail and changing her diapers became his responsibility.

Lola grew more beautiful each day. Her dull coat took on a shine under Bernard's diligent grooming. Then one day she groomed herself. From that moment on, gratitude was dead. She forgot she owed us anything. Her appealing, almost self-effacing nature morphed into that of a little tyrant. Lola emerged from her pitiful shell to become a spoiled and unmanageable child, given to sneaky thefts and pouting when reprimanded. Worse, Bernard became head honcho, and I the lowest person on our totem of three.

When Bernard yelled at her, she'd either spend hours complaining to me or slap me hard on my leg. Lola spent hours grooming Bernard. She inspected every hair on his legs and arms. From time to time she'd stop, inspect her fingers, and appear to slip a speck of something into her mouth. For the life of me, I could see nothing and couldn't imagine what she was harvesting.

He in turn spent hours grooming her in the same manner, pretending to pick something off her coat and putting it into his mouth. It was a ritual that gave her great pleasure and kept her out of trouble for the moment.

On her more expansive days she groomed me. Every inch of my scalp was inspected under her nimble fingers. And as she'd do with Bernard, she'd stop from time to time as though she'd found some questionable living thing on my head that she had to dispense with. I used to look forward to those rare moments of intimate pleasure when she would groom me. After my grooming, she'd sit on my shoulder and stare at my hand, watching it create odd symbols on blank sheets of paper. Writing both fascinated and perplexed her. She felt I was most in need of an inspection when I was hunched over the little table in the aft cabin writing in my journal.

She followed Bernard everywhere and became agitated if he left for any length of time. She could distinguish the sound of our dinghy from all the others in the harbour and, when she heard him returning from shore, she'd dance in excitement and dash up the galley stairs to greet him.

An issue we had to deal with was cigarettes. Bernard rolled his own. Lola decided to roll her own also. She became pretty good at it. I was constantly picking up bits of tobacco and paper and at first thought it was very funny. When she started handling the matches, the scene lost its humour. Tobacco, paper, and matches had to be locked away. And that wasn't easy, as Lola could open anything and inspected the contents of the lockers daily.

Aside from feeding her, everything related to Lola was Bernard's responsibility. She saw me as an intruder on their boat. I was tolerated but not indulged. My duties were relegated to housekeeper and cook. All acts of food preparation held her enthralled, and I couldn't turn my back for a second. To keep Lola out of trouble, I fed her peanuts while I cooked. She stuffed them into her cheeks until she looked liked a chipmunk and kept begging for more. When her ploy for more didn't work, she scurried into a corner and took them out of her mouth to be eaten one by one, her back to me in case I might want her to share.

My status improved when my father-in-law came for a brief visit. There was now a lower person in the hierarchy. So low in fact, that he was subject to bites after a Lola/Bernard brawl. I felt sorry for him. He had to endure his wife Dède at home, and now on vacation, he had another self-centred female to deal with. The poor man spent his entire vacation hanging on to a flashlight to ward off attacks. When he saw Lola coming, he'd bop her on the head. She got the message and kept her distance, but it was an uneasy truce.

I tried to make his visit as comfortable as I could. It touched me that he spent hours looking for a nice gift for his wife, knowing how much ill will she had towards him. He was a caring man who embraced my sons, and I thought he deserved better.

During a day's sail to Malaysia, Lola and Bernard had words. The sails were up and a light breeze pushed the ketch at a nice speed. Lola was having a fine time jumping from mast to mast, something she liked to do when the boat was moving with the sails unfurled. But she couldn't let go of that last argument they'd had. At one point, she swooped down and grabbed the flashlight from my unsuspecting father-in-law and threw it into the sea. Bernard went after her and Lola took off. Just as Bernard was about to grab her, she jumped overboard. To this day, I don't know how she did it, but she managed to climb up the stern and there she was — soaking wet and triumphant.

We later discussed what we were going to do with her. It was a delicate subject. Bernard was in love. But this couldn't go on. She couldn't be trusted around matches, had already eaten the teak on one of the lockers under the galley sink and was starting on another. We couldn't leave her behind when we went out. We had tried that by putting her in a bucket with a net over it suspended from the ceiling of the salon by a rope. While we were gone, she managed to swing the bucket from side to side and with a hand stretched through the net, shredded the curtains covering the portholes. And because she had no papers, we had to hide her in a shoulder bag when we took her with us. I wanted her gone. Bernard couldn't do it.

That changed when we were invited to a party at the home of one of my colleagues. We brought Lola with us with the idea of tying her to the bedpost in the bedroom of our host, making sure to check on her from time to time. Within minutes of her confinement she ripped apart the entire bedding. Feathers were strewn everywhere. Our host wasn't amused. Lola had gone from a novelty to a liability. Even Bernard acknowledged she had to go.

The next day, we took her to the Singapore zoo. The zookeeper told us they generally didn't take domesticated monkeys because they couldn't adjust, but Lola was still young enough, and she might get adopted into the group. We went with her to her cage and saw there were about a dozen monkeys that looked like her. We felt the adjustment would be easy. Lola saw it differently. She looked at her fellow Macaques and froze. She had no idea what they were.

The zookeeper tried to reassure us. "She'll be okay," he said, but we weren't so sure.

"We'll be back in a few days to see how she's doing," Bernard said.

When we returned a week later, Lola was part of the pack. It was hard to differentiate her from the others, and she had lost all interest in us. Bernard was crushed.

"She's ignoring me," he said. "Do you think she's already forgotten us?"

"Yes," I said. "She's a monkey."

I knew Lola had a special place in Bernard's heart, and I knew she had felt something for him, the man who saved her from the sea, but I wasn't very sympathetic. It's hard to be generous when your coffer is empty. A smile, a look, a touch would have filled me, but I had not received that. I had nothing to give.

During Christmas vacation I went for a two-week holiday to Bali with one of my colleagues from work. I wanted to sail there with Bernard, but he wasn't interested in going anywhere. He had relaxed into a daily routine of boat maintenance, TV watching, and evening socializing. It wasn't how I had envisioned sailing, and I found this lifestyle boring. The thought of a change of scenery excited me. Little did I know how exciting Bali would be.

My travel companion, who was from Australia, and I decided to forego Kuta Beach with its hordes of tourists and high-rise hotels and head directly for Ubud, the cultural centre of the island. Hotels weren't allowed in Ubud, so we booked a one-room house in a private garden. Once inside the grounds, we felt as though we had left the real world and stepped into a canvas by Rousseau. Hibiscus grew over our heads, and the leaves were at least a foot and a half across. Our little house was of carved stone.

The owner told us he had brought each stone up from the river himself and then chiselled the intricate relief carvings we saw on its outer walls. We had no running water, but an opening in one of the walls was set with a stone basin that ran from the outside in. Every morning hot water was poured in from the outside so that we could bathe. After bathing, we'd open our door to a huge bowl of mango, banana, and papaya sprinkled with coconut shavings that had been left on our doorstep.

The owner was a rice farmer, but he was also a skilled stone mason and sculptor. "I tend my rice fields," he said, "but I'm an artist."

That was true of everyone we met in Ubud. They worked the land, but this was not what they told us when we questioned them. They were dancers, or musicians, or sculptors, or artists. It was not unusual to see children being trained in their compounds by their parents in one of the arts. In the evening we joined the locals to listen to male frogs serenading females. If the performance was good, the people clapped. We were told the gamelan, a musical instrument peculiar to Indonesia, was inspired by frog vocalization, Bali having many species, each having its own sound. Some evenings we attended Kecak performances, a hypnotic series of sound and ritualized movement executed by men who seemed to be in a trance, and soon put us there; or watched the exquisitely graceful Legong dance performed by young girls who were certainly in a trance-like state.

Grace came easily to the Balinese. I remember climbing a narrow mountain path on my hands and knees trying to keep up with a young woman in a sarong who was carrying a table on her head and moving before me like a mountain goat. In processions that were almost a daily occurrence, women carried huge baskets of fruit on their heads with total ease. Their lithe, sinuous movements were a beautiful sight, but then everything in Ubud was beautiful.

One time we passed a stream that widened into a small pool where an older woman was bathing, naked from the waist up. A man had stopped to talk, perhaps a friend or neighbour. A few years earlier the government had passed a law saying blouses had to be worn but old habits die slowly. I felt privileged to be there at the end of an era.

I loved everything about this island — the brilliant green, terraced rice fields, the elegant bamboo structured homes, the physical drama of an island carved from a volcanic aftermath with its varied landscape of mountains, rivers, and fertile plains, and the fact that a man could only enter a temple wearing a sarong with a hibiscus behind each ear and a woman had to enter the same way but with only one hibiscus.

"It's disgraceful," the local tourist guide said to me on seeing two young Australian men enter a temple in shirt and jeans. "Would they enter their own church that way?"

Yes, I thought, but didn't say. The tourist guide hadn't travelled out of the country, but his English was good, so I imagined there must be a language school on the island. I played with the idea of teaching English, and settling in Bali forever. It wouldn't be unheard of. Many artists came to visit and never left. Others arrived with no artistic talent, and were now selling Balinese craft all over the world in order to stay. They built their homes along the shore of a local river.

I met a young graphic artist from Saskatchewan who came on holiday shortly before me, and like me, was mesmerized by this other-worldly paradise. He was determined to stay. He took me by motor-cycle into the mountains to meet the craftsmen and to look at some of the wooden pieces of sculpture and furniture he was selecting to send back. He had already spoken to the government about doing this and was in the process of filling a container. In the early eighties there was a huge market for Balinese craft. I couldn't wait to get back and tell Bernard. This could be our survival.

While I spent my time checking out Balinese craftwork, my Australian travelling companion filled her days with a young Balinese gentleman she'd met in a restaurant. "He's in love with me," she said, gushing. "We have a connection."

"I'm not so sure." I reminded her of our cab ride from the airport to Ubud.

"I'm available," the cab driver had said. "Australian and Swedish women like us. They come to Bali for sex."

"Are you married?" I had asked him.

"Of course, I have two children — a very nice wife."

"Why do you do this?"

"Do what? We are a tourist country. We fill the needs of our tourists."

"Doesn't your wife mind?"

"No, why should she mind?"

"This is different," my travelling companion retorted.

One night she didn't return to our room. I assumed that she and her soul mate had decided to consummate their "connection."

That morning she stormed into our little guesthouse. "That bas-tard," she shouted. "He asked me for money. I refused and he got upset. Imagine — HE got upset."

My colleague and I still had a few days of vacation, but I was now the only one enjoying our trip. We left Bali on the day of a mass cremation — five rich men and a bevy of poor were to be cremated at the same time with no cost to the poor. Many families had waited for months for the rich to be cremated to be able to join the procession carrying the remains of their own dead to the place of cremation. Five huge, black, ornately adorned papier mâché bulls led the procession, one for each of the men who would be put into them before the actual burning.

The procession wove in and out of streets in the hope of confusing the spirits so they wouldn't return home. Gamelan music was also employed to disorient the spirits while the women of the village swayed elegantly in their colourful batik sarongs carrying huge baskets laden with fruit and flowers on their heads. Men accompanied them in their black and white chequered sarongs, hibiscus behind each ear and Nike running shoes. It seemed to be the official male dress of Ubud.

I knew I'd mourn leaving a place with so much physical beauty and cultural richness, and I thought how fitting for my last day in Bali.

Back in Singapore I tried to talk Bernard into buying crafts from Bali and selling them in Western markets. He wasn't interested. It was my last attempt at trying to use the *Santa Rita* as a vehicle for our future. Now, more than ever, I wanted to make it to Europe where there would be a better market for selling yachts.

I gave my notice of resignation to the British Council and looked forward to the day we'd be able to sail out. I had made good friends in Singapore, knew I would miss them and promised to stay in touch. Still, I felt a great excitement at the prospect of lifting anchor and heading towards unexplored waters. I hadn't lost my wanderlust, and felt more secure having put some well-needed money into the kitty. Bernard was as excited as I was to continue the journey. As soon as my teaching contract ended, we lost no time in provisioning and preparing the *Santa Rita* for the next leg of our voyage.

Chapter 21

FROM DOLPHINS TO DHAL

<hr>

Winter 1984: From Singapore To India

> *It is good to have an end to journey toward;*
> *but it is the journey that matters in the end.*
> — ERNEST HEMINGWAY

As luck would have it, or so we thought, a fit Barbie and Ken look-alike couple approached the *Santa Rita* and asked if we needed crew. "We're on our way home to Switzerland," they said, "and if you're heading towards Europe, we'd be happy to work in exchange for passage."

With Stefan no longer on board to give us a hand, it seemed like a good idea. "Glad to have you," Bernard said.

Early next morning, the couple arrived at the water's edge with their backpacks, and waved at us to pick them up with the dinghy. Barbie cradled a ten-kilo bag of carrots.

"Nice of you to share," I said as I extended my hand to help her aboard.

"You make a mistake," she answered, clutching the carrots tighter to her chest. "This is mine. Food for the skin."

The carrots went into their cabin along with the couple, and were never seen again.

We soon learned that besides the periodic squalls, possible pirate attacks, and half-sunk containers that always gave us stress in the Malacca Strait, we now had the burden of an unseasoned crew, and worse, an unseasoned crew who refused to learn anything. The Barbie and Ken look-alikes viewed sailing as an opportunity for endless sunbathing and room service. At the first sign of work, they disappeared into their cabin and didn't resurface until mealtime.

"In place of getting two extra hands, we got two extra mouths," I said to Bernard. "At least they can help with the night watches — not much skill required there."

On our second night in the Malacca Strait, we were sideswiped by a sudden squall. We roused our crew in an effort to get them to participate in reefing the sails. Bernard tried to shout directions to the clueless duo, but they lurched about the deck like pin balls in a pinball machine. Ken finally managed to grab hold of the boom. He then swung it in the direction of Barbie, knocking her to the deck. I secured the boom while Ken carried Barbie below deck and disappeared for the night.

The next morning Ken surfaced to tell us that Barbie had a concussion. "I'll have to take care of her until we reach a port."

Bernard's face showed concern. "I'd like to see her," he said and started towards the cabin.

"She's resting," Ken said. "It's better that you didn't."

Our concern melted away when Barbie appeared later that day to take her usual sunbathing spot in the bow of the yacht. There was a slight bruise on the side of her forehead but nothing more. The accident did nothing to cut her appetite or change her daily routine of sunbathing, eating, and reading in her cabin while munching carrots.

Meanwhile Ken, who didn't have a concussion, followed her precise regimen. "I have to be with my girlfriend," he informed us, "in case of complications." Now there was not even the remotest possibility of either of them sharing the night watches. Bernard and I were furious. But at sea you learn to control your anger.

I relaxed once we sailed past Sebang, the small island at the tip of Indonesia that marked the end of the Malacca Strait and beginning of the Indian Ocean. We were now past the threat of pirates and half-submerged debris waiting to damage the boat. But eight hours later the wind died, and Bernard couldn't start the engine. After a quick check, he discovered a corroded heat exchanger and gearbox flooded with water. We had no choice but to backtrack to Sebang. With little wind and the current against us, the trip took a day and a half.

In Sebang, we patiently waited three days for the heat exchanger to be repaired at a local machine shop. Barbie's bruised forehead had healed by then, but neither she nor Ken made any effort to leave the yacht as they had threatened to do on the night of the accident. Bernard and I didn't force the issue although we would have loved to have seen them go. International law states that if you take someone aboard your boat, it's your responsibility to repatriate them, and we weren't about to finance their trip back to Switzerland. We were stuck with a bad deal.

Once again on the Indian Ocean, Bernard and I took turns doing the two-hour night shifts. We no longer asked our crew, and they didn't volunteer. The nights were so fresh and the sailing so smooth that I didn't mind. It was the only time I was totally alone, and I savoured the privacy — my mind empty, my body moving in sync with the yacht, and my ear tuned to the soothing sounds of swishing water.

During one of my watches, on a starless night, I lost all sense of boundaries. The sky and water were black, and there was no horizon line or point of reference to ground me. I was suspended in space. The auto-helm held a steady course, and without needing to give it attention, I drifted off like stardust in the Milky Way.

The sudden onset of a deep, throaty "ahhh-hahh, ahhh-hahh" startled me from my trance. The heavy, rhythmic breathing resonated through the hull of the yacht, and sounded as though the planet was having an asthma attack — or maybe heavy sex. I peered over the starboard side, and saw nothing but a small window of black water ruffled by the wind. I moved to the prow and still saw nothing. The sound stopped when I got up to investigate.

I relaxed. Whatever it was had gone. I wasn't going to give it more thought, and returned to the cockpit. As soon as I sat down, a soft, persistent thump started to beat against the side of the hull. It was followed by more heavy breathing. For the second time I went to investigate, but again the breathing stopped before I reached the stanchion lines. I couldn't find the source of the sounds. They came out of nowhere, and I felt vulnerable in the vast darkness. I imagined I was going to be sucked into something unpleasant, but I didn't know what. After several bouts of trying to locate the sound, and convinced it was something threatening, I inched my way below deck to wake Bernard. I didn't want to be out there alone with whatever it was.

I knew he wouldn't be happy to be awakened before his shift, but I didn't care. "There's something out there," I said.

His eyes flashed open. "What?" he said. "A tanker? A trawler?"

"No, I don't know what it is." I could sense his irritation rising. I felt pretty stupid. "It's a sound — really eerie — and it's all around us, also some weird thumping on the side of the boat."

"There's nothing there." He rolled over and tried to fall back asleep.

"I will not go back up there alone." I tugged at his undershirt.

He sighed. "Did you see anything?"

"No."

He tried to turn away again, but I wouldn't let him. And then I heard the soft thumping inside the cabin. "Did you hear that?" I asked.

"No," he answered.

"Listen."

This time he heard it and went for the large projector light. I followed behind him. As we entered the cockpit, he heard the heavy breathing.

"Now, do you believe me?"

Bernard walked over to the stanchion line and shone the emergency searchlight out over the water. I was terrified that whatever was out there might pull him in and would probably come for me next — maybe some giant underwater creature with uncanny intelligence, one not yet discovered, because there's never been a survivor. But that didn't happen. Instead Bernard burst out laughing. I walked over to where he was standing and gasped at the sight. A huge school of dolphins surrounded the yacht. I had been listening to the heavy breathing of a bevy of dolphins circling the boat. Bernard caught them by surprise before they had a chance to dive under. Their game was up.

They knew what they were doing. As soon as their plot was discovered, they stopped hiding and were content to swim beside us, sometimes in front of the prow, sometimes along the side, leaping into the air, diving under, and in general having a good time. I could barely see them until light started to define the horizon, but it was comforting to hear them splashing about. I didn't feel so alone.

A steady seven-knot wind carried us from Sebang to the coast of India in nine days. The night before we entered Cochin, the port entry to the state of Kerala, we found ourselves surrounded by hundreds of tiny fishing boats stationed in the dark. Without being aware, we had moved into the middle of their fishing grounds. Bernard turned on the big searchlight to illuminate our way through.

It angered the fishermen. I never knew whether it was because we disturbed where they had positioned themselves in the water, or if the light frightened the fish away. One of the fishermen took a long, wooden pole and tried to break the searchlight. The others shouted things that were probably just as well I didn't understand, but we had no choice if we didn't want to hit one of their fragile boats. We slowly threaded our way through until we left the area, and began to breathe easily again.

As we approached Cochin's harbour, an enormous sea of swimming crabs with claws in the air raced past the yacht like a huge floating island pushed by wind. We had no idea where they came from, why they were in a rush, or where they were going, but they gave the impression that the water beneath the yacht was teeming with life.

In the morning light, we feasted our eyes on enormous nets that lined the harbour, each one at least thirty feet high and sixty feet across, their filigreed interior held in place by arched bamboo and teak poles. Teams of fishermen worked the nets, slowly lowering and then raising them from the water. The men acted as a fulcrum between the massive structures and roped stones at the other end. It was a beautifully choreographed performance, but the catch never seemed to equal to the size of the nets, though I don't think it mattered. The ephemeral delicacy of the giant nets against the light of the rising sun gave a charm to Cochin that compensated for the small amount of fish caught.

We learned that these Cheenavalas, as they were called, had been in use since the thirteenth century when they were brought to Cochin by a Chinese explorer named Zheng He during the reign of Kublai Khan. Until then I had thought that Kubla Khan and Xanadu were figments of the poet Samuel Taylor Coleridge's imagination. I now knew that that he'd misspelled Kublai and the Mongol lord was real, as was Xanadu. The magic of the harbour whetted my appetite for exploring more of India, but it wasn't to happen.

You cannot leave the city of Cochin," the immigration officer said, curtly handing back my American passport. Then he turned to Bernard. "Welcome to India," he said as he stamped Bernard's Canadian passport and returned it with a smile.

Unbeknownst to me, there was tension between India and the United States. I was confined to Cochin as a questionable alien. Bernard, the Canadian, was a welcome guest. As Swiss citizens, Barbie and Ken had free run of the country. They left for the tourist haven of Goa, leaving their gear behind to ensure we'd still be there when they returned.

Because I couldn't leave the city, Bernard suggested we explore Cochin together. The *Santa Rita* was safely moored in a harbour within the city, and he felt comfortable leaving her for a while, but I think it was the culture's vibrancy that lured him. Cochin's narrow streets were filled with a colourful patchwork of people moving about its tiny shops and make-shift stalls in search of clothing, jewellery, produce and spices, oblivious to the motorcycle taxis weaving in and out among them.

We sampled the local cuisine and found it to be pure ambrosia, India being the home of cinnamon, cardamom, turmeric, chili, and mustard seed. Kerala grew coriander, tamarind, garlic, ginger, and coconut, and the blending of these ingredients with the spices created a mouth-watering array of memorable dishes. We gorged on curried shrimp and fish, fresh daily from the sea and at an unbeatable price. Food was almost given away. When I bought produce in the market, I had to buy far more than I could use because with our American dollars, the smallest unit of exchange bought an overwhelming amount. In spite of the obvious poverty, the people of Kerala, for the most part, ate well.

I learned they had the highest level of education in India, which meant the state of Kerala was more privileged than most, and should have had a higher standard of living. But we visited a factory that made hemp rugs and the conditions there were appalling. Men in thread-bare *dhotis* worked in extreme heat inside a primitive structure that looked like a workhouse scene from the late Middle Ages. Perhaps they eked out enough wages to keep from starving, but quality of life had a long way to go.

Happy to stretch our legs after so many days at sea, we took in a few tourist attractions that weren't too far from the *Santa Rita*, One of our outings was to a Kathakali dance performance, native to south India. This dance form, performed by men, tells stories taken from the Mahabharata, a Sanskrit book of poems dealing with royalty, war, and ethics. Though I had never seen Indian dance, I studied dance when I was young, and had done a paper on dance in India when I was in college.

I was excited to see a performance of one of the schools I had written about, but in spite of the elaborate costumes and eye-catching make-up, the stylized movements of the dancers failed to engage me. I knew it took years to perfect the intricacies of this dance form, but I had to admit I was disappointed. What my imagination had envisioned as a young student in search of unique experiences was something quite different from what I now saw.

The other touted tourist attraction was the Paradesi Synagogue, rebuilt in 1568 on land donated by the Rajah of Cochin, who welcomed Jews escaping from persecution in Portugal and Spain. The Portuguese had burned down the original synagogue that belonged to the Malaberi Jews, a darker skinned people who had come to Cochin in the fourth century or possibly before. At the time of our visit, we were told there were only ten Jews left in Cochin, but the synagogue was still functioning.

Blue and white hand-painted Chinese tiles covered the floor of the interior giving it a unique charm. The brass trim and lacquered woods in the main sanctuary created a pleasing counterpoint to the slew of coloured glass lamps and elaborate crystal chandeliers hanging from the ceiling. The space looked like a theatre in the round before a play was about to begin. It was barely used, yet so well cared-for. In contrast, the exterior of the compound was nondescript, the history of the building and its people being far more interesting than the architecture.

Having taken in some of the tourist sites of Cochin, and with our virtual crew bronzed and back on board, we prepared to set sail for the Red Sea. Bernard pointed to a location on the nautical chart spread before us.

"I think we should head for Aden on the coast of Yemen," he said. "From there it's a short sail through the Bab-el-Mandeb Strait to the Red Sea."

"Bab-el-Mandeb," I said. "What a great name! It conjures up images from those *Dune* books by Frank Herbert." Bernard smiled. Years before, we had read and enjoyed the science fiction trilogy. I later learned Bab-el-Mandeb meant Gate of Grief in Arabic.

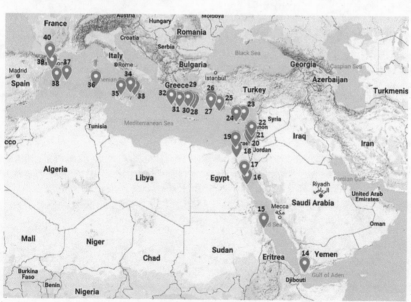

From Yemen-Aden to Andorra

Chapter 22

STORMS BREWING ON THE HORIZON

~~~

Spring 1984: To Yemen and Sudan

> *Though we travel the world to find the beautiful,*
> *we must carry it with us or we find it not.*
> —RALPH WALDO EMERSON

After fourteen days on the *Santa Rita* crossing the Arabian Sea from India, Bernard and I were ready for a break. We also needed provisions. The Barbie and Ken couple continued to be a pain in the butt. They spent the two-week crossing locked in their cabin, appearing when hungry or to sunbathe on nicer days. After a week of cooking for them with no effort on their part to participate in the handling of the yacht, I no longer called them for meals.

"When do we eat?" Barbie asked on the first day of the new regime, when she noticed I didn't knock on their cabin door at lunchtime.

"You don't," I said. "If you don't contribute, you don't eat."

"You have to feed us. It's the law."

"Is it?"

The pouty little princess marched back to the cabin and slammed the door. She reappeared in bikini, with sun hat and towel in hand, and strutted her way to her favourite sunbathing spot. Later that evening when Bernard and I were on deck, I heard the couple rummaging below, looking for what they could find to put their own meal together.

"Let them scrounge around for whatever they can find," I said to Bernard. "They wouldn't dare use the stove, and I doubt if either of them know how to cook." I hoped our new arrangement would encourage them to jump ship once we docked.

We made it clear they weren't welcome. Nevertheless, they had no compunctions about having opinions on where we should sail.

Ken pulled a sour face when he saw us entering Aden, the port city of Yemen. "Why not Socotra?" he said, not aware that we had already passed the archipelago.

"It's a pirate hangout," Bernard said. "It's not safe for boats. But if you'd like to go, you can always fly."

Ken didn't take the bait.

I had been excited about exploring Aden, knowing that Yemen was one of the oldest civilizations in the Middle East. Not only did it control the spice and incense trade from the twelfth century BCE to the sixth century CE, it was also rumoured to be the home of the biblical Cain and Abel.

Even before dropping anchor, my illusion of finding remnants of the country's historical past was shattered. The heady smell of fresh earth that often uplifted me as we entered other ports was missing. Oil replaced the spice trade, and the stench from refineries was sickening.

Before leaving Cochin, I had sent letters to friends and Jonah telling them we'd soon be in Aden, and I'd pick up the next batch of mail there. When we arrived, a number of letters were already waiting for us at the post office. I opened Jonah's first, looking forward to his entertaining stories about life at Oxford. I had hoped to see him before he returned to Middlebury for his senior year. Now it looked as though it could happen. His spring break was around the time we planned to pass through the Suez Canal. I was ecstatic. It had been almost three years since I'd seen him off at the Manila International Airport. I wrote to him suggesting we meet up in Israel. Having heard about the vagaries of the Red Sea, I wasn't sure we'd make it, but Bernard seemed pretty certain, and he was usually right.

The second letter I took out of the packet left me amazed at the effectiveness of the "Poste Restante" mail system. It was easy to receive mail from one country to the next using the local post office as a mailing address, but what a surprise when the packet held a letter addressed to "Rita Pomade/Aden" without the name of the country. I had another surprise when the stamps I bought pictured guerrillas with machine guns pointed directly at the purchaser.

Little did we know that in 1983 escalating tension between Palestinians and Israelis resulted in a mass exodus of Palestinians to Yemen. Anger towards Israel was palpable, and I could feel it in the streets. Also, tension between British-held North Yemen and Russian-supported South Yemen was threatening to erupt at any moment. Each time I licked a postage stamp, I was reminded we were in a dangerous environment, but then I forgot. Until something happens, there's the feeling that nothing will happen. So in spite of the charged political environment, we thought the port was too interesting to lift anchor and leave.

We headed for the office of the Harbour Master to announce our arrival. Endless rows of empty shoes covered the port's streets, giving the feeling of people mysteriously lifted out of their footwear into an alternate universe. I later learned it was the custom never to enter an establishment in shoes.

The Harbour Master's office bustled with people coming and going. When it was finally time for us to state our business, Bernard had hardly made his request when the sound of the Muezzin's call penetrated the office. Everyone dropped to the floor and prayers began. We stood there, above the lumps of bodies wondering whether to go or stay. We waited awkwardly for the office staff to take their seats and for business to resume. The sudden change of tempo and then return to business as usual had the surreal feeling of our being extras in a science fiction movie. It was the first time I felt culture shock since our first weeks in Taipei four years earlier.

Aden's streets were a tapestry of texture and colour. Tribesmen, coming into town from the mountains, still dressed in their native clothes. The women wore colourful dresses, their headscarves lined with coins, and diaphanous veils covered their faces. The men wore skirts and had turbans wrapped around their heads. Daggers with carved blades called *jarbiyas* were tied around their waists. They were a small and wiry people with handsome, weathered faces.

There were also tall, lithe women who seemed to glide as they walked. They were too dark to be Yemini and must have been from Somalia or Eritrea, a stone's throw across the sea. These women wore flowing black robes, their faces and heads covered with the same material. Only their slender hands and feet were visible, finely tattooed with intricate patterns that looked like lace. The women moved together in a group, and at one point I found myself on a bus with them, the only Westerner. Their slow and graceful movements made me feel like a bulky sack of potatoes, but I have no idea what was hidden behind those long robes. They were as mysterious to me as they were alien.

Barbie and Ken had gone their own way for the week of our stay, and it was a relief for us to have the yacht to ourselves. We spent the time readying the *Santa Rita* for the voyage up the Red Sea, Bernard always on maintenance and me provisioning. Food, abundant and delicious, sold for a pittance. European agencies had been sending food aid to Yemen, a third world country, for years. Instead of the food reaching those in need, it was sold by private vendors in the marketplace. For the first time, I was filling the lockers with tasty European fare from roast duck to scrumptious whole chickens packed in cans.

The day we were to sail, Barbie and Ken arrived with packages given to them by Palestinians they had befriended. They had been asked to take these up the Red Sea and deliver them to a third party. They had no idea what was in them. Bernard was furious.

"Get that stuff off the yacht," he demanded. "You have no idea what you're carrying and you don't know where it's really going. Return it and tell them the captain won't let you aboard with unknown cargo."

The two looked at each other and made irritated faces — then reluctantly left to return the goods.

Bernard was visibly agitated. "Idiots," he mumbled.

I couldn't be more in agreement. As owners of the *Santa Rita*, we were responsible for anything that came aboard. If we were stopped and searched, ignorance wouldn't get us off the hook. We couldn't take a chance like that, and they should have known better. When they returned we lifted anchor and headed for Sudan, only a day's sail away.

Several months later, we learned by VHF radio that fighting broke out in Aden between North and South Yemen, and all the ships in the harbour were at risk. The *Innocent Bystander*, a yacht we had encountered when we were anchored there, was caught in the crossfire. The crew spent several tense hours lying on the floor below deck, while bullets sped overhead.

In contrast to Aden, Port Sudan was one of the most serene places I had ever visited. Against a backdrop of undulating dunes peppered with round mud huts, tall, slender black men in flowing white *djellabas* glided by. Even the camels moved in graceful motion quietly nuzzling their way through mounds of garbage heaped along the edges of dusty lanes. Mud walls functioned as outdoor toilets and every so often a man would squat near one, and protected by the flow of his robe, he would pee. I was curious as to what the women did as their cotton skirts wouldn't permit the same luxury of discretion.

Couples strolled towards the outdoor marketplace where there was no sense of bustle, and families sat at small tables and drank tea together. It was the first occasion I witnessed time not measured by output of productivity, but defined by community where family and friends sat about and chatted without an agenda. I felt the Sudanese had a lot to teach us. But I knew there was no going back. More so today in our wired world, computers ubiquitous — cell phones and Twitter our virtual community. Still, when I'm most in need of serenity, I go back in my mind to Port Sudan in 1984 — as it was then.

But even then, I was already looking at an illusion or the last remnants of what may have been a gentle world. Civil war had just broken out in the south of the country, although we didn't know it. Soon after, the conflict escalated into a blood bath of massacres, rape, and enslavement. The country's plight became so horrendous the UN declared that the war against the country's non-Arabs constituted genocide. I feel sad every time I read about Darfur or the Janjaweed militias.

We didn't stay in the port long. After buying a few twigs to use as toothbrushes (never figured out how), we headed back to the *Santa Rita* for the next leg of our journey. On our return, we discovered that Barbie and Ken had jumped ship. Our joy, however, was short-lived. We were headed towards some of the most troubling experiences we were yet to have, distress we couldn't have imagined.

Chapter 23

UNDER THE GUN IN EGYPT

~~~~~

Spring 1984: Along the Coast of the Red Sea

Fear is as deep as the mind allows.
—JAPANESE PROVERB

Off the coast of Sudan, the wind picked up to gale force and the erratic movement of the yacht shook and jerked us in all directions. We were trapped in a sandstorm that forced grit into our ears and mouth and coated our skin with salt. I could hardly see, and coral was everywhere, waiting to tear out the bottom of the keel. French sailors call the Red Sea the *Merde Rouge* because its narrow passage makes the waves short and unpredictable.

We had one advantage over the majority of yachts trying to make it through the Suez Canal to the Mediterranean Sea. We had no high-tech equipment aboard. There was no satellite system that could clog with sand, no short wave radio to go awry, and no electronic log that could fizzle out while measuring speed and distance.

Bernard got his bearings by using a sextant to measure the angle between the horizon and the sun — something many of the pleasure sailors couldn't do. The only damage that might have befallen our equipment would be the sextant falling overboard, which never happened — or fish biting through our log line, a one-inch steel cable pulling a bomb-like hunk of steel that measured the speed of the boat. A fish had done that earlier when we were crossing the Indian Ocean; judging by the power of its teeth, probably a barracuda.

For two days, we made little progress against the wind. On the third day, even with full throttle of the engine, the *Santa Rita* inched backwards. We decided to wait out the storm by taking shelter off El

Quseir, a small town mid-way up the Egyptian coast. Within minutes of our dropping anchor, two clean-shaven but tough looking men motored out to us and demanded a harbour fee.

"Any port in a storm," Bernard said. He refused to pay. Fees are not asked for when you anchor offshore in a storm. This was common sailing courtesy.

The men weren't happy. They returned at daybreak carrying machine guns and took Bernard away. Fear cut my breath. I felt pressure in my chest. For how long he was gone, I couldn't say. It could have been an hour, two hours, maybe five. It felt like an eternity. At no time was it ever clearer to me that my never having learned to use a sextant or the two-way radio could endanger our lives.

Later in the day, my heart jumped when I heard a dinghy motoring towards us. I raced on deck and waited anxiously for the boat to pull aside the *Santa Rita*. A wave of relief came over me when Bernard scrambled aboard, and I actually smiled at the two men as they took off.

"Did they hurt you?" I asked.

"No," he said. He sort of smirked. "When I saw them coming, I knew what it was for and stuffed some money in my pocket. They took me to a shack near shore, sat me in a chair, and demanded that harbour fee. I took out what I had and gave it to them. They wanted more, but I told them it was all I had on board."

His coolness astonished me. I watched in awe as he took out his pouch of tobacco, rolled a Gitane cigarette, stuck it into the side of his mouth, and then took out the chart for the Red Sea.

"Where next?" I asked.

"Hurghada." He pointed to a speck on the chart. "It's a larger town up the Egyptian coast and has a marina."

On entering Hurghada's harbour, we spotted *Cloud Nine*, a familiar yacht from Singapore. The captain had the reputation of being a Captain Bly for the strict way he dealt with his crew, but they were an interesting mix of people. One was the actress who played Miss Moneypenny in a James Bond movie. Another, a dead ringer for the actor Richard Widmark, was a young guy from Wisconsin with whom we had become friendly.

As soon as we dropped anchor, "Richard Widmark" motored over to exchange stories about the Red Sea. Everyone knew it was a bitch to navigate, and everyone had a story or knew someone who did. Over several refills from Bernard's store of saki, we told him about the money grab in El Quseir.

"Speak to Captain Borai," he said. "He controls this harbour and has good connections with the police."

We contacted Captain Borai and lodged our complaint. His outrage at our extortion endeared him to us. The following day he boarded the *Santa Rita* with half the money Bernard had lost the day before.

"I couldn't get it all," he said. "I came too late and half of it was gone. They're a gang of criminals that control the southern part of the coast. We know who they are, and we'll get them."

When we related the incident to the captain of one of the other yachts in the marina, he told us Captain Borai was in a turf war with the hoodlums to the south. He said Borai had control of the northern part of the coast and had ambitions to take over the whole area. "Getting your money back," he went on, "was to show them he had more power. He probably pocketed the missing half before returning the rest."

Two days later Captain Borai came aboard the *Santa Rita* with an interesting proposition.

"You're Westerners," he said. "You haven't our fear about crossing the desert. I have an engine that needs to be taken for repair in Alexandria, but my men are superstitious. Deliver it for me, and I'll send you with a note for my brother to be his guest at his villa. Stay as long as you want. He's a generous man. I'll look after your yacht."

I couldn't believe our good fortune. Laurence Durrell's *Alexandria Quartet* danced through my head. I remembered Durrell's sensuous description of the city during the 1940s with its host of exotic characters set against a background of poetic decay. And now I'd actually get to see this ancient wonder with its famed library and historic ruins, already cultured when the West was still ploughing through the last days of the Iron Age.

With Captain Borai as our neighbour and a guard with a machine gun at the entrance to the port, we felt safe in Hurghada's dreary, makeshift marina. For the first time since we started this adventure, Bernard was willing to leave the yacht for more than a day.

At sunrise we were on Captain Borai's luxury yacht waiting for him to finish writing a note to his brother so that we could get started. Two of his crew stood behind him watching him pen the note. The one on his left snickered which made me suspicious. The note was in Arabic so there was no way I could tell what it said.

"What are you writing?" I asked.

Captain Borai looked up and smiled. "I'm telling my brother what nice people you are and asking him to extend you the most hospitable of receptions."

He handed Bernard the note, shook our hands, wished us a safe journey, and then walked us to a derelict pick-up truck punctured with bullet holes that he explained were sustained during the Six-Day War with Israel. Bernard balked.

"I can't drive that!"

"Not to worry," Captain Borai said. "The gas tank leaks, but there's plenty of fuel." He pointed to a number of jerry cans that had been packed in the back of the truck along with the boxed engine.

Bernard seemed to nod his approval, and that reassured me.

"One last thing," the Captain said. "There are checkpoints along the way. Drive through quickly. No one will stop you."

Bernard nodded again, as though this were an everyday occurrence, and jumped into the truck. I jumped in beside him. If it was all right with him, it was all right with me. I believed Bernard had a sixth sense about danger and would never put us in harm's way.

As I was about to shut the door, two of Captain's Borai's henchmen pushed into the front seat beside me. Neither man spoke French or English. Body language told me I didn't want lengthy conversations with them anyway.

Bernard looked at Captain Borai.

"They'll accompany you," he said. "It'll be safer. They know the desert."

Didn't he tell us locals were afraid and that's why he was asking us to go? Still, I was desperate for this experience and wasn't willing to back out now. Bernard must have felt the same way because a moment later he stepped on the gas pedal and we were off.

It took a day and a night to drive through the Sahara with nothing to see but paved road, sand, and the occasional checkpoint that we sped through — unmolested as Captain Borai had promised. The day was blisteringly hot and we froze at night. I sat stiff, upright, squeezed thigh-to-thigh with the two silent men whose only conversation was to shout in English "go, go" as we neared each checkpoint. The man to my right kept moving his hand over various parts of my leg while I strained to get as far to the left as possible.

Our only stops were to relieve ourselves behind the truck and refill the gas tank; that is, until we came to the last checkpoint before entering the outskirts of Cairo at about five in the morning. Two soldiers planted themselves on the road in front of our headlights. They each held a machine gun pointed at our windshield.

"Go, go," one of the brutes with us shouted.

"Are you crazy?" Bernard said.

I was beginning to think they were — as well as the two of us.

One of the soldiers asked for Bernard's driver's license. He looked at it upside down and declared it not to be a license. Back then there were no photos on Canadian licenses, and this was unheard of to the guard. He yanked open the truck door and beckoned Bernard to follow him into the guardhouse. Our two passengers went along. I was left with a small, pudgy looking soldier who couldn't have been more that seventeen or eighteen.

Pudgy pointed his gun through the window towards my stomach.

"Baby, baby," he said.

"Yes," I answered. "Two babies — big boys now." I gestured with my hands to show "big."

He shoved the gun further toward my stomach and shouted this time: "Baby, baby."

I suddenly had the shocking revelation that he was planning to rape me. A few days earlier, I had learned that ballpoint pens were new in the area and the locals were fascinated with them. There was a pen on the dashboard, and I picked it up.

"Pen," I said. I held the pen in front of his face and kept repeating the word while taking off the cover and putting it back on. Each time he said baby, he brought the gun closer to my stomach. I forced a smile and kept repeating "pen." I was trembling and at the same time out of my body watching my idiotic behaviour. I felt foolish but couldn't think of anything else to do.

Finally, my ploy took hold. The soldier put down his machine gun and grabbed the pen from my hand. "Pen," he said over and over while repeating my act of inserting and removing the cover from the pen.

Shortly after, Bernard, the soldier, and our two unwanted passengers came out of the guardhouse. They were accompanied by the commander of the check point, a dishevelled man in blue and white striped pajamas with scuffs on his feet. He watched as the men scrambled back into the truck and then in French wished us a safe journey. There were "feel good" smiles all around, and we were waved on our way.

The first half of our adventure was behind us. I braced myself for the next leg of our journey. About two hours later, on the outskirts of Cairo we found the highway heading towards Alexandria. On our right was a drive-in coffee shop, the first of many that dotted the barren, sandy landscape along the road.

"We stop for coffee," Bernard said.

"No, Go. Go," the two men demanded, vehement in their insistence, the moment so tense I was sure they were going to throw us out of the truck and drive off. But they didn't. They fell silent and sat, immobile, like two hunks of granite. And then it dawned on me. They probably couldn't drive.

In the ensuing silence Bernard let them know he was exhausted from having driven all night without a break. "If I don't get a coffee, we won't make to Alexandria," he told them.

The men didn't respond. Bernard got out and returned with four espressos. The two men drank their coffees with obvious relish. I couldn't figure them out. I was guessing wildly as to why they were with us, and knew I wouldn't rest easy until they were gone.

The drive to Alexandria was harrowing. The wide highway stretched before us with no lanes and no speed limit. Littered along the sides of the highway were animal carcasses, some huge, bleaching in the sun.

Crowded in among the animal bones were abandoned wrecked cars, rotting with rust. The landscape had the dream-like feel of a Dali painting. The traffic was so chaotic that I suspected no ambulance ever got to any of the accidents in time to save anyone. I was sure bodies still sat in the cars, desiccating in the heat.

Although Bernard and I couldn't speak freely, I felt his tension and knew he wanted to dump our escorts and the engine as fast as he could. Still, the carrot of that villa in exotic Alexandria held us.

As soon as we entered the city, Bernard asked the men to take us to Captain Borai's brother.

"Machine shop," one of the duo said.

"Borai's brother," Bernard said.

"No, machine shop. Go. Go."

Bernard pulled over to the side of the street. "First, Borai's brother," he said.

"Machine shop first. Go. Go."

Bernard didn't move.

The two men, after a short conversation in Arabic, relented.

"Okay, okay. Drive."

They led us through some of the worst slums and filthiest streets I'd ever seen. Through the windshield, I could make out a number of once stately homes, now derelict, their beautiful doorways and balustrades covered in grime and in disrepair from centuries of neglect. We passed blocks of broken down storefronts in cement block edifices with ragged children and surly looking men squatting in the doorways.

Where was Durrell's Alexandria? Could it have changed so much since the Second World War, the setting for the *Quartet*? Recently, I re-read *Justine*, the first of the four volumes of the *Quartet*, for some hint or foreshadowing and found ... *unaware that their mother city was dying, the living still sat there in open streets like caryatids supporting the darkness, the pains of futurity upon their eyelids.* The message had always been there, but embedded in so much florid, descriptive prose that I hadn't seen it. *The dusty, deathward drift of the city,* he wrote.

And now I saw it, and if I were to read the complete *Quartet* again, it would be with different eyes. The city I had envisioned as wickedly alluring with its patina of antiquity was not so much decadent as decayed — in fact, a rotting corpse.

Finally, on one of those bleak, squalid streets, Bernard was told to stop the truck. One of the men pointed to an unpainted, concrete building that had a large sign in Arabic over the entranceway and motioned to him to go there. My first thought was that perhaps it was where Captain Borai's brother worked. Bernard took the letter Captain Borai had given us and disappeared into the building. He was out in less than five minutes.

"What's up?" I asked.

"It's a youth hostel," he said. "The director is an old friend of Borai's, and the letter tells him that we're two hippies looking for a place to stay for the night. It suggests that he put us up."

Stories we'd heard about Captain Borai from people around the port came back with full impact. Stories I had dismissed because of Borai's elegant appearance and perfect English, and because stories of his outrageous criminal activity were unimaginable to me. The worst was the one about his luxury yacht belonging to two Italians who had mysteriously disappeared. The unclaimed yacht was seized by Borai. Everyone assumed that Borai had them drowned, but that seemed too much like a Hollywood thriller to me. I dismissed it all as jealousy and hearsay.

I should have known better. I'd already been witness to stolen yachts and disappearing people. It was inexcusable that I would be taken in by this gangster — and just because he returned half our money.

"We've got to get back to the yacht fast," Bernard said.

My head was spinning with questions. Why did Captain Borai send us on this trip? What was really in that boxed crate in the back of the truck? Was he planning to seize the *Santa Rita*? I'd never know the answer to the first two questions, and I feared that the third could be true. It was obvious that Bernard had the same thought.

He drove the truck to the garage at full throttle. Once there, the two thugs refused to let us drive the truck back. We didn't argue. We left as soon as we could and searched for the fastest way out of Alexandria. I no longer had any interest in this run-down city. It had lost its soul a long time ago. I wondered if Durrell's Alexandria ever existed.

We eventually found the local airport, but when we got there, we learned that planes flew out only twice a week, and this wasn't one of the days. There were no trains or buses to Hurghada. We located a taxi and were gouged fifty American dollars to be taken to the nearest town where we could catch a bus. When we got into the taxi, seven men piled in after us.

"It's a private taxi," Bernard said to them.

"These men are going where you are going, but they can't afford the fare," the taxi driver explained. "You are doing them a favour." A quick glance at the characters told us it would be best not to push the subject.

A miserable hour later, wedged next to sweating bodies in sweltering heat, we arrived at the bus station of a small town where we could catch a bus to Hurghada. Once on the bus, I noticed that I was the only woman and tried my best to melt into Bernard. Seats lined each side of the bus with the passengers jammed thigh to thigh.

At one stop, a middle-aged man in a spotless, white *djellaba* and carrying a walking stick got on board. He approached an old man seated across from me and spoke a few words to him in Arabic. When the old man didn't move, he beat him with the stick and shoved him to the floor. He then took the seat and stared at me all the way to Hurghada. No one reacted to the incident. Everyone continued to focus blankly into space. Pressing closer to Bernard, I did the same.

In Hurghada we jumped off the bus and raced to the marina praying that the guard at the gate wouldn't give us a hard time. Entering and leaving was always a game of nerves. Sometimes he would let us out but not back in even though it was clear that we'd only gone for provisions. We'd walk about aimlessly and try again every so often until he'd suddenly let us through. Sometimes he'd send us back to the boat at gunpoint when we wanted to leave the marina. Other times he'd ask for our passports, kiss them, and wave us through. This day he was in an expansive mood and welcomed us back with a wave of his hand.

I collapsed in relief when I saw the *Santa Rita* anchored exactly where we had left her. We checked everything on board and saw that nothing was missing.

There was barely time to savour our good fortune before Captain

Borai boarded the yacht. "My men kept an eye on things," he said. He was effusive in his praise for the way we helped him by delivering the engine. "I am inviting you for dinner at the Club Med — very elegant, delicious food. How better can I thank you?"

Bernard and I knew it would be a mistake to refuse his invitation or to bring up the deceitful way he had treated us. We no longer had any illusions about the gentlemanly Captain Borai, and we didn't want to be out of favour with him.

That evening we were treated to a sumptuous dinner surrounded by a lot of stiff, pretentious people in formal dress, holding drinks and barely moving. Everyone looked as though they were waiting for something but nothing happened. Somewhere in the background a comedian was performing, but nobody laughed.

I thought that perhaps this was where Alain Resnais vacationed before filming *Last Year in Marienbad*. I remembered the arty 1961 movie filmed against a static background dotted with elegantly dressed people, who moved about in a somnambulistic state making a point of going nowhere. Renais filmed emptiness well, but I thought of it as metaphor. Here I was experiencing it as the real thing.

In spite of, or maybe because of the atmosphere, we ate well and drank a lot. After thanking Captain Borai for his gracious hospitality and for looking after the *Santa Rita*, we rushed back to the yacht to prepare for leaving Hurghada at daybreak.

We had talked earlier with "Richard Widmark" from the *Cloud Nine* yacht about heading for Port Said. He said they were as anxious as we were to leave Egypt. Mrs. Moneypenny had found the stay in Hurghada unsettling, and while we were in Alexandria, she flew back to England. Others in the crew were also getting antsy. We arranged to sail out together.

Aside from wanting to get away from Captain Borai, we had another reason for moving on. We were supposed to meet Jonah in Israel for his spring break from Oxford. Bernard calculated the approximate time it would take us to get through the Red Sea. He figured Jonah's vacation would coincide with the time we'd arrive in Israel. We had arranged to meet him there, but we were behind schedule. I wanted to send him a telegram saying we were on our way.

Our first port of call on the way out of Egypt was the marina in Suez to pick up fuel and send the telegram. It was a windless morning, and we had to motor all the way, but at least we made good time. As night approached, it became tricky. The sea was full of odd debris, hunks of metal and huge tankers due to the oil exploitation along the coast. The smell of oil was suffocating.

We dropped anchor in the harbour at about ten at night. There were already a number of yachts at anchor waiting to pass through the Suez Canal. Bernard, along with the Richard Widmark look-alike and some of the other yacht owners, took their jerry cans and in *Cloud Nine*'s dinghy headed for a fuelling station. That's the last I saw of Bernard until six the next morning.

I couldn't believe this was happening again. In El Quseir, I'd at least had some clue of what was happening. This time he just disappeared. I'd experienced enough to know Egypt was a dangerous country outside the prescribed tourist route. Bernard could disappear without a trace. Officials could confiscate the yacht on any trumped-up charge, and expel me from the country. With no witnesses, they could do whatever they wanted. I remembered hearing about incidents like this in the yachting community. The worst scenario was that Bernard could be dead. I took comfort in the fact that the Richard Widmark double had also not returned. At the same time, I knew this was no consolation.

When Bernard finally returned, I was too distraught and spent to react. I had sat frozen in one position all night, my eyes glued to the companionway. When I heard the dinghy's engine stop alongside the boat, I was so stiff I couldn't unravel myself to get up. Seconds later, completely high on his adventure, Bernard stepped below deck.

"What a wild night!" he said, dancing around the salon. "We were at the police station. I think the police officer fell in love with 'Richard Widmark.' He kept telling him he looked like a movie star and wouldn't let us go. He was trying to seduce him. No charges were laid, and he finally released us."

I didn't know what to say. I wasn't as amused. "I have to go into Cairo to send that telegram," I said.

"Sure," he said. "I'll go with you. It's not safe to go alone."

I wasn't going to argue or make a scene about how casually he took my distress at his all-night absence. I wanted to get to Cairo, and I didn't want to go alone.

In Cairo, the bus took forever to get downtown. The main artery through the city was in absolute chaos with cars going any way drivers felt like taking them. Traffic jams were the only thing that permitted pedestrians to cross the street. Teeming with people, the congestion was so thick, the city was reduced almost to a standstill.

On every corner a soldier stood guard with a machine gun aimed at the cars. Before we arrived in Egypt, I'd never seen a person with a machine gun. Now, I saw them everywhere. When Hosni Mubarak came into power in 1981, he declared emergency law to combat Islamist extremists who were responsible for former president Anwar Sadat's assassination. He'd never lifted the law.

In 1982 Israel invaded Lebanon, but Mubarak promised to uphold the treaty that Sadat had signed with Israeli Prime Minister Yitzhak Rabin at Camp David. It angered a lot of his countrymen. We arrived in 1984, in the midst of the Israeli-Lebanese conflict. Probably, for all these reasons a huge number of armed soldiers were on the street. We hopped off the bus where we were told we might find a telegraph office. Bernard said he'd wait outside the building for me so he could smoke.

"Can I borrow your pen?" I asked.

Inside, it took forever before I was served. When my turn came, I asked about sending a telegram to Israel.

"There's no Israel," the clerk replied.

"Are you sure?"

He pointed to a large map of the Middle East behind him. "Find me Israel."

I looked. It wasn't there. The whole area was called Palestine.

"Palestine," I said. "Jerusalem."

He smiled and handed me the telegram to write my message. In the confusion of our disconcerting conversation, I forgot where I had gotten the pen.

"Is this yours or mine?" I asked.

"Mine," he replied.

When I left the building, Bernard asked: "Where's my pen?"

"Forget it," I said. I didn't want any more hostility than I had already experienced inside, but Bernard insisted on getting his pen back.

To my surprise, after a few rounds of the clerk's denial and Bernard's insistence, the pen was returned.

Pleased with his victory, Bernard suggested we try some of the local cuisine. Aside from the lavish western feast that Captain Borai had treated us to, we'd been eating from our provisions on the *Santa Rita*. Cairo seemed like the right place to try the local cuisine. We found a small restaurant nearby and ordered the only plate on the menu — a wilted salad of chopped lettuce and tomatoes with some *foul*, a local bean, on the side. The disappointment in our only meal out was soon replaced by the uneasy feeling of having eaten lettuce that probably wasn't washed. We'd been incredibly healthy through the voyage, and I hoped we'd stay that way.

Bernard was exhausted from his night away from the yacht, and I was feeling queasy from our lunch, so we decided to head back without visiting the city. All we saw was a distant view of the Sphinx, impressively large and stately, even with its broken nose, and the monumental presence of the pyramids of Giza rising behind it through the bus window. Today we both regret that we didn't get off the bus at Giza or make it to the Egyptian Museum.

On the third day of our stay in Suez, we felt rested enough to move on to Port Said and through the Canal. That entailed endless documents to sign and a pilot coming aboard. Agents motored from vessel to vessel in the marina offering their services for both. Officials also motored from boat to boat with one excuse or another to demand money. We were asked to inform them of our next port of call, and Bernard repeatedly answered: "Cyprus." As always, his instincts were right, as we would eventually learn.

The pilot we hired stayed with us for the two days it took us to go through the Canal, leaving at night on a motor boat that came for him and returning in the morning, always with prayer rug in hand. He never missed his hour of prayer and Bernard, fed up with having been constantly hassled for fees, including the one for the unnecessary pilot, deliberately changed the yacht's direction ever so slightly making the poor fellow constantly shift his rug to face Mecca.

As soon as we unloaded the pilot, we were again besieged by officials pulling up to the yacht and demanding money. This time Bernard refused. One of the officials pulled out a gun, but Bernard motored out into the Mediterranean without looking back. Free at last.

Chapter 24

UNHOLY IN THE HOLY LAND

Spring 1984: Israel

> *People say that what we're all seeking is a meaning for life.*
> *I don't think that's what we're really seeking. I think that what*
> *we're seeking is an experience of being alive, so that our life*
> *experiences on the purely physical plane will have resonances*
> *within our innermost being and reality, so that we actually*
> *feel the rapture of being alive.*
> —JOSEPH CAMPBELL

The first port outside the Suez Canal was Ashkelon on the southern coast of Israel, thought to be the home of the biblical Canaanites and then the conquering Philistines. It was also where Delilah was said to have shorn Samson's hair, thereby divesting him of all his strength. Under layers of Ashkelon's parched earth lay a treasure trove of ancient artefacts that could validate these stories, and led to many archaeological digs. We thought Ashkelon would be a good place to drop anchor and explore the sites before moving on. I planned to call Jonah, who was already in Jerusalem, and have him meet us there. As we approached the harbour, a woman's voice came through the VHF radio: "Wind power, wind power. Stay where you are."

At first, we thought she was calling the name of another yacht and didn't pay attention. When the voice insisted, we gleaned that this might be a call to us and cut the engine. Within seconds, divers in flippers and underwater gear surrounded the yacht. They searched the underside of the hull and then came aboard to finish the inspection.

"What are you looking for?" Bernard asked.

"Bombs," the diver-in-charge answered.

My mouth went dry. Hadn't a peace treaty been signed between Israel and Egypt in 1979? Until we entered the Middle East, I hadn't fully grasped the extent of the animosity the Arab world held towards Israel.

"You sailed from Egypt. Did you tell the authorities you were coming to Israel?"

"I thought it wouldn't be a good idea," Bernard replied. "I gave them Cyprus as the next port of call."

The diver nodded his approval. He went on to explain that, when the Egyptians know a yacht is coming to Israel, they plant explosive devices underneath the hull without the knowledge of the people aboard.

"All vessels passing through the Suez Canal," he said, "have to be inspected before they're allowed into Israel."

I wondered how often an unsuspecting yacht had blown up in these waters, and why I had never heard about it.

Because Ashkelon was a military zone, we weren't permitted to visit, and were asked to move on after the divers finished their job. Farther up the coast, we passed Ashdod, one of the oldest cities in the world dating back to the seventeenth century BCE. I couldn't imagine a city that old, and was tempted to visit, but didn't want to lose more time before seeing Jonah. We dropped anchor in Tel Aviv, and spent the night aboard the *Santa Rita* waiting for a channel to be dug to the marina so the keel of our yacht could pass through. Storms often filled the channel with sand, and periodically it had to be dredged. Once berthed, we hastened ashore.

The contrast between Cairo and Tel Aviv was like the difference between a film noir and a high-tech cinemascope Hollywood production. Cairo was drab with narrow streets and shadowy corners. Tel Aviv was lit up like a neon sign. The sudden blast of colour and light, along with the expansive movement of people, overwhelmed my senses.

The waterfront swarmed with people — families sitting in groups, children chasing each other, athletic young men preening themselves along the water's edge, and young women with model-perfect bodies sunbathing in bikinis. I was amazed at how fit these young adults were and attributed it to the two-year military service required of Israeli citizens between the ages of eighteen and twenty. It had been so many years since I'd seen so much skin on a public beach that I felt slightly embarrassed. My discomfort didn't last long. I soon found the free, unselfconscious lifestyle exhilarating.

I phoned Jonah who was in a hotel room in Jerusalem waiting to hear from us.

"Hey, Mom," he shouted into the phone. "Guess what? A bomb just exploded near my hotel!"

"Oh my God," I said. "Are you okay?"

He laughed. "Of course, I'm okay. I wouldn't be on the phone if I wasn't."

He found the experience more interesting than frightening. I didn't feel as nonchalant, and without any rational reason for it, felt he'd be safer with us. I had so many mixed feelings as I watched Jonah approach the *Santa Rita*—overwhelming love for the little boy I raised, guilt for having sent him so far away to college, and immense pleasure that he was able to spend time with us.

I hugged him hard and patted his back. "It's good to see you," I said, feeling my words were so inadequate.

Bernard first shook his hand and then gave him a bear hug. "So you're now an Oxford man." He pulled away to size up the young man.

I had last seen Jonah when he was eighteen. He was now twenty-one. The child who left us in the Philippines was now an adult. Too quick, I thought, but how grateful I was that he found his life full and productive. He regaled us with stories about Middlebury College and his junior year at Oxford.

"I'm majoring in English Lit," he said, "but I decided to minor in Mandarin because I already knew the language from when we were in Taiwan. Middlebury paired me with a great roommate from Beijing. And here I am now at Oxford. What a difference from Middlebury! My bed gets made every morning, and I have sherry with my professors. The best part is that no one can place my accent, so I have easy access to being friends with everybody. There's still a class system where you get accepted or rejected depending on how you speak."

Jonah had found his niche and was comfortable with his life. He and Da Shing, his roommate from Middlebury, remain good friends to this day. Da Shing was Jonah's best man at his wedding. And Jonah is godfather to two of the children of friends he had made at Oxford.

"We were a little late getting here," I said. "What did you do with your time?"

"I went to Eilat to spend a day on the beach and go swimming. On the bus, crossing the desert, I sat next to a young guy who had just come back from fighting in Lebanon. He wasn't happy about that. When we arrived at the sea, he took off all his clothes and walked into the water. I thought I'd wait until morning, but the weather turned, and I never went swimming."

Recently, I asked Jonah what he remembered about his time in Israel. Along with finding the people pushy but generous, and Jaffa, an ancient Palestinian suburb of Tel Aviv, picturesque, it's that young man walking into the sea that has stayed with him.

Tel Aviv bustled with small outdoor cafes and falafel stands. I ate falafel wrapped in a pita for the first time and decided the long wait in line was worth it. I noticed everyone ate a lot of salads. All the produce looked fresh, clean and inviting, but the biggest surprise was how beautiful the young people looked. The mixing of the gene pool from so many different ethnic backgrounds produced striking off-spring. It helped that they were in such good physical condition. Obesity was not a problem in Israel.

With its art galleries, cultural activities, financial district, and nightlife, Tel Aviv was totally western. Only the food with its hint of the exotic gave a clue that I might not be in any European city. It was hard to believe that in 1909 this area was nothing but desolate sand dunes. The story goes that sixty-six Jewish families settled there. One hundred thirty-two seashells were gathered — half grey, half white. A boy was to select one of the white shells that had a family name on it. A girl was to pick a grey shell that had a plot number assigned to it. The two shells were paired. From this unique beginning, the city grew into the party capital of the world with a huge international presence.

We spent a few days gorging on fresh salads, browsing the shops and people watching in small street cafés. Then we lifted anchor and the three of us sailed north to Haifa. It was closer to Jerusalem, a city we wanted to explore before leaving.

We arrived in Haifa to what appeared to be a huge celebration and discovered we were the honoured guests. In 1984 there weren't many yachts that entered its port, and we were received like royalty. The Israelis, who lined the dock, besieged us with every manner of question, from who we were, to why we were doing this, to the measurement and cost of the yacht.

Our dream became their dream, and they expressed interest in wishing they could make such a journey. One couple planned to do it. They pushed themselves forward, and a short, solid-built young man introduced himself. "Hello," he said. "I am Bebe. This is my wife, Ilana. We're also going to sail — as far as Martinique. That is our dream."

Bebe and Ilana led us to the steel-hulled yacht they had been building over the years and introduced us to their four beautiful young daughters who were going to sail with them — all still in grade school.

"We're almost ready to sail," Bebe said.

"We'll meet you in Cyprus," Bernard replied.

"I look forward to seeing you there," I said, but I didn't think I'd see them again. I couldn't believe they'd undertake this adventure with four young daughters on board.

In spite of our tumultuous welcome, Haifa was more subdued than Tel Aviv. It was grittier and had none of the buzz. I was surprised that in such a small country there could be so much contrast from one part to another. Israel was a mosaic of many disparate parts, socially and emotionally — a cauldron of tension and anger, feistiness and compassion.

A striking difference between the two cities was the cultural divide. Tel Aviv felt Western. Haifa was still a Middle Eastern city where Muslims, Druze, Christians and Jews lived together in an easy let-live harmony. Though few of the Baha'i faith live there, Mount Carmel in the centre of Haifa is home to the Baha'i World Centre. The Bab, the founder of the faith, is buried in a gold domed shrine on the mountain, and his followers have planted elegant gardens laid-out in terraces around his shrine.

They've also built houses on the property that are architecturally imposing, including the stately house of justice. Through their efforts they transformed what had been a barren mountainside into an oasis of colour and ordered calm. It cheered up Haifa's otherwise drab look. The gardens, since our visit, have been extended into nineteen terraces up the slope of the mountain and are maintained by six hundred Baha'i volunteers and one hundred full time gardeners. I can only imagine how splendid they must be now, for even in their smaller design, they were a vision that stays with me.

The adrenaline of so many new sights and the energy of the people kept us buoyed up, but we couldn't sustain the momentum. After leaving Egypt, we had been on a roller coaster of high energy followed by longer periods of lethargy. At first, we thought it was a question of recuperating from the stress of our experiences in Egypt, but we kept getting weaker. We finally had ourselves checked out at a hospital and discovered we had picked up worms in Egypt. Knowing I had live creatures laying eggs in my intestines turned me into a wobbling mass of Jello.

I was glad this parasite was well-known in Israel, and the cure was a quick one two punch; first to kill off the parents and then to catch the babies before they hatched. After the first dose of medication, we started to feel better, but I refused to look in the toilet for weeks after. I couldn't bear the thought of coming face to face with one of my visitors.

As soon as the medication took effect, the three of us set out to explore more of Israel. Bernard was still paranoid about leaving the yacht for any period of time, so we stuck to day visits. Fortunately, Israel is so small we could go anywhere within a day.

Our first visit was to the old section of Jerusalem, squeezed inside thick, ancient stone walls. After entering through one of its eight gates, we strolled the Arab sector with its bustling merchants, got lost in its labyrinth of messy alleyways and colourful souks, and found our way to the quiet Armenian sector. We then back-tracked through the Arab sector to the Christian quarter to walk the stations of the cross that ended in a visit to the Church of the Holy Sepulchre, where Christ was said to have died, been buried, and rose from the dead. We eventually arrived at our final destination — the clean, relatively new Jewish quarter rebuilt after its destruction by the Jordanians in 1948. I couldn't believe how much history was inside these walls, an area no more than a square kilometre that can be walked in an afternoon.

We spent another day visiting the area around the Wailing Wall where we caught a glimpse of the Temple Mount with the beautifully built Dome of the Rock and the Al Aqsa Mosque, both sites sacred to the Muslim community. We weren't allowed to enter them, but had no problem visiting the Wailing Wall, the last remnant of the second temple, so long as our heads were covered and we walked backwards upon leaving.

The wall, the holiest of Jewish sites, was in constant activity with the ultra religious, mostly men, praying and swaying in long black coats, their heads covered with stiff, broad-rimmed black hats, their faces bearded and framed by long side curls. The less religious of the orthodox wore normal street clothes but covered themselves with prayer shawls. Chinks in the wall held bits of paper on which prayers were written. I found a small piece of paper in my handbag and wrote my own, which I carefully folded and inserted into a tiny crevice that I found among the ancient stones:

Please God, let Bernard's good will towards me continue.
Please exorcise whatever that demon is within him that is
pushing him further away from me and the world around him.

One day, we visited Ein Gedi, a desert oasis that's a national park where wild animals, natural to the habitat, roam. The ruins of Masada are located in Ein Gedi, and we hiked up to the top. We learned that this had been Herod's fortified palace taken by the Sicarii, an ultra religious Jewish sect. The Romans stormed the fortress to reclaim it, but the Sicarii committed mass suicide rather than surrender. I believe this story carries a powerful message for the Israelis.

The day before Jonah left for England, we visited The Church of the Nativity on Manger Square in Bethlehem. In 1984 Bethlehem was under the jurisdiction of Israel and was a quiet town with a mixed Moslem/Christian population. I noted that, wherever we went in this ancient land, its history revolved around birth, death, and resurrection, whether by supernatural means or human will. Its history from its first recorded time to the present day has been one of strife. Every site and centre we visited was a reminder of the intense energies at play in this area. The epochs change, the architecture changes, the alliances change, but the story is always the same. It brought to mind Escher's drawing of stairways that lead in many directions but go nowhere.

When Jonah's brief visit came to an end. I gave him the last of his things that had remained on the yacht — a small bamboo stool and plaster statue of the God of Wealth, both purchased in Taipei and still with him, and a collection of books that he'd carted all the way from Montreal when our journey commenced. It symbolized the last time we'd ever live together, and was a heartbreaking moment for me.

"Goodbye, sweetie," I said. "I promise I'll make it to your graduation from no matter where we are."

He still had his senior year at Middlebury to do, and I hoped we'd have the *Santa Rita* sold by then, so I'd have the money for plane fare. If not, I'd do whatever was necessary to make the trip. As I watched him go, I was taken aback at how much it hurt. I felt the loss in every part of my body but knew it was good that he felt secure enough to forge his own road.

Bernard wasn't with me to say good-bye. He stayed behind on the *Santa Rita* while Jonah and I lugged Jonah's books to the airport. Jonah seemed all right with it, or at least he didn't show disappointment or annoyance. I think he was looking forward to getting back to Oxford. I wasn't all right with it, and more than a little annoyed. I decided not to make it an issue with Bernard because I didn't want to spoil the memory of the wonderful days we had together. But he had started to drink again, and that made me uneasy.

Bernard and I took one last trip before leaving Israel — this time to the Dead Sea. When we left Hurgada, he accidentally tipped over a kettle of boiling water that scorched one of my legs around the ankle and Achilles heel. I had huge water blisters that I didn't want to burst for fear of infection, but they weren't disappearing.

"Maybe a soak in the Dead Sea would help," he said.

"I don't think so," I said. "With all that salt, it'll hurt."

"Maybe not. It's a closed wound."

He kept insisting. I knew his insistence was a peace offering. The accident had been the result of nervous agitation during one of his sulking periods. Bernard could not apologize. This was code. I could accept it or not without our ever discussing the real issue of why I was a scapegoat for his frustrations.

"Okay," I said, which meant that for the moment all was forgiven.

I took my bathing suit with me in case I wanted to give it a try. I did. I figured if it hurt, I'd get out fast. The water remained shallow no matter how far out I went. The tepid water and lack of depth felt like a sticky mud puddle. Finally, I let go of my resistance and lay on my back as I saw others doing, amazed at how buoyant I was. It was impossible to sink. Most people who've floated in the Dead Sea have found the sensation pleasant. I found it disconcerting. It didn't seem right that without effort I could lie on top of the water. I also didn't like the density of the water mixed with mud.

Much as I tried, I couldn't get settled, but I was determined to stay for the sake of my blisters. About fifteen minutes later, I got out expecting no change. But in that short period of time, the bloat of my blisters had started to subside. If a few minutes could do so much for my blisters, I fantasized what it could do for my whole body. I regretted I hadn't stayed longer, but felt no urge to return.

On shore, Bernard met me with a huge bag of the sweetest and most succulent cherries I had ever eaten. We sat on a bench, tucked into each other's folds, and savoured the fruit. I felt cherished and loved. I recall that moment with a bittersweet sharpness because the situation changed a few days later.

Looking back, what I most remember about Israel are the Baha'i gardens in Haifa and the juicy sweetness of those succulent red cherries I ate near the shore of the Dead Sea. And I'm reminded it's the senses that carry the deepest memories, not history or stories or the edifices built during a certain period. It's in our visceral centre that our truth lies, not in what's fed to our brain. Perhaps that is why Israel with its thousands of years of history did not engage me as I had thought it would. But the small sensual pleasures of the country are still with me.

Israel revived us. We indulged in the country's sun-ripened fruit and fresh vegetables like insatiable rabbits. We showered luxuriously in the private homes of generous and outgoing people, and slept a great deal without the threat of pirates or gun-happy harbour masters. Towards the end of our visit, we felt a renewed vigour and looked forward to setting sail for Cyprus, Larnaca being our port of entry.

Chapter 25

THE PLAN IS NOT TO GET ANYWHERE

Summer 1984: Cyprus

> *All changes, even the most longed for, have their melancholy;*
> *for what we leave behind us is a part of ourselves; we must die*
> *to one life before we can enter into another.*
> — ANATOLE FRANCE

Thirty to thirty-five knot winds on our bow all the way from Israel to Cyprus meant constantly tacking while trying to brace ourselves against a turbulent sea. But because the crossing was done in a single night, I arrived in Larnaca in high spirits. I looked forward to sharing "war stories" with yachties who had sailed through the Suez Canal before us. We knew a number of them were moored in Larnaca, trying to rest up before moving on.

Soon after we docked, Bernard and I went in search of two couples we had met earlier in our sailing adventure and found them together on one of the yachts, along with another couple we didn't know. Over some finger food and local wine that was surprisingly good, they took turns sharing the woes of their journey up the Red Sea.

"The satellite system got clogged with sand," one of the couples told us. "We couldn't see anything. We didn't know where we were."

"Strong winds blew us off course. We were blinded by sand," the other said.

"We got stuck on a sand bar, but managed to break loose," piped up the pregnant half of the yachtie couple we didn't know. "We were afraid to go ashore and ask for help in case they'd confiscate the yacht on some trumped-up charge." She then went on to relate an incident that happened to one of their sailing buddies. "They ran aground and had to be towed into port. The fee to reclaim their yacht was so high they couldn't pay it. They were forced to leave Egypt without their boat."

We were surprised to discover that the two couples we had met earlier were now parents. While we talked, they passed the babies from one to another, and the mothers casually nursed whenever the babies fretted. I marvelled at the ingenuity of these freewheeling couples who, without any forethought, suddenly found themselves parents. Instead of giving up their adventure, they took it in stride and made do with whatever they had at hand.

Makeshift strollers were constructed from plastic storage containers onto which they wired small wheels. I saw them pulling their offspring along the pier by ropes tied to holes in the containers. Their ingenuity was impressive, but I was curious as to what they'd do as the children grew older. I wouldn't want the responsibility of a rambunctious two-year-old or an independent-minded three-year-old on a fast-moving yacht.

I was fascinated that the three women became pregnant while in the grip of terror at sea. It reminded me of stories I'd heard about London during the Blitz when Nazi bombers were overhead. People in the bomb shelters mated like rabbits, so the rumour goes. And I wondered if there wasn't a genetic component built into our DNA to propagate life under dire circumstances, as I now knew of two children and a third on the way who wouldn't have been conceived if not for the vagaries of the Red Sea.

If there was such a gene, I didn't have it. The last thing I thought about during that harrowing Red Sea passage was having sex. My focus was on survival — my survival — not the species. The bulk of my energy went into coping. I was sure it was the same for a retired teacher we met by chance along the pier. He told us he had been diagnosed with having had two strokes while on the Red Sea. His yacht was to be his retirement home. I wondered if he still felt that way.

A few yachties we met in the harbour, who like us, had travelled the old spice route across the Indian Ocean and through the Bab el-Mandeb Strait, had t-shirts printed that read: BEEN THERE. DONE THAT. I understood the meaning behind the slogan. We were tired of assimilating the "exotic." We'd seen so much in so few years that we'd reached saturation. It was like going to a museum where after a while you become weary and your eyes glaze over. The senses become over stimulated, and everything starts to lose value. I needed to stay put for a while to give my wanderlust a rest.

Life along the pier was one big party. The tension between the Turks and Greeks who'd split Cyprus in two under a fragile truce didn't concern the yachties in the least. I remember writing to my friend in Belgium: "I've changed my diet to gallons of wine. It's so cheap here. And I'm gorging on cheese — both items the price of gold in the East."

Our healthy regime in Israel drifted into a dim memory. At first, I thought it was a release from the tension of traversing the Red Sea that put everyone in a festive mood. I soon discovered it was a way of life among yachties in Europe. The plan was not to get anywhere. Very few talked about heading to the next port. No one spoke of seeing the world. The idea was to hang out in the Mediterranean, and frankly, it wasn't a bad place to be.

The exceptions were our new Israeli friends Bebe and Ilana, who had left Israel for Larnaca a few days after us. I had been wrong about his ever making the voyage. Bebe held on to his dream of making it as far as Martinique with his wife and four daughters. Within the next two years, the family made it to Martinique and back. The dream held, but the marriage didn't, not uncommon among sailing families.

Ilana was a bundle of energy, and she often invited me in the evening to troll the local stands to gorge on *souvlakis*, a local favourite made with pieces of grilled pork wrapped in pita bread and topped with a yogurt dressing. She told me she wasn't kosher but didn't eat pig. "Pigs aren't allowed on Israeli soil," she said. "The one pig farm there is on raised wooden planks so that the pigs don't touch the land."

One evening Ilana, Bebe, Bernard and I went for a bite. "Meze is good," Bebe announced. "We order that."

"That's a mixed grill," Bernard said. "I thought you didn't eat pork."

"We eat pork," Ilana replied. "The only meat we don't eat is pig."

"Pork comes from the pig," Bernard explained.

"No, no, no," the two insisted. "Pork is not pig!"

Bebe may not have known cuts of meat, but he was right about the meze. Dish after dish arrived at our table that could titillate any palate. Spread before us were small plates of olives, tzatziki, hummus, fried eggplant, grilled meats and grilled halloumi cheese, a specialty of Cyprus made with goat and sheep milk. Among the assortment of meats was marinated pork and what looked like fried pork sausages.

"That's pig," Bernard said pointing to the two dishes.

"No," Bebe said. "Pork."

Bernard tried again. "Pork comes from pig."

"No, pig is pig. Pork is pork,"

"You're right," Bernard said. "Let's enjoy."

When I order a *souvlaki* in downtown Montreal, I think about Ilana, and I wonder if she ever gave up *souvlakis* after Bernard tried to burst their bubble. Memory is fickle. It's impossible to predict what will remain with us and what disappears. I've had catastrophic incidents, or so I thought, that are vague today. But small moments, such as eating at a stall with Ilana, reappear; though at the time they seemed to have had little significance.

The French writer Marcel Proust in his novel *Remembrance of Things Past* expounds on the power of involuntary memory and its relationship to the senses. He felt it to be far more powerful than intellectual memory as it is complete immersion rather than recalling a linear series of events. Involuntary memory always comes up spontaneously induced by some outside stimulus to the senses whether through the taste of a certain dish, or the sound of a certain piece of music, or an object we've held from an earlier time, or the aroma of something wafting through the air. This is the only explanation I have for why Ilana and *souvlaki* are irrevocably tied forever inside my head.

Johnny Baumann was another frequent visitor on the *Santa Rita*. We had last seen Johnny in Puerto Galera in the Philippines. Back then, he was a fairly prosperous middle-aged ex-pat from Germany. He had married a Filipina and started a small business hiring local crew for German ships. Since we last saw him, his wife had taken over the business and had him thrown out of the country. He was still middle-aged, but no longer prosperous.

Wine flowed freely aboard our yacht, and Johnny was always there to imbibe. One evening, while under the influence, he told us he had been part of Hitler youth, though thrown out as not good material. "My father," he told us, "made his fortune by denouncing a rich Jewish neighbour, a friend. He stole his property." There was a long pause while Johnny poured himself another drink. "My mother couldn't deal with what he did. She went crazy and was committed to an asylum."

He went on to say that, while he was still a teenager, Germany fell to the Allies, leaving his generation caught between Nazi ideology and that of the newly-formed democratic state. The government put into practice regulations designed to find and debrief his generation. "Anyone picked up three times for drunk driving was considered to have confusion about what to believe and sent for therapy," he said.

Before this was put into practice, Johnny left Germany and was never properly rehabilitated. He renounced his country, and buried his pain in alcohol. He was one of those wounded souls we sometimes met on our journey, who chose to live without social constraints and took to the sea as refuge. Some were ex-Viet Nam vets, and I already knew their stories without having to probe. There were others, who I'm sure had stories, but we didn't ask and they didn't say.

Bernard was now only communicative during "happy hour" which started to invade more and more of the day. When not socializing with his drinking buddies, he was distant and silent, focusing all his attention on the boat. In the midst of Bernard's withdrawal from me, my cousin Shirley wrote and asked if she could come and stay with us for a week's vacation. I jumped at the chance to have lighter company. I also thought it might help draw out Bernard to have someone other than me or his yachtie gang to talk to. The day Shirley arrived, we decided to go to a nice restaurant for dinner. It would be a treat for me not to eat my own cooking and a welcome change from the local stalls. When we were ready to leave, Bernard decided he had work to do on the engine.

"Go on," he said. "I don't mind. Bring me back something."

I hadn't eaten in a fancy restaurant in Larnaca before Shirley's arrival and had no idea I had to reserve a table. We waited forever in line before we got seated and served. During the meal, I felt a gnawing in my stomach. I couldn't trust Bernard's moods. He was becoming edgier and more paranoid by the day. The emotional warmth and good-will we shared in Israel had become a wishful memory. I sensed that my ploy to bring Bernard back to civility by having someone from the outside visit wasn't going to work. I regretted my decision to let Shirley come.

Shirley noticed my nervousness while we waited for Bernard's dinner to be prepared.

"What's wrong with you?" she asked.

"Nothing," I said. "They're taking forever to wrap that take-out." I didn't want to get into a conversation about my personal life.

We'd hardly stepped on deck when Bernard came up from below. "You bitch," he shouted. "You took long enough with that dinner. I knew you'd try to get even if I didn't go with you."

Shirley tried to intervene. "It wasn't her fault. We had to wait for a table, and then it took even longer to get your meal."

"I know her. You don't. This was deliberate."

He wouldn't stop shouting. I couldn't get a word in. And even if I had, I knew he wouldn't have heard.

Robert, an Australian three yachts farther down the pier, came out on his deck. "Will you shut the hell up," he shouted. "We don't have to hear you all through the harbour."

I was utterly humiliated. Every cell in my body felt on fire. I ran below deck and threw myself onto the berth in the aft cabin. Shirley came in after me and stood beside the berth saying nothing for a long while. "He needs you," she finally said.

I couldn't believe what I heard. At that moment, I hated her. "I certainly don't need him," I replied. I turned away from her to make it clear that there was no more conversation to be had on the subject.

I lay on the berth without moving until morning hoping she'd leave during the night and find herself a hotel room. She didn't. When I left the berth the next day, I found her and Bernard having coffee at the salon table. I got my own cup of coffee and forced myself to sit, making sure to have eye contact with neither of them.

Shirley turned to me and chirped in an irritatingly pleasant voice: "I spoke to Bernard about the idea of sailing to Paphos, and he agreed. Some of the oldest mosaics in the West are there. And I don't know if you know, but it's the birthplace of Aphrodite — the very place where she rose from the sea."

Who gives a damn, I thought.

"Yeah, great. It sounds interesting," I said.

In truth, I was intrigued. As much as I'd have liked to spend the day on my own processing what had happened the night before, I was aware that if I didn't visit this site, I might regret it later on. I had troubling feelings about my marriage, but I wasn't going to let it destroy this once-in-a-lifetime adventure. I had invested too much. Maybe Bernard would shift back to his old self, I told myself, once we had less stress on the sea. I was still willing to give our relationship a chance. I was caught by good memories of our past life and his seductive charisma when he reverted to his old self.

The sail along the coast of Cyprus to Paphos was pleasant. Bernard displayed none of the animosity towards me that he had shown the night before. I discovered years later that his emotional distance, anger, argumentativeness and paranoia were all indicators of alcoholism — as was his sudden reversal to good will.

Once in Paphos, the three of us visited the ruins of Roman villas dating back to the third and fifth century. I saw mosaics of such fine quality and exquisite detail that I doubted I'd ever see work of that calibre again. I was astonished at how much history passed through here. Remains from both the Hellenistic and Roman periods were in evidence as well as ruins going back to the twelfth century BCE. The cult of Aphrodite had its origins here, the foundation of her enormous temple still discernible.

Paphos, I learned, was the site where Saul of Tarsus became Paul after converting the Roman governor, Sergius Paulus, to Christianity, and also where the oracle spoke wise words to seekers of the truth. *Where was the oracle now*, I thought, *when I needed her*?

So much early history that I believed had taken place on mainland Greece and in the Middle East had actually happened on this tiny island of Cyprus. What had once seemed beyond the veil of time when I studied history in school no longer felt distant. I walked on the foundation of Aphrodite's temple, and linear time collapsed. The old goddesses from Ishtar to Astarte along with the titan, Hekate, and now Aphrodite came alive here.

I felt them under my feet and wondered that I hadn't picked up that early, rooted connection in Israel, home of our three great western religions. It then struck me that all three were male religions. In Paphos I felt the power of the goddess, and I identified with that energy. It awakened a fire in my belly, and gave me a heightened sense of personal power.

On Shirley's final day in Cyprus, the three of us took a bus trip to Choirokoitia, an archaeological site with ruins dating back to 2300 BCE, and then continued on to Kourion, to see the performance of a Greek tragedy in a second century Roman amphitheatre. So many layers of history on this small island, I thought, but I wasn't fully engaged with that insight. I was too focused on Aphrodite and intrigued by the hold she had on me.

As soon as Shirley left, I felt my limbs loosen. Only then did I realize how tense I had been during her stay. All through her visit I had braced myself against another of Bernard's outbursts knowing I couldn't bear to go through another one of those episodes while she was visiting. The irony was how civil he had become after that attack and how well she and Bernard got along. I hardly joined their conversations and was glad they didn't notice. At one point, I tried to engage Shirley in a discussion about the goddess.

"God is male," she countered.

So I pondered my discovery on my own and left them to their chitchat, finding it a blessing to have time to myself.

After Shirley left, we trekked to the Stavrovouni Monastery located on one of the peaks of the Troodos Mountains, formally Mt. Olympus until it lost its name to a higher peak. The monastery was said to have been built over an ancient temple by St. Helena, the mother of Constantine, to house a fragment of the holy cross. I found it ironic that the mother of Constantine had the monastery built but no woman could enter. I had to content myself with the bookstore and a superb view of Larnaca spread out below. I thought again about Paphos and wondered what happened to that vibrant feminine core that raised the island from obscurity to a centre of worship in pre-Christian times. And I wondered what brought about her demise.

Our one-month stay in Larnaca slipped into two. By the end of the second month, I was feeling antsy. I was bored with our drinking buddies, and didn't have the temperament to lose myself in drifting time and small talk. I wanted to work, and I wanted Bernard to look for work, and there was no chance of finding employment in Cyprus. I was tired of provisioning and cooking and cleaning while Bernard sat around with his pals and drank. I was also tired of walking on eggs never knowing what I might say that could suddenly anger him.

I needed to take some physical distance from this relationship, not that it would be noticed. But I thought it might make a difference in our rapport if we weren't together every day, twenty-four hours a day. If we both had a commitment off the *Santa Rita*, that could improve the relationship.

"Isn't it time for us to move on?" I asked.

"Maybe," Bernard answered.

"I think we should move on," I said a week later.

Bernard simply shrugged his shoulders.

A number of our fellow travellers had already left for other ports. "When are we going?" I insisted on knowing.

No answer.

One day, without any discussion and for no apparent reason, Bernard took out a couple of nautical charts stored in one of the lockers behind a settee. It meant we were about to sail, though I had no idea where we were going. Perhaps this should have upset me, but it didn't. I was happy we were finally on our way. It wasn't in my nature to sit around going nowhere. It's not how I envisioned life at sea.

Chapter 26

CROSSING THE GREAT
EAST/WEST DIVIDE

Autumn 1984: Turkey/Greece

> *Though we travel the world to find the beautiful,*
> *we must carry it with us or we find it not.*
> — RALPH WALDO EMERSON

Bernard sat at the chart table, hunched over a spread-out nautical chart, carefully studying the Turkish coastline, his ever-present hand-rolled Gitane dangling from his lips and dripping bits of black ash onto the chart. *God, that annoys me*, I thought. At one time I over-looked his messy habits and found them endearing. Something was shifting inside me. I felt on edge, but wasn't ready to face my growing resentment. I had thought of us as soul mates. I couldn't admit I might have been wrong.

"Why don't we do some of the islands first?" I suggested, trying to refocus my mind. "There are a number of them on our way to Turkey."

I had an atlas open in front of me and was eyeing some of the Greek islands known as the Cyclades. I visualized our Mediterranean journey as pleasant island hopping with no worries about pirates or unpredictable squalls, but Bernard reminded me that the winds are never predictable, nor is the sea.

"Not a good idea," he said. "The sea is too rough this time of year." He reminded me how seasick my cousin Shirley had become just sail-ing down to Paphos. "It's better to take a coastal route along Turkey's edge and take shelter in Marmaris. There's a good protected harbour there. We can wait out the winds."

He was concerned about the Meltemi, a summer wind off the

Aegean Sea that could reach gale force and trigger waves up to ten feet high. We were leaving Cyprus mid-summer, at the height of the Meltemi season. It wasn't a good time to explore the Cyclades.

I knew nothing about Turkey, but I'd always felt excitement entering places I didn't know. Even eating in restaurants for the first time gave me a rush. I wondered if this thirst for experience wasn't triggered by an off-hand remark my mother made when I was ten.

"The only things," she had said, "that belong to you are your life experiences. No one can take memories from you."

Today I wonder about what had brought her to that view. She was a private person, and I knew little about her.

With a steady five-knot wind, the sail holding at its set angle, and the *Santa Rita* under the guidance of the autopilot, we sat back and took in Turkey's powerfully rugged coastline and pine-clad mountains. The *Santa Rita* cut through a sea that shimmered turquoise in the sun, and I felt completely at one with the yacht's movement and the water around us. Towards the end of July we entered the bay of Marmaris, the point where the Aegean Sea meets the Mediterranean, and tied the *Santa Rita* to a pier.

In 1984, Marmaris was a quiet fishing village, and we were one of few yachts in the harbour. Later, it became hyped as part of the Turkish Riviera and was transformed overnight into a bustling tourist mecca, but at that time we had this quiet paradise to ourselves. Looking back I think how fortunate we were. We stumbled on many picturesque harbours by chance, having no idea they were there. Today many of these quiet out-of-the-way places are major tourist centres, complete with scuba diving clubs, discos, and group charters with, I feel, something precious lost.

Bernard followed his usual pattern of hibernating aboard. After a small foray to a castle re-built by Sulieman the Magnificent in the 1500s, he was content to stay ensconced on the yacht. He spent hours fiddling with the hardware but neglected the upkeep. Ropes were strewn all over the deck. Odd pieces of acquired junk lay about. It depressed me to see the elegant, clean lines of the *Santa Rita* hidden under so much rubbish.

A young American couple strolling along the pier stopped and called to Bernard who was on deck. "That's a beautiful 'character' boat you have."

Bernard didn't acknowledge their presence, and they walked on.

"Idiots," he spat out. "They can't tell the difference between a Peterson-designed ketch and a character boat."

No they can't, I thought. *You've sufficiently trashed this boat.*

"Think so?" I said.

There was no point in suggesting he clean up the deck or throw away the junk he'd acquired. I had already tried. It only irritated him and didn't change the situation.

Since Cyprus, wine had become ubiquitous and cheap. Bernard was now drinking all the time, but I still wasn't putting all the pieces together. I only noticed he became more sociable if I drank with him. The wine is good and he's French, I thought. Of course, he's drinking more. It's cultural. I was flip-flopping about the extent of his problem.

I had hoped his moodiness would abate when the stress in our travels lessened. I missed the companionship — the pleasure of sharing the uniqueness of our adventure. He didn't talk about where we'd been. He didn't discuss future plans. He charted our course, announced our next port of call, set the sails, and ate the meals I prepared, mostly in silence. He wasn't aggressive. He just wasn't there. When we were crossing the Indian Ocean, he had once again informed me he didn't want to share the aft cabin.

"It's better I sleep in the salon," he had said. "That way I'm alert for any danger."

Now we were no longer in danger and he still hadn't returned to the aft cabin.

Then suddenly one night I opened my eyes found him standing beside the berth. "Do you mind if I sleep with you?" he asked, as he had on other occasions. Each time he made it seem as though I'd been the one who arranged our living conditions.

That night the memory of all his transgressions diminished to what I decided was over-reaction on my part — their impact lessened by hope. But the next day, there was no morning glow, just morning coffee.

Bernard was already on deck fussing over a broken shackle, and that night he was back in the salon.

I took pleasure in the small trips I made into the heart of Marmaris, buying provisions and talking to the local people. I found them interesting both physically and in temperament. The mix of Slavic-looking Turks with light hair and blue eyes, and darker more Semitic-looking Turks was fascinating. Their openness was more European than Middle Eastern. Yet, there was a graciousness about them that struck me as more Middle Eastern. As a whole they were the most hospitable, accepting, and generous people I'd met anywhere on our voyage.

I sought out one small rug shop whose walls were covered with Kilims. Their rich, jewel-like patterned colours — at once mysterious and accessible — hinted at stories from earlier times that seemed just out of reach of consciousness, as though I once lived them but couldn't access them. I wanted to bathe in the colours and lose myself in their mystery.

"You like my carpets?" the shopkeeper asked.

"Yes, very much."

"I'm brewing tea," he said in his soft accented voice. "Share a cup with me."

"No, I couldn't. I'm only looking. I wish I could, but I can't afford to buy."

"Still, have a cup of tea."

"No, really, I can't buy, much as I'd like to."

"Your appreciation is enough."

I was sure this was a ploy. I remembered the shopkeeper in France, who ordered me out of her shop when I went in to admire the elegant chocolate sculptures she had on display. If you do not wish to buy, she had said, please leave.

"Really, you don't understand," I said more emphatically. "I won't be buying."

The shopkeeper pulled over a low wooden stool and placed a small glass of tea in my hands. "Drink," he said.

The next day I returned to the shop for my afternoon tea. I returned on and off for the next three weeks until we set sail, and each time I came I was welcomed.

I visited the village often. If not to see the Kilim vendor, to pick up tubs of yogurt sold in unlabeled buckets, with swinging metal handles that made the tubs resemble paint cans. I could live on that yogurt, and did, for the length of our stay. No ice cream was ever as rich and creamy, and the texture so thick, the spoon stood straight up. Sharing that sensual experience with Bernard was one of my fondest memories. No matter how removed he became from everything else around him, his pleasure in good food was a constant. Long after we left Marmaris, I yearned for that yogurt. And as I write, I can feel its cool, unctuous texture on my tongue.

My life became revolved around the subtly blended flavours of Turkish mezes and broiled kebabs, and the intricate, patterned universe of Turkish carpets. I felt comfortable with the local people and wanted to embrace the country. The yacht had become too small a world for me.

"Let's make a trip to Bodrum," I suggested. Bodrum was another coastal village a short bus ride away, with a rich history going back to early Greece. A trip to visit its historical sites would be a good excuse for journeying out.

"You go," Bernard said. He dismissed my request with an impatient nod of his head. "Show some independence." He didn't say this with anger, but more as though he didn't want to be bothered.

My feelings were hurt. Why couldn't he understand that part of the enjoyment of travelling was sharing the experience? Part of me still held on to the hope that I could spark a mutual interest that might bring us together again.

"I'm getting on a bus to Bodrum in the morning," I said.

Bernard didn't comment although I knew he heard. He had stopped interacting with me and was focused on finishing his monkey knot, an elaborately knotted ball of cord that weighted one end of a rope to be thrown to shore for someone to catch. It's rarely used in sailing today, but its construction is still a good meditation piece and a nice challenge. He was pleased he had mastered the technique.

The bus heading for Bodrum was packed, every seat taken. We started early, and much to my surprise, passed through miles of dense, pine forest. I had no idea Turkey was so green. I had lumped it together with the dry, desert climate of the Middle East. Everything about the country was a surprise for me. At one point, we passed a bear sitting by the side of the road. Bears in Turkey?

About a quarter of the way to Bodrum, the bus stopped to pick up a very pregnant woman. The man in front of me hastily got up to give her his seat.

"Oh, no sir," she insisted.

"Yes, madam, for you."

"No, no."

"Yes, yes."

It was all in Turkish and I could only surmise this is what passed between them. I just know that he kept insisting on giving her his seat, and she kept refusing. The bus driver sat there patiently waiting. No one seemed annoyed or in a hurry though perhaps five minutes passed in this back and forth dialogue.

Without a word, the bus driver got up and left the bus. That's it. He's fed up. Who knows how long we'll be stuck here. From my window, I saw the driver open a door in the side of the bus and pull out a small folding chair. He re-entered the bus and placed the chair in the aisle next to the arguing couple. The man promptly sat on the stool. The woman took the man's seat, and the bus driver continued towards Bodrum with no further words exchanged.

Every gesture was kind. Every person on the bus participated in their own way. I don't know when I've ever seen a more gracious people. Someday, I told myself, I'll return and explore more of this country.

Bodrum was a pleasant, European-looking resort town with gleaming white buildings, posh shops, and high-end yachts moored in the marina. Standing across the harbour in bold contrast to this pretty, up-market town was Bodrum castle, built by the crusaders in the 1400s. The massive fortress-like structure seemed like an aggressive intruder on this airy, whitewashed vacation playground.

Looking over at the castle and then at the streets of Bodrum lined with picture-book palm trees, I recognized that I had left behind my gritty, sea faring existence and was about to enter an easier, more up-scale lifestyle within the boating community. The medieval castle represented an earlier part of our adventure where we sailed into countries that were steeped in history but not travelled as much by Western yachties. Most of the yachts we had encountered so far were manned by adventurous Australians or New Zealanders, and a handful of Europeans to whom sailing rather than lifestyle was the main objective.

The town of Bodrum represented a dividing line, its history no more than a quaint backdrop for tourism. The high-end luxury yachts and huge motorboats in the harbour supported my perception. I felt a sense of loss and relief. I knew the world I had passed through would not be there much longer, and that if I were to go back one day, it wouldn't exist. At the same time I felt a lightness knowing that life would now be more predictable — and more comfortable, that wherever we went from here on, there would be a marina with showers.

The castle didn't hold much interest for me as I had seen enough in the way of stone fortress- like walls in the churches of Cyprus. But another ancient site in Bodrum did — the tomb of King Mausolus. I had learned about the Mausoleum in school. It was one of the Seven Wonders of the World built in the fourth century BCE by Queen Artemisia whom I learned while in Bodrum was Mausolus' sister as well as his wife — a relationship I found a bit shocking. The ancients, it seems, knew how to take nepotism to its extreme.

The Mausoleum had been a marble tomb almost forty feet high surrounded by imposing columns, and housed detailed, life-like sculptures done by famous sculptors of that period. What was left by the time of my visit was a field of rubble surrounded by a scattering of low, unimposing walls. An earthquake had toppled the Mausoleum in the twelfth century, and the crusaders had taken much of the marble for their castle two hundred years later, the embedded blocks still clearly visible in the castle walls.

Bodrum had been called Halikarnasseus in ancient times. It was a Greek city state. What was it doing in Turkey? King Mausolus was Greek. I was sure I had learned that in school. What was he doing in Turkey? On the bus ride back to Marmaris, I thought about Greek history and how much of it I found centred in what was now Turkey.

I learned that not only was Mausolus born in Bodrum (Halikarnasseus), but so was Herodotus, considered today the father of history. Other illustrious names born on now Turkish soil were Homer,

Pythagoras, King Croesus, Midas, and even Rhea, the mother of the gods. Turkey was littered with ancient Greek sites and history. I discovered Troy is in Turkey, as is the temple of Artemis at Ephesus in Lydia, Lydia being where coins were first minted under government control.

The minting of coins was a boon to trade taking place from East to West along the Anatolian coast of Asia Minor. Phoenicians, Egyptians, and Persians travelled this route, and it's likely that this confluence of cultures fed Greece's Golden Age; the country barely separated from Turkey by a narrow slice of the Aegean Sea. I felt that I'd touched the tip of a historical treasure, and it reinforced my desire to return to Turkey one day to explore more of its buried past.

Three weeks later, Bernard charted our new route, and I bought as many buckets of yogurt as I could store without them spoiling, to the exclusion of a number of other provisions. Our plan was to head towards Rhodes by way of Kas and Castellorizon, two neighbouring islands, one Turkish, one Greek.

Kas came into view within hours of our leaving Marmaris, its craggy terrain rising from the sea like the hump of a petrified whale. A jumble of red tiled houses inched up its side layer by layer and flowed back down to the waterfront. It was charming, comfortable and laid-back. Bernard seemed relaxed here. He was even willing to explore some of the town with me. I didn't know what had shifted his behaviour. Maybe it was because we sailed without mishap in a pleasant five-knot wind, maybe because he could explore without the *Santa Rita* being out of view for any length of time. I had no idea what changed him, but I appreciated the company that I had missed so often on our adventure.

We wandered the narrow streets, took in the sweet scent of jasmine that flowed out of pots, and marvelled at the light filtering through the mauve bougainvillea that hung off terraces and climbed walls. We sipped coffee at one of the small cafés that lined the waterfront and whiled away the time watching other people doing the same.

Our rhythm was shifting from hyper vigilance to sybaritic self-indulgence. It seemed fitting. Sybaris was an ancient Greek colony, and we were heading towards that part of the Mediterranean. The luminous light, the clear azure water, the welcoming climate lent itself to a more hedonistic lifestyle. Scent and colour are missing at sea and it heightened our pleasure ashore.

The next morning we lifted anchor for the Greek island of Castellorizon, so close to Kas a strong swimmer could easily have swum the distance. While musing on the physical closeness of the two countries, I was shaken from my reverie by an astonishing sight. Spread out below me, buried in the sea bed, was an ancient city. We glided over its ruins in water so clear that it looked like a scene in one of those heavy glass paperweights that snow when turned over. It was so unexpected and otherworldly that I couldn't believe it was real.

"Bernard," I shouted. "Is this what I think it is?"

Bernard looked over the stanchion lines to where I was pointing. "It's a Roman town," he said. "Do you see those huge amphorae? They're ancient wine vessels."

"My God, yes, I do."

I had become jaded, having seen so many ancient sites and was reluctant to see another, but this was something special. It was not part of a tourist-planned excursion. There were no roads leading to it, and it could only be seen from this particular location on the water. The surprise of the find and the uniqueness of the view brought home once again how fortunate I was to be at this moment in this place. It pleased me that the discovery of the city brought Bernard further out of his shell.

I cast my eyes towards Castellorizon with anticipation of what might await us there.

Castellorizon was the most remote of the Greek Islands with a population of around five hundred people. From the moment we tied the *Santa Rita* to the pier, I was seduced by the unhurried, immutable atmosphere that permeated the waterfront. There was no feeling of the layers of history so evident in Turkey, though I learned that the island had changed hands many times and was devastated during the Second World War. Perhaps because of the small population, the island had managed to keep a timeless feel as though nothing had changed for eons.

Most of the people lived in colourful houses on or just behind the waterfront that was lined with low-key shops and restaurants. I wanted to remember the seductive lure of this out-of-the-way place, and bought a small embroidered cushion cover made on the island. It came with a broken zipper and still has a broken zipper. But the small, multi-coloured geometric pattern, stitched onto the course fabric in measured but graceful lines, makes up for the defect. It makes me think of Castellorizon with its soft charm, coloured houses and wounded past.

Before we sailed out, we had an excellent fish dinner with some good local wine. I started to believe that old adage about the way to a man's heart being through his stomach. It was over a good meal that Bernard and I connected once again.

Rhodes was our next port of call. I knew little about it except that it had housed the Colossus, another of the Seven Wonders of the World. I hoped to see some remnants of the statue, but whatever remained of it after an earthquake around two hundred BCE had been carted off long before we arrived.

We entered Mandraki Harbour, where the Colossus, almost a hundred feet high, was said to have stood guard, a foot anchored on a pedestal on each side of the harbour. Its straddling the harbour turned out to be a myth, though the Colossus was not, and people came from all over in ancient times to see it, even after the destruction. It must have been an impressive sight, since early records say that the thumb itself was so big that few people could wrap their arms around it.

Instead of the Colossus, a couple of deer, a stag and a hind, stood on pedestals on each side of the harbour. They were a disappointment after my envisaging the great feet of the Colossus anchored where the deer now stood.

But Rhodes got better once we left the harbour. Entering the old city was like stepping out of a time machine into the Middle Ages. Everything was made of stone — the streets, the houses, the alleyways, the square with its Grand Masters' Palace and the Church of St. John — all built by the Crusaders. Time warp is what I think of when I think of Rhodes. I remember thinking how young North America was, and how flimsy our structures were. Rhodes felt anchored and forever. It was humbling to know it was already thriving before the birth of our Western religions.

I wanted to visit Lindos, with its temple of Athena on the acropolis, but as always, Bernard was reluctant to go too far from the yacht, and as always I felt sad to see it alone. Like a turtle, his head had come out for a brief moment and then retreated back into that dark shell, of which the *Santa Rita* had become an extension.

As we travelled farther west, we no longer saw yachts from Australia and more appeared from Europe and North America. Anchored near us in the Mandraki Harbour was an American couple who had sailed from the States. "Your main sail looks pretty worn," the young man said.

"The Red Sea," Bernard replied. "It took a beating. Those tears, I've got to get them repaired. No way it'll take a heavy squall."

"We've had a few tears, but we've got a sewing machine aboard. My wife made our sails."

She made their sails? For a moment I felt inadequate, but I rose to the occasion and let my pride go.

"Can she repair ours?" I asked. "We're short of funds, but I read palms and can give you both a reading."

Until the Harbour Master in Colombo's harbour in Sri Lanka had asked me to read his palm and then praised me for my skill, I hadn't thought of using it to barter on the yacht. But his words boosted my confidence and, when we sailed back to Galle, I exchanged a palm reading for a flute lesson for Bernard. Much later while moored in Larnaca, I gave a reading on my birthday for a dinner for both of us at a high-end restaurant.

With the agreed-upon exchange made and the repair done, the *Santa Rita* could once again handle rough weather. We left over-priced Rhodes for what we hoped would be the less expensive Cyclades, the group of Greek islands sprawled across edge of the Aegean Sea.

But our departure was short-lived. Soon after we left port, we heard a noise coming from under the hull.

"Something isn't right," Bernard said. He stripped off his shorts and dove into the sea.

"It's the propeller," he said surfacing. "The security pin's fallen off and the nut's come loose. I've tightened it but it won't hold for long. It's brass and corroded. We've got to head back. I need to find a stainless steel nut in one of the harbour shops."

Within a day the yacht was repaired, and we again set sail for the Cyclades. But I was more aware than ever that to depend on a tiny object floating in water to secure my life was a naive fantasy. If Murphy's Law that states that *"Anything that can go wrong will go wrong"* exists anywhere, it's at sea. I first heard about Murphy's Law when we moored in Hong Kong, and then many times over wherever yachties gathered.

Sailing came with a price, but it didn't dampen my enthusiasm. I looked forward to the Cyclades. I'd been interested in visiting this group of islands since I was a child, and read their names in stories that brought to life magical creatures and naughty gods; and later as an adult, in stories that conjured up sensual pleasures and poetic angst.

Chapter 27

WESTWARD HO!

~~~

Autumn 1984: Greece

> *There can be no boredom with anything that varies in such*
> *a way as always to tip one's thoughts just over the horizon;*
> *and the absence of boredom must be one of the main*
> *attributes of happiness.*
> —FRIEDA STARK

Before visiting the Cyclades I had imagined this circular array of Greek islands to be alike, but each one we visited was different. They all had charming whitewashed houses with blue window trim, narrow winding streets and cascading bougainvillea. All were drenched in Mediterranean light, but each had enough difference to give a feeling of discovery and offered a hint of surprise and something to anticipate as we sailed from one island to another.

Santorini, our first destination, was made up of a large island called Thera surrounded by several smaller ones. Thera was the rim of a gigantic water-filled caldera, the aftermath of a huge explosion that took place thirty-six hundred years ago. Some archaeologists believe that the blast was so powerful the backlash from its tsunami wiped out the whole Minoan civilization on the island of Crete.

We sailed into a quiet bay that held one of Thera's satellites named Nia Kameni, which translates as Burnt Island. Nia Kameni, as the name suggests, was a chunk of lava in the middle of the caldera brought up from the sea floor by a volcano that erupted about four hundred years ago and has remained active. The bay offered a safe haven from the sea, but Bernard's eyes were on the depth sounder. "It's too deep to drop anchor," he said.

"Does that mean we can't stay?"

"Um ... no," he said.

With ropes knotted to the stern and bow of the *Santa Rita,* he tied the yacht between two lava rocks jutting out of the water. With the yacht secured, we jumped into the dinghy and were off to visit Fira, the capital of Thera.

Fira sat atop Thera's steep cliffs that rose up nearly a thousand feet. I felt dwarfed by their height and at the same time protected, enclosed as we were, from the open sea on three sides. I remember feeling like a tiny embryo tucked inside the womb of the earth. Looking up towards Fira, I saw a number of homes built into the sheer face of the cliff, some with only their terraces visible to the sea.

I thought about Lord Tennyson's *Lady of Shalott* confined by magic to a tower and only allowed to view the world through a mirror. She wove stories into a tapestry until she spied Sir Lancelot in the glass, was besotted by love, and defied the curse. Escaping the tower, she found a boat to follow him, but died in a storm before reaching Camelot.

I loved the poem, saw some relationship to my own story, but planned to write a different ending. Coming back to earth, I took a closer look at the perched houses and wondered how the dwellers got around. Perhaps they used the donkeys that waited patiently at the foot of the cliff to take passengers up to Fira. There were a number of donkeys, but no one around but us. Santorini hadn't yet been inundated by honeymooners and cruise ship tourists.

"Ready to ride?" Bernard asked. "We can keep an eye on the *Santa Rita* from the top."

"I'm not riding a donkey!" I said. "They look sad enough without me on their backs."

We hiked up the 588 steps stopping now and then to look out over the wide expanse of azure sea. The sight made the exertion worthwhile and encouraged us to continue the steep climb. When we made it to the top, Bernard took my hand, something that hadn't happened in a long while. My whole self melted into the soft cushion of his flesh. It felt like coming home to a warm hearth, and I hoped we'd find again the early part of ourselves that brought us together.

We strolled along narrow, stepped streets, browsed the small shops, and perused the menus of tasteful but over-priced restaurants crowding the cliff's rim. The jumble of whitewashed buildings appeared etched into the brilliant blue of the sky. Walking along the rim of the caldera, with the sea on one side and the narrow sliver of town anchored on the other, felt as though I was crossing a great void on a tightrope. The sensation made me think about my relationship with Bernard and the way it swung precariously between unexpected moments of affection followed by rejection. Yet, if I were to have given my impression of paradise, it would have been that moment in Fira when Bernard took my hand. Reflecting back, I don't think I could have visualized paradise so strongly without that feeling of the devil nipping my heels.

We found a small restaurant with open windows facing the sea and ordered a Greek salad with Santorini tomatoes and a side dish of fried tomato balls called *keptedes*. Santorini's tomatoes are tiny and sweet, and can be found only on the island. I asked for a dish with the island's eggplant, which could be found nowhere else, and we washed it down with local wine. The waiter told us the island had no water and its produce and wine were watered by dew. Volcanic soil and the island's dryness gave the produce a special taste not found elsewhere in the world. His story conjured up Thera as an enchanted island with hidden gardens tilled by elves.

"I love this place," I said.

"We have to go," Bernard replied.

I'd felt his agitation growing from the moment we entered the restaurant. He had gone silent and hardly listened to the waiter's stories about the island. "The yacht's too isolated and too far from shore," he said. "If the wind picks up, the ropes won't hold."

"Whatever you say," I mumbled, but I would come back. I needed more time to absorb the allure of Fira.

Throughout the night Bernard was anxious about how well the yacht would hold tied between the two rocks. In the morning he suggested we motor further up the island where he thought it would be safer. Another yacht, owned by a French couple, was already there when we arrived at the new anchorage. As we were the only boats in the vicinity, we agreed with the other couple that we'd feel more secure being near one another. With the yacht safely anchored, Bernard and I went ashore to further explore Thera's storybook terrain.

The town overhanging the cliff was Oia. We trekked up the stairs to Oia and explored the stores along the lone cobbled street that wound through the town. Oia was more laid-back than Fira, with a plethora of galleries and small artsy shops overflowing with handicrafts and handmade jewellery. Its many homes carved into the cliff had blue domed roofs that gave an appealing contrast to the completely white town, and offset any possibility of visual fatigue. The layered buildings flowed one into another, and looked as though they were sculpted from sugar icing with the cliff as the cake that held them.

At my insistence, we hopped a bus to Fira and took in the basket-shaped vineyards and various cave houses along the way. The striking landscape of the countryside seen from the bus window reinforced for me that Thera was a special place. But our visit to Fira was too short to savour the uniqueness of the area. With the *Santa Rita* out of sight, Bernard was too nervous to relax. We took the next bus back to Oia and ate an early dinner before heading down the cliff for home. Halfway down the steps, we stared in disbelief as a ferry entered the harbour and passed near the *Santa Rita*, unsettling the water in its wake. On what had been a flat sea, a huge swell rolled in sideways and passed under our yacht and the neighbour's causing them to collide. We watched in horror feeling totally impotent before the sight. My heart pumped wildly as we raced down the remaining steps, taking them two at a time. Back on the *Santa Rita,* we were relieved to see there was no damage to our hull, but our yacht had gouged out a sizeable chunk of wood from the railing of the other boat. Fortunately, there was no blame. I think they were as pleased as we were that the damage hadn't been worse.

Although the *Santa Rita* wasn't hurt, watching the approaching collision of the yachts from our helpless position midway up the cliff unnerved me. I tried not to think about how vulnerable our sailboat was or how we'd ever find the funds if the collision had been serious. Words from one of the sea shanties I'd heard Ewan McCall sing when I was a young girl popped into my head. Back then, the rollicking tunes of sea shanties held promise of freedom and adventure, and I used to play them over and over. But now the poignancy of the lyrics held greater meaning for me. I felt their undertow.

Oh the times was hard and the wages low
Leave her, Johnny, leave her
And the grub was bad and the gales did blow
And it's time for us to leave her
I thought I heard the Old Man say
You can go ashore and take your pay
Oh her stern was foul and the voyage was long
The winds was bad and the gales was strong ...

Most sailors were fishermen who went to sea out of need, not for adventure. I wondered if I was daft to have chosen this life. As for Bernard, there was no way he could have known he had anchored in a ferry lane until that fateful moment. It exacerbated his already well-defined anxiety about something happening to the *Santa Rita*.

Finding a safe spot for the yacht was iffy, and he didn't want to chance another mishap. I shared his unease, and agreed when he suggested we sail on rather than spend more time exploring Santorini. We missed Oia's sunset, touted as the most beautiful in the world, but that didn't bother me. On the sea we had seen many sunsets, utterly breathtaking in their colour and intensity. I was sure they matched those of Oia.

My one regret was that we never made it to Akitori, a Minoan settlement in the north of the island that had been preserved in volcanic ash. Akitori homes had pipes with running hot and cold water and flushing toilets, the oldest ever found. That was enough for me to give credibility to Plato's argument that Santorini was the site of the lost continent of Atlantis believed to have supported a civilization more advanced than any today. When I was a child, outhouses were still in use in parts of America, and here was an ancient civilization that had indoor plumbing long before the birth of Christ.

By noon we arrived at the small port of Karavostes on the tiny island of Folegandros. Its humped, rocky back rose high above the sea. Along the edge at its highest point, the capital city of Chora glowed a brilliant white under the Mediterranean sun. Chora was known for its old section, but I questioned whether it was worth the hike, though it had been my original plan.

"What do you think?" I asked Bernard.

"Let's do it," he said. "If we tie up along the pier, we'll be pretty secure."

In the short sail from Santorini to Foligandros, Bernard's mood as well as his enthusiasm had picked up. Sharing some good time together in Foligandros seemed possible, and I looked forward to the walk.

Before trekking up to the old quarter, we settled in at one of the outdoor cafés along the waterfront for a light lunch of grilled sea-bass and indulged in a bottle of wine. The street was crowded with small cafés and shops selling novelties, but no one pressured us to enter or buy. The relaxed pace of the locals gave the island a gentle feel in spite of its jagged, almost barren landscape. While checking out the Cyclades, Bernard and I decided not to visit the most travelled islands, and Folegandros seemed to have been entirely overlooked by the tourist crowd—perhaps overshadowed by its bigger, more glamorous neighbour, Santorini. Their loss, as Folegandros offered tasty cheap fare, less crowding, and a languid lifestyle that made the place seductive and worth the visit.

Chora, like Fera and Oia, was perched on the edge of a cliff with whitewashed houses and narrow streets—all of it wrapped in that warm Mediterranean light that turns whatever it touches luminous. The old section known as the Kastro was built in the thirteenth century, its houses knitted tightly together, their backs to the sea, creating a solid wall of defense against marauding pirates. This jumble of connected white houses, with their stone paved streets and paved steps leading up to the front doors, has been in continuous use since they were built.

It impressed me knowing that my own country had only been around for a little over 250 years, and the 150-year-old house I was raised in was considered a historical site. I couldn't conceive of a people staying put for so many generations. Bougainvillaea, jasmine, and potted plants along steps and beside doors softened the stone and enhanced the elegance that the patina of age had given the area.

Bernard was as pleased as I to take it all in. I warmed towards him as I watched him ease into being more adventurous and accommodating since our arrival on the island. I marvelled at how effortlessly he drifted into the relaxed lifestyle of the local people. He reverted to the partner with whom I had wanted to share this journey, and lulled me into my old affection for him.

Our next port of call was Milos, the home of Venus de Milo, the beautiful lady whose marble body sans arms was now ensconced in The Louvre in Paris. A number of sculptures belonging to the island had been confiscated by other countries and are now seen in their museums. It attests to the early development and wealth of Milos, a place blessed with a plethora of mineral deposits coveted by many countries going back further than the Bronze Age. I knew none of this before arriving, other than from having seen the Venus de Milo at The Louvre. The wealth of knowledge I acquired through our travels was one of the real joys of our adventure. And the history of a place became so much more alive and relevant after I'd visited where an event occurred.

Milos, like the rest of the Cyclades, was a volcanic island but ceased its rumbling about 90,000 years ago. Unlike Santorini, there had been no cataclysmic blast, but a series of small eruptions over millions of years that left layer upon layer of mineral deposits in its wake. And though it had the usual array of charming whitewashed houses set high above the sea, its attraction was in the topography of the land. While Folegandros had a rugged crudeness offset by gracious people and a gentle dusting of age, Milos had drama. Almost devoid of vegetation, the island looked as one might imagine a distant planet in the outer reaches of our solar system. Huge rock formations, pushed up by sheer will from the bowels of the sea, rested at the water's edge like behemoths taking the sun.

We circled a coastline composed of undulating rock formations that looked like bleached pelvic bones of prehistoric animals fused together. In places it looked as though stone had been melted and moulded into organic shapes by a gigantic furnace. I envisioned a giant sculptor commissioned to arrange the massive hunks of rock into these aesthetic shapes. Had I been a sculptor, I would have used

Milos as my inspiration. Mineral deposits coloured some of the terrain in shades of burnt umber and sienna, and the sea in places had hints of emerald, crimson and violet. We sailed past small beaches tucked around the stone, but neither Bernard nor I felt compelled to visit them.

The following afternoon we left the Cyclades for the Peloponnese Peninsula on mainland Greece, but not before a final lunch of fried sardines at one of the waterfront taverns in Adamas, the main port of Milos. I had become addicted to dawdling at outdoor eateries over cups of coffee or a glass of wine — a relaxing habit I still indulge in.

We sailed for a day and a half before reaching the port of Gefira on the southeast coast of the Peloponnese. From Gefira, a short causeway led to Monemvasia Island, a huge slab of rock that had broken off from the mainland during an earthquake in the fourth century. We had spotted the island from the *Santa Rita* as we sailed towards Gefira.

"Why don't we visit?" I suggested. "The island's within walking distance of the port."

Bernard agreed.

Monemvasia supported an intact medieval village that had been carved into its rock. The remains of a fortress dominated the apex, and stone houses with red tile roofs cascaded down to the sea. Much of the town was in ruins and many of the houses empty. The few inhabitants who still lived there seemed determined to preserve its twelfth century architecture and earlier way of life. The quiet, contemplative aura that infused the town captivated me, and I played with the idea of leaving the *Santa Rita* in the harbour and spending some months in Monemvasia. I envisioned myself in one of the stone houses, gazing out over the clear, turquoise water while writing profound thoughts inside my hardly-used journal. The town was the perfect writer's retreat.

But I didn't think about it for long. Monemvasia had no electricity, and I was too dependent on my few creature comforts. I couldn't give up my late night reading in the aft cabin or hot sponge baths however meagre my water supply. We didn't have many amenities on the *Santa Rita,* but electricity was essential for quality of life. After a good night's sleep and re-provisioning at a market in Gefira, we set sail again, this time for Pylos on the southwest coast.

After sunset, we found ourselves becalmed at the southern tip of the Peloponnese near the lighthouse of Faros. The sea was flat and there wasn't a shred of wind.

"Let's call it a night," Bernard said. "The wind will pick up in the morning. Why don't you take the first watch?"

"Sure," I said. "Get some sleep. I'll wake you in two hours."

It must have been about ten at night when Bernard went below deck. I looked around and saw nothing but a sky full of stars and an empty sea. After a while I drifted off into a light sleep, lulled by the gentle bobbing of the boat. A disquieting sensation of something nearby jolted me awake. In front of the *Santa Rita,* and almost upon us, was an enormous wedge of steel at least sixty feet high. Oh my God, a tanker! I hadn't seen it approaching, and it was moving fast.

"Bernard!" I shouted, paralyzed by the implication of what I saw. "Bernard!"

Alerted by the urgency in my voice, Bernard raced onto the deck and leaped towards the ignition. In a split second he started the engine and swerved the yacht aside. The tanker raced past us never knowing we were there. It came so close I could have reached out and touched its hull. For a split second I drifted out of real time. Everything appeared in slow motion, even a fantasy of my reaching towards the tanker. And then I came back to my senses. I was shaking. We could have been split apart and sunk.

Bernard was speechless for the next twenty-four hours. His refusal to acknowledge my presence shouted louder than words that I had shirked my responsibility, and he was right. I made myself as invisible as possible, and stayed out of his way.

Late afternoon the following day, we arrived in Pylos and entered the main harbour in the Bay of Navarino. The waterfront, shaped like a large horseshoe, was protected on its sea side by a long, narrow stretch of island called Sfaktinia. The *Santa Rita* was in a circle of safety. After the experience of the night before, it offered us security until we got our bearings. The town hugged the semi-circular shoreline and was a comforting sight with its huge, umbrella-like trees and many outdoor cafés. I hoped it would settle our nerves. However, still traumatized by the night before, neither of us was in the mood to explore.

As we motored towards the pier, we discovered the harbour was filled with hulking tankers. With good reason, Bernard remained vigilant. At one point a wine tanker came into the port and decided to tie up next to us. As it swung around to come along the pier, it was about to bump us. Bernard leaped on shore and pulled the yacht only a fraction, but that small move averted a collision. We no longer had to worry about pirates as we had in the East, but the Mediterranean would present its own set of problems. I was reminded again that the sea was not a stable home.

We spent a week in Pylos gorging on olives and watching truck after truck arrive in the harbour to fill those enormous tankers with wine. Wine was more plentiful than water in this part of the world, and to Bernard's delight, it had become cheaper at each port. He was indulging more. I wasn't concerned because it seemed to relax him, and that helped me relax.

Our week of self-indulgent leisure put enough distance from our near collision to restore my will to go on. When I saw how close we came to annihilation, my energy had drained away. Bernard never berated me for my sloppy handling of that night watch, but I knew I shouldn't have drifted off to sleep. I waited for his reproach, but it never came. I think he had been too stunned to bring it up, and I certainly wasn't going to. Under the warm sun of Pylos with its easy lifestyle, the angst of that night faded away. Bernard seemed to have revived as well.

One morning he went ashore in search of a packet of Gitane tobacco, and returned more animated than I had seen him in a long while. "I was talking to some sailors," he said. "Calabria is only two days from here, and there's a sheltered port with nobody there."

It was the most he had spoken to me all week. I felt relieved and absolved of guilt.

"There's a big industrial harbour with a defunct factory. We'll have the place to ourselves."

That afternoon, we set sail for Calabria, a fertile region of Italy located at the bottom of its boot.

Chapter 28

SENSUAL PLEASURES

Autumn1984: Italy

> *With a contented stomach, your heart is forgiving,*
> *with an empty stomach; you forgive nothing.*
> — SICILIAN PROVERB

S ailing from Pylos to Reggio Calabria was a two-day pleasure ride under a gentle breeze. As we entered the harbour of the city, I felt the fragility of our small yacht, eclipsed as we were by an immense empty pier, towered over by a cavernous rusting structure that may at one time have been a factory or warehouse.

The deserted landscape had all the elements for a blood-curdling thriller where the good guy and bad guy shoot it out, but I liked the fact that we had the place to ourselves. As soon as we stepped ashore, Bernard took my hand as he had done in Fira. At a small kiosk a short distance from the harbour, I discovered the creamy ecstasy of gelato, the most sensually satisfying ice cream I'd ever eaten.

"Do you want whipped cream?" the vendor asked.

"Yes, please."

I'd never had an ice cream smothered under mounds of freshly whipped cream. I loved the rich excess of it. With our ice creams in hand, Bernard and I walked along the sea, and stopped to rest at an outdoor café. We lingered over tiny cups of espresso, and had fun commenting on the local inhabitants who passed by.

Reggio, already a flourishing city before the time of Christ, was a melting pot of many cultures, each one leaving behind some of its influence in spite of several devastating earthquakes. Statues of dour-faced saints shared the city with nubile nymphs and anatomically correct gods, and hinted at the diversity of its cultural legacy. Remnants of ruins were another reminder as was the archaeological museum stuffed with the remains of what was left after the quakes.

But neither of us had any interest in exploring Reggio's past. We craved sensual pleasure more than culture. The juicy taste of fresh fruit, the aromatic scent of flowering trees, the feel of grit under our shoes — these sensations took priority over the edification of the mind. Had we stayed longer, I might have had a change of heart, but we were only there for two days. Our destination was Mallorca in the Balearic Islands. We'd heard it was a haven for yachties and one of the less expensive spots in Europe. We hoped to winter there.

On the morning of our third day, Bernard and I left for Sicily, our destination Palermo, where we planned to pick up provisions before leaving Italy. We didn't know as we sailed into the Strait of Messina that high cliffs bordering this narrow body of water separating the toe of Italy from Sicily created a wind tunnel. High winds swept down on us and shredded our mainsail. We struggled against the wind to get what was left of the sail furled, and then turned our attention to the mizzen and stay sails. Luckily, they had weathered the blast of air, and Bernard was able to stabilize the yacht. Once out of the Strait, the smaller sails proved adequate for sailing, but we still had to find someone who could repair our main sail.

"Why don't we take a break on one of the Aeolian Islands?" Bernard suggested. He had a chart of the area spread out on the table. "They're close by. It doesn't matter when we arrive in Palermo."

We were in the sun-drenched Tyrrhenian Sea north of Sicily. With a clear blue sky above, rolling waves beneath, and the luminous Mediterranean light transforming our surroundings into a pastel world, it was hard to conceive we'd been through a hair-raising episode less than an hour before. Lingering a bit longer in Italian waters seemed like a great idea.

"Sure," I said. "We'll probably never pass this way again."

Bernard showed me the Aeolian Islands on the chart, and pointed out the seven main ones, two of which were still volcanic, Stromboli and Volcano. We opted to sail for Lipari, the largest and most developed of the group. At another time, Stromboli with its active volcano that spit fire into the night sky would have captured my imagination. But I was still under the spell of the sybaritic pleasures that seduced me in Reggio Calabria. Stromboli would have been more rugged and exerting.

Lipari, by contrast, was tourist friendly with its endless ribbon of hotels, restaurants, outdoor cafés, and cheesy tourist gift shops that followed one after the other. I could see its appeal for anyone in search of a beach holiday, especially with its azure water lapping the shore. And perhaps, if I held a job and needed a break, it would have appealed to me. But sailing into this man-made vacationland made me wish we had chosen Stromboli because of its singularity. I'd been to many resort towns, but I'd never been close to a fiery volcano.

My one shot of adrenaline on this serene island was the local car scene. Lipari was the only island that had cars, and the people drove insanely. They followed no rules, but had extraordinary reflexes. My most memorable experience during our stay was car gazing and watching the drivers — fast, precise, reckless, and alert. In Lipari, driving seemed to be a sport much like hockey in Canada.

In the afternoon of our arrival, I visited the local archaeological museum with its impressive collection of Greek theatrical masks, some dating back to the fourth century BCE. The early inhabitants of Lipari belonged to the cult of Dionysus, the god of theatre. He was also the god of ecstasy and intoxication, but it looked as though the locals had managed to put out that early passion — except behind the wheels of their cars.

I had seen too much antiquity and too many beaches over the years, so nothing seemed fresh or out of the ordinary as I made my way back to the *Santa Rita*. Yet, having said that, I still have shards of obsidian and feather-weight balls of pumice that I picked up along the shore. The dry, tactile feel of the pumice takes me back to Lipari, and in spite of my jaded response at the time, I feel nostalgia for the island. It's in retrospect that I've embraced the uniqueness of experiences that I will never have again.

In Lipari, we tied ourselves to a row of four or five small yachts strung out like peas in a floating pod, each one carelessly tied to the other. The first yacht was attached to a tiny pier, and to reach land, we had to climb across each of the other yachts. During the evening, the wind rose, and the first yacht came loose. Being the only ones aboard our yacht at the time, we spent hours running our engine to keep the row of boats, with us tied at the end, from drifting out to sea.

When a few of the owners returned to their crafts, we helped them tie up more securely and were finally able to get some sleep. Had we not been there, that little group would have drifted out to sea. I couldn't believe how casual these Sunday sailors were. They would never have survived our adventure unless they learned quickly about how unpredictable life at sea could be. Bernard and I agreed there wasn't much to hold us in Lipari, so the following afternoon, we decided to set sail for Palermo. It was time to see about having that mainsail fixed, and Lipari was too small a place to find a sail maker.

We dropped anchor in Palermo early the next morning. Bernard asked around and acquired the name of a Frenchman with a workshop not far from the port, who repaired sails for a reasonable price. The Frenchman told us that our sails were worn out. If we wanted to do a major crossing, we'd have to refit the *Santa Rita* with new ones — an expense we weren't prepared for with our funds dwindling.

Bernard was concerned. He told the Frenchman he was thinking of taking the trade winds across the Atlantic to North America. His comment surprised me. We had talked about selling the yacht in Europe. He had even written his brother to find where a good market might be. It was one of the reasons we were heading for Spain's Balearic Islands. Now it seemed he was having second thoughts. I didn't question him about it. We were in one of the happier interludes of our journey, and I didn't want to break the spell.

Bernard was living impulsively, changing his mind from moment to moment depending on the circumstance and how he felt at that second. In retrospect, I wonder if this was due to his having no parameters that defined his life, no boundaries that channelled him into any direction. When he held a job, he was disciplined and super responsible to the people who worked with him. Do we need defined boundaries in order to make decisions? What happens to commitment? Inside me there was a growing knot of unease.

While we waited for the sail repair, I visited Palermo's outdoor market, so vast it seemed to take in the whole city. I'd never seen such variety of fresh produce in my life. Stalls overflowed in a patchwork of every shade of green, purple, red, orange, and yellow. Only the colour blue was missing, but the Mediterranean sky made up for that. It was the first time I had seen green and yellow cauliflowers among the white, or carrots in a riot of colours, or many odd-shaped veggies I had no name for.

We ate every meal off the yacht, and our indulgence bordered on the obscene. In the various countries we had travelled through, each had its gastronomic specialties, but here everything was a treat for the palate. I had my first taste of hand-made cannoli stuffed with ricotta, now a common restaurant entree, but back then mostly confined to Italian homes. And I discovered Sicilian pizza with its thick satisfying crust, still hard to find in North America though many places offer a poor imitation. I miss the stuffed rice balls or *arancine* that were sold on every street, and would love to re-experience the joy of eating there, a pleasure enhanced by the vibrant culture and warmth of the people. Sadly, food seems to lose something outside its country of origin. We eat with all our senses, and environment heightens the enjoyment of eating.

Sicily's location as a crossroad between the Middle East and the West not only gained gastronomically, but its blend of cultures gave a unique character to Palermo. The jumble of architectural styles — Byzantine, Arabic, Norman, wedding cake Baroque — interwoven with stiffly sculptured saints and sensuous, naked nymphs frolicking with naked gods (a paradox we also noted in Reggio) gave an interesting texture to the city. I wondered how the people came to terms with their historical legacy of sensual indulgence and religious restraint. Unfortunately, we weren't there long enough to indulge in all the city had to offer. With our mainsail repaired, we quickly departed though I hoped to be back one day.

With Italy behind us, I looked forward to Spain's Balearic Islands, our resting place for how long I didn't know. We'd heard stories about Ibiza's popularity with the rich and famous and tentatively picked neighbouring Mallorca as the better choice for our modest lifestyle. Each island in the Mediterranean offered something different.

"We're going to pass Sardinia," I said peering over Bernard's shoulder. He had just unrolled a nautical chart and was plotting the course for our sail. "We could make it a stopover on the way. What do you think?"

The prospect excited me. I had wanted to visit Sardinia since my university days when an anthropology professor gushed over the island and told me she imagined me there. At the time, I had no idea where Sardinia was, and here we were, so close. I thought I was fated to go there.

We anchored off the south side of the island, where there weren't many yachts and none of the large luxury ones Sardinia was noted for, only to discover we needed boat insurance. In all our years of sailing this was the first time insurance was mandatory. It brought home how much more regulated the West was than the East. On our way to the insurance broker's office, we decided to pick up fuel for the boat and discovered that, in Sardinia, wine was sold out of the same type of gas pumps that are used to fuel cars. Bernard was ecstatic.

"We've got to come back with jerry cans," he said.

I felt my stomach tighten and push up into my chest. My stomach was a barometer that always foreshadowed when something not good was about to happen. I tried to dismiss the sudden spasm as over-reaction. I'm a high-strung person, I told myself. I worry too much.

Later that day, I watched with dismay as the price on the wine meter barely moved up. Bernard filled two jerry cans from the converted gas pump, wine in Sardinia being cheaper than water. Over the past few weeks, Bernard had stopped drinking heavily and our relationship improved proportionally. I couldn't tell if his better mood was because he felt more at home in Europe or because he was drinking less. I feared the latter. I knew it wouldn't be long before I'd know for sure, but my body told me I already knew.

To my disappointment, Bernard didn't want to see more of Sardinia. He was happy with his purchase, and wanted to move on. I wish I had insisted. Had we explored the island, I might have met Chiara Vigo, the woman who spun silk from the saliva of clams to weave into bracelets as protection against bad fortune. She gave them to anyone who asked at her door. Perhaps my anthropology professor was thinking of someone like her when she oriented me towards Sardinia. I wondered if she saw something in the earthy, mystical energy of the island that related to my nature, or sensed I'd be in need of a lucky charm, or maybe she only sensed my longing for the exotic and the unknown.

I didn't know why a professor's offhand remark so many years earlier had such a hold at that moment. I only knew that I felt a strong pull towards the island when I saw how close we were. I wanted to know what this teacher saw in me that I didn't recognize in myself.

Each country we visited had its unique character, and each brought out a different facet of my personality, in the same way that different people did. A subliminal dialogue is always at play between ourselves and our environment, and if we pay attention, it can lead to greater self-knowledge. So perhaps some undiscovered part of myself was awaiting me on Sardinia.

Living so many years at sea with no roots and no permanent community gave me a wealth of experiences, but constant adjustment without a goal made it difficult to internalize and process experiences. Bernard's identity came from being a sailor, but it was too narrow and claustrophobic for me. I had wanted an independent life, free of constraints, but with some sense of direction that would ground me. Instead, I found myself the handmaiden of a small yacht at the mercy of an unpredictable sea and in a precarious relationship.

Sardinia, with its primordial energy, felt rooted in the sea, and had a power that held its own against whatever onslaught the sea delivered. It felt stable and eternal whereas I felt adrift. Perhaps this awareness of what it felt like to be rooted was all I needed from Sardinia. It shocked me into finally acknowledging that Bernard was comfortable with drifting while I wasn't. I didn't share my thoughts with Bernard. What could I have told him? He was thrilled with his wine purchase and in a good mood as we sailed towards the Balearic Islands.

Chapter 29

RESETTING MY COMPASS

Winter 1985: Balearic Islands

> *There is nothing more enticing, disenchanting,*
> *and enslaving than life at sea.*
> —JOSEPH CONRAD

After a two-day sail from Sardinia, we arrived in Mahon, Menorca's capital, just as the sun was rising. Palma de Mallorca was still our destination for the winter months, but it seemed a shame to sail past this smaller island without acknowledging its presence. A short hike to the nearby beach revealed the same white sand as the beaches of Italy's Lipari, but the ambiance had none of the buzz. Instead of chic outdoor cafés and boutique hotels, Menorca offered basic, motel-style lodgings with good value for the dollar. The beach swarmed with British and German tourists on family vacations. A nice place to bring kids, I thought, but not very interesting.

Before leaving for Palma, we decided to eat at a small waterfront restaurant. Our lunch of omelette *bocadillos,* fried egg sandwiches with mayonnaise on French bread, was interrupted by the restaurant's chef.

"Mayonnaise comes from Mahon," he solemnly announced after a quick inquiry as to where we were from and an assurance that we liked his *bocadillos.* I'd never given mayonnaise much thought other than to assume it was invented by the Hellman's Mayonnaise Company in a food processing lab. "Don't let anyone tell you differently." The chef looked at me accusingly. I wondered if he could read minds. "This salsa is Spanish, not French."

A mayonnaise war, I learned, has been fought between the two countries for centuries. Menorca had such a small footprint on the world stage; I wondered why the French couldn't let them have this victory. I assured the chef that I would spread the word.

After lunch we sailed the short distance to Palma de Mallorca, and tied up along the Paseo Maritimo, a sprawling waterfront walk crammed with high-end yachts and luxury motorboats. Bars, restaurants, clubs, outdoor cafés, and a gigantic Continental Hotel faced the moored yachts, while the Seu Cathedral and a castle overlooked the bay. "Quite a contrast from Menorca," I said to Bernard.

We berthed alongside moneyed boat owners, a very different breed from the rugged yachties we encountered in the East. The Australians who dominated the China Sea prided themselves on their sailing skills and self-sufficiency. Many of these European and American yacht owners generally hired crews to do the work while they supervised. What both groups had in common was hard drinking and a limited interest in their host country.

I did, however, encounter the occasional fascinating outsider. Along the Paseo Maritimo, I met an ex-Viet Nam vet who became a Buddhist after the war and kept to himself. I watched him every morning as he did Tai Chi in front of his small yacht. Gossip among the local inhabitants, who stopped to observe his practice, hinted at it being a form of devil worship. In Taipei, I had seen whole neighbourhoods doing Tai Chi before opening their shops. I had taken lessons from a Chinese woman in Singapore, who was in her late sixties but didn't look a day over thirty. I wondered if through Tai Chi I could also push back time. One morning I asked my neighbour if I could join him, and we became friends.

Alexandra, a young French girl, not yet twenty, whose parents had chartered a yacht for a family vacation on the Mediterranean, provided another story along the Paseo Maritimo. Alexandra, to her parents' dismay, remained behind. She'd fallen in love with the handsome captain of the yacht and was living with him aboard his boat tied up not far from us. Alexandra played classical guitar. I'd sit on deck and listen to her move effortlessly from Bach to Handel to Verdi to earlier Baroque composers. I loved the classical guitar. Under Alexandra's skilful fingers, I lost myself in the music. My son Stefan had left his guitar behind when he returned to Canada. I worked up the courage to approach her.

"Could you give me lessons?" I asked.

Aside from endless scales, I learned to play a passable *Ode to Joy* from Beethoven's *Ninth*. It became the only piece in my repertoire, but I never grew tired of it. Bernard, to his credit, didn't complain through my endless attempts to perfect it. Over the course of the guitar lessons, I became Alexandra's confidant and only friend. This shy, romantic, wisp of a young woman with the big glasses and limp hair had no one else to talk to.

"I love Patrick," she confided. "But he has no money. A yacht is so expensive."

I tried to be sympathetic, but it was hard. Patrick was the spoiled only child of an aristocratic French family. His mother had bought him the yacht.

Alexandra went on. "He wants me to work in a topless bar."

"What did you say?"

"I didn't want to. But he told me it's not a big deal. I go topless on the beach. It's the same thing."

"It's not the same thing," I said. "There are only men in a topless bar."

"I don't feel comfortable," she said. "I hate the idea."

But she did it anyway. "It pleases Patrick that I'm doing something useful to help him maintain the yacht."

One day she started to cry during my guitar lesson. "A man asked me to go with him," she said. "I pushed him away. The owner was angry I'd refused. So was Patrick when I told him."

"Get off that boat," I said. "Patrick doesn't love you. He's using you. Go home. Go back to your parents."

I saw her several days later.

"I went with the man," she said.

She curled up on my settee and lay there for a long time.

"Don't do this," I said. "Patrick is no good. He's a pimp. He loves only his boat and maybe his mother."

Alexandra took her guitar and left Patrick, but when she returned to France, her parents refused to let her back in the home. They disowned her. She had many difficult years trying to find her place in the world, and never married. We stayed in touch and only recently stopped sending each other Christmas cards. Or rather, she stopped answering mine. Perhaps she's finally put away her past and moved on.

Our first winter in Mallorca was said to be the coldest winter of the century. We hadn't prepared for this and didn't have winter clothes. We also didn't have money to buy any. Many of our neighbours, including a Swedish couple that I thought would have been immune to harsh winters, docked their yacht and returned home. We had nowhere else to go and spent most of our days huddled around a kerosene lamp in the salon.

I cooked non-stop to warm the air. Moisture from condensation on cold, humid nights was our biggest problem. It crawled down the salon walls and lodged in our bedding. At night, we slept wrapped around each other. It felt good to be so close to Bernard.

"You wet the bed," Bernard teased one morning when we awoke entangled in dank, musty sheets. He had a wicked sense of humour that still endeared him to me.

"I did not," I said, laughing.

"Yes, you did. I bet you were too cold to make it to the head."

Brook and Jenny, a British couple we'd met soon after our arrival in Mallorca, lived in Binissalem, a small town near Palma. One evening Brook picked us up for dinner at their recently renovated farm house. Riding in Brook's car was the warmest I had been for weeks. I daydreamed all the way to Binissalem about the comfort of living in a home like theirs, and was taken aback to see their king-sized bed squeezed into their tiny kitchen. In that unforgiving winter, there was no place to hide.

Winter wasn't our only problem. Money was becoming a real issue. Bernard kept talking about taking the trade winds across the Atlantic to North America.

"It's our easiest sail. The winds are constant and steady and we'll get there in little more than a week."

"It's unrealistic," I said. "We need new sails. Our sails are too worn to get us across. And anyway, how would we live once we got there?"

Bernard didn't disagree, but wouldn't face reality. His drinking increased, affecting his judgement, but I didn't want to say. For months there had been no unexpected outbursts or undermining comments. I wanted to sustain the harmony as long as I could.

"Cheaper than water," he kept repeating every time he opened another bottle of wine. It didn't help that every café meal came with a glass of wine. If you wanted water, you had to ask for it. And sometimes it came with a service charge.

Bernard's reputation as a whiz with anything mechanical spread quickly throughout the waterfront. Yachts always had problems. He was the "go to" man. It meant we could buy provisions, sit long hours in cafés lingering over coffee or glasses of wine, and always have a stash of wine aboard. Without the usual expenses connected with onshore living, life in Mallorca was cheap. He liked working on other people's boats, sometimes not even charging them or asking for next to nothing, talking forever to them about the mechanical difficulties associated with boat life, and commiserating about it over countless glasses of wine. I felt like trailer trash afloat.

Our plans to use the *Santa Rita* in some kind of enterprise had disappeared. Our dream of finding that special place on the planet where we would settle never materialized. Even the plan to sell the *Santa Rita* in Mallorca was drifting away. Bernard seemed quite happy to live hand to mouth doing odd jobs and repairs but never really turning his skills into a business.

In early spring, a letter came from Middlebury College in Vermont, an invitation to my son Jonah's graduation which was to take place that June. I was desolate.

"How can I go?" I said knowing there was no money for a plane ticket." I felt a knot in my stomach. "I promised him I'd go. And I want to be there."

Bernard drifted away from me, and focused on some piece of metal he'd found that he thought could be useful on the yacht. When he finally spoke, it wasn't with much interest. "A lot of the luxury yachts need housekeeping. It won't pay much, but it'll pay something."

"I hate cleaning," I said. "It's a thankless job that you have to do over and over. I don't even like doing it for myself, and I certainly don't want to do it for others." I was livid that he'd even make the suggestion.

"Where do you expect to get the money?" he asked.

So, for the next few weeks I found myself cleaning toilets on other people's boats. With each plunge of the brush into a toilet, I imagined plunging it down Bernard's throat. I resented his living as though he were one of the privileged or one of the retirees with sufficient income to sustain this lifestyle. I couldn't understand why he wouldn't look for work. And worse, why he did "favours" repairing other people's yachts instead of making a business out of it for himself. Who did he think he was? And worse, who did he think I was? I couldn't help thinking about Alexandra and Patrick. If I were younger, would he have suggested I go work in a topless bar?

Then I remembered that I could read palms. I'd done it in Taiwan, Sri Lanka, and Cyprus. Why not Mallorca? I had an article from a Taipei newspaper where I'd been interviewed about my skill. It was in Mandarin, but it used my name and I could show it to potential clients. I also had a letter from the harbour master in Colombo in Sri Lanka, who was impressed with the reading I had given him. The East believed in palmistry, and I thought their recommendation would go far with a Western clientele.

I was right. I charged thirty US dollars, which included two palm prints and a typed analysis. I read the palms of most of the people along the waterfront and, with the help of Brook and Jenny, who had a lot of ex-pat friends on the island, I had as much work as I could handle. In two months I had earned enough for a plane ticket and more. I took the money I made cleaning toilets and bought myself a white bikini. I needed a reward to clear my head of the anger I had felt doing it.

"You look awful in that," Bernard said the first time I wore it. I never put it on again. When we sold the yacht, I gave the bathing suit to the girlfriend of the new owner as part of the package.

I had lost all illusions about the yachting life. My disillusionment was reinforced when Jenny told me about a rummage sale one of the churches was having a week or so before I was to leave. "I've a good eye," she said. "We'll get you something real classy to wear for Jonah's graduation."

As soon as we entered the church basement, I had the uncomfortable feeling that I was being watched. I noticed the same woman behind me wherever I went. "Why is that old lady following us around?" I asked Jenny.

"Don't you know? Yachties steal all the time. They can spot you as soon as you walk in."

I wanted to crawl into a hole.

"Let's go," I said. "I'll buy something to wear in Vermont."

Chapter 30

SETTING A NEW COURSE

~~~~~~~

Spring 1985 — Summer 1986: Palma de Mallorca

There is nothing permanent except change.
— HERACLITUS

I left Bernard in charge of the *Santa Rita,* and flew to Montreal to see Stefan before taking the train down to Middlebury College for Jonah's graduation. When I greeted him at the airport, I had no sense that three years had passed since I last saw him. It could have been the day before. But since his return to Montreal, he had found part-time work and an apartment while earning the credits necessary to be accepted as a full-time student majoring in physics at Concordia University. And he had established a relationship with a lovely girl who was to become his wife. During those years his life had moved ahead. Mine, I felt, was at a stand-still.

The girlfriend was a surprise, but a pleasant one. I was happy he'd found someone with whom to share his life. "I'd like to get the two of you a gift," I announced shortly before leaving for Jonah's graduation. I wanted to give them something as a memory of the visit since I had no idea when I'd see them again.

"How about a set of dishes?" Stefan said.

"Dishes?"

"Yeah, why not? We could use them."

I'd forgotten how practical Stefan was. I hoped his girlfriend shared this trait. "Sure, why not?" I answered.

Today when I visit them, more than thirty years later, and reach for one of the odd pieces remaining from the set, it takes me back to their old apartment in Montreal.

On the train down to Middlebury, I thought about my boys. Before leaving Mallorca, I received a letter from Jonah saying he'd been awarded a two-year scholarship to do a Master's of Philosophy at Oxford University. It reassured me that both my sons were making good decisions about their futures. Knowing how unconventional their childhood had been, I felt relieved, and because well-meaning people had told me over the years that I was making a mistake in how I was raising them, I also felt vindicated.

When Stefan and Jonah were young, it sometimes felt as though they'd be with me forever and I wished they'd grow up faster. Then one day they were gone, and I wished I could bring back those years. I was glad they had the confidence to venture out, but it was also painful. I hadn't realised how much I missed them until an acquaintance in Mallorca asked how they were doing, and I suddenly burst into tears. I was finally able to let in that feeling of loss, and in time, I let it go. My boys had moved on with their lives. It was time for me to move on with mine.

At the graduation, one of Jonah's professors made a point of letting me know how much he enjoyed having him as a student. "I've rarely had a student so focused on his work, yet so socially amenable and integrated into college life," he said. It was another confirmation that my son's exposure to different cultures and people broadened him and opened him up to new experiences, and that the independence that came with the sea life gave him a remarkable discipline for his age.

I mingled with other parents and found the time spent with them stimulating. They were engaged in the world — earning their way, making a difference in their communities, participating in social affairs. There was a dynamic between their personal lives and the greater world at large. I valued my experiences at sea, and what I'd learned from other cultures and about myself. Now I wanted to use what I had learned in a challenging and meaningful way.

I was determined that Bernard and I put the *Santa Rita* on the market. Just "hanging out" during my most productive years seemed like a waste of a life. Before we had embarked on this adventure, I had envisioned the transition from land-living to water as a change in lifestyle, not as an escape from life. We would test our strengths, explore different worlds, and grow from the enrichment of our expanding awareness. I saw our journey as a book with many chapters waiting to be written in life experiences. I had assumed Bernard saw it the same way. What I discovered was that, for Bernard, there were no chapters to be written. Acquiring the *Santa Rita* was the last chapter of his book, not the first.

"Just having a yacht," I kept insisting on my return to Mallorca, "isn't an end in itself. We wake up the next day and there's still a whole life to live." But I was talking to myself.

While we were sailing I could feed my sense of adventure, test my resourcefulness, and feel an integrated wholeness in my body that empowered me. But now that we were anchored in Mallorca and no longer moving, I felt the full weight of living a parasitic life. I told Bernard I couldn't go on drifting from day to day. "I want a stable home on land," I said, "and I want to do something productive with my life."

"You never loved the boat," he said.

"It has nothing to do with loving the boat. I don't love our life. I want us to have a shared life. We don't. Your whole world is wrapped up in this yacht."

He didn't answer, but nodded as though he understood what I was saying.

"Look," I said, "if you want to continue living this way, you can. Sell the yacht. Get a smaller one — more to your liking. You're always saying there are things you would do differently if you built again. Or you can crew on other people's yachts, without the responsibility of ownership. You have great skills, and you can easily earn your way doing boat maintenance. I can get a small place somewhere and restart my life."

Bernard didn't object to what I was saying, but he made it clear he wasn't going to actively pursue the sale of the yacht. "We can't get a good price here," he said. "It would be better to sell in the States."

"It'll take us a long time to make the money for new sails," I said, "and we can't sail across the Atlantic without them." I had reminded him of this several times before, and each time he just nodded and said nothing. "Maybe we should charter," I blurted out in frustration, knowing he wouldn't, but still hoping. After our one try in Singapore, he vowed never to do it again and so far stuck to that mind set.

"Sure," he mumbled in a half-hearted attempt to appease me, and put an end to the conversation.

A few days later a voice called us from the shore. "*Santa Rita, Santa Rita*. Anybody home?"

I came through the hatch and found myself face to face with a slim, stylishly dressed but severely bruised woman in her mid-sixties. Her face, arms and legs looked as though someone had repeatedly punched her. I was sure it was a case of domestic violence, and I wondered what yacht she'd just run away from.

"Can I help you?" I asked.

"Do you mind if I come aboard?"

I nodded, and she deftly manoeuvred along the four-foot long, two-by-four inch beam that was our walkway from the cement pier to the bow of the yacht, and hopped over the stanchion lines onto the deck. I led her below deck prepared to hear a tale of woe.

"Hi, I'm Kit," she told Bernard and me. "I heard about you from some friends of yours when I was looking for a yacht to charter. I was on another yacht, but a mistral hit us. The boat and captain were badly damaged. They're both being tended to, but I'd like to go on with my trip and was told that you people might be willing to take me."

So this wasn't domestic abuse. Those bruises came from her being tossed about when that yacht she hired got caught in the squall. I knew how nasty a mistral was, and most sailboats were reluctant go out when one was brewing. I admired her spunk, hoped I had it at her age, and immediately liked her.

"How about it, Bernard?" If he was serious about selling the yacht in North America, this charter could go a long way towards making the money for the sails.

"No," he said. He gave no explanation.

I was furious but held my temper. I didn't want to make a scene in front of a stranger.

"I've seen most of the Balearic Islands," she said. "I'm just missing Menorca."

"Not interested," he said and brushed past her to go on deck.

She turned to me. "Do you want to go? I don't feel like going alone. There's a ferry we can take. I've already paid for a room and rented a car."

I had no idea there was a ferry on Mallorca. It reminded me how little we had explored the island even though we had been here several months.

"Didn't you know?" she said. "It runs from Alcudia, on the other side of the island. But I can drive us there."

"How soon can you get ready?" I asked. I wanted to get far away from Bernard as soon as I could. I needed time to settle my fury. I also welcomed the opportunity to explore Menorca by car. Perhaps it had more to offer than what we had seen when anchored there.

Unfortunately, Menorca didn't improve on second viewing, but it was nice to have a car and be driven around the island looking at something other than boats. I learned that Kit was an interior designer from New York who had just retired and was looking for an island in the Mediterranean where she could bask in her memories of an old lover.

"I'd loved to have settled in Capri," she told me. "It's the most romantic of all the Mediterranean Islands. Thirty years ago I had a ten-year affair there with a man I was deeply in love with, but it ended badly, and I returned to New York. It would be too painful to go back. Besides, after all these years, it wouldn't be the same, and that would be a disappointment."

She was looking for an island equivalent. Menorca didn't do it for her. Neither did the other Balearic Islands. After a short liaison in Palma with a minor noble, she packed her bags and returned to New York.

Kit and I remained friends until she died. It was an odd relationship. We had nothing in common. But she liked my writing. "I'm only interested in talented people," she said after reading something I had written. As for me, I loved hearing stories about her past bohemian episodes, all unfortunately with tragic endings. The greatest of her loves, the man from Capri, called her just before he died. He phoned to say she had been his greatest love, but he could never leave his wife and children. He wanted her to know. She never fully recovered from his phone call and died a few years later.

A few weeks before she died Kit confided in me: "Without romance in one's life, one has nothing. I'm now no more than a fag hag."

"Fag hag?" It was the first I'd heard that brutal expression.

"I only attract gay men," she explained. "It's not what I want to be."

She lived for and defined who she was through her ability to attract and bring lovers into her life. For whatever reason, I was the vessel she poured her stories into. In return for my "ear" she left me a Persian carpet that runs the length of my hallway. It ties me to this unique friendship that had such an odd beginning.

On my return to the *Santa Rita* after spending the week with Kit, Bernard informed me that his mother, along with his eighty-year-old aunt, was coming for two weeks. This was his mother's oldest sibling whom she claimed to hate. But then, Bernard's mother didn't like anyone except for her son and her dead neighbour's mistress, who I was pleased she wasn't bringing this time.

Our strained relationship didn't improve on her arrival, as "Madam" was quite a princess and never happy. But this time, no longer willing to accommodate her whims or placate her desires, I felt prepared for her antics. In Sri Lanka she was determined to make me feel like an outsider in my own home, and made it clear that I was not the woman she would have picked for her son. I thought the best solution was to leave her to her son and be away as much as possible with friends I had made on other yachts along the waterfront. By the second day of her arrival, she became aware that I wasn't going to cater to her as I had during her visit to Sri Lanka. She called to me from the salon as I was about to go out the hatch, her voice saccharine-sweet.

"Oh, Rita, aren't you going to introduce me to your new friends? You're always running off somewhere."

I turned around and smiled. "No, Dedé, stay here with your son. You see him so seldom. And your sister is here to keep you company. You're such a good cook. Why don't you make them a little something for lunch?"

She was taken aback by my change of behaviour, and this pleased me. The other upside of her visit was that I got to see parts of Mallorca other than Palma. The women wanted to explore the island and that meant renting a car, something Bernard had been unwilling to do until his family came. The four of us set out together, Bernard and me in the front, Dedé and her sister Suzanne in the back.

For the duration of our motor trip, I ignored the mother, was kind to the aunt whom I had always liked, and without any expectation found myself enjoying the adventure. Travelling along the coast through the rugged Tramuntana Mountains invigorated me. It called to mind how much I loved mountains. We stopped at the Carthusian Monastery in Valldemossa, where Chopin had stayed with George Sand. We took the winding roads dotted with olive and citrus trees to the town of Deia, the last home of Robert Graves. With its beautifully aged buildings and winding, cobbled streets, Deia was home to an astonishing number of writers, painters and musicians. I could see myself living there quite happily. I played with the idea of returning after we sold the yacht.

Once Bernard's family left, he withdrew further from me. Everyone else was his friend. I had become his enemy. Even worse, he considered the *Santa Rita* as only his. I was treated as guest on board, as though he had picked me up in some port and let me stay due to his good graces. My wanting to sell the *Santa Rita* made for a tense relationship, in which the yacht took precedence over any personal commitment he might have felt toward me.

"How nice that Bernard let you and your children sail with him," an emaciated, thin-lipped British woman of "a certain age" said to me over dinner at the home of one of the ex-pats. Our yacht was a calling card for dinner at various homes by people who thought it was "interesting" to know yachties.

What was he telling people? I was the one who encouraged him when he had doubts. I was the one who invested the money that helped make the sea voyage possible. Without me this adventure might never have happened. That's what he told me in New York when we went there to buy some yachting equipment before leaving for Taiwan. "I know I owe a lot to you to have made this dream possible," he had said. "I'll never forget that."

These thoughts raced through my head, but I was tongue-tied, too shocked to find the words to reply. To this day I regret not setting the record straight. And this woman will live in my head forever because I could not vent my rage.

This same brittle woman, who was so enraptured with the dashing Captain Bernard, told us about a classical guitar concert in town. We went several evenings later with Ann, an Australian woman sailing with her husband Robert, and my artist friend Jenny from Binissalem, a twenty-five minute drive from Palma. I had invited Jenny to spend the night aboard the *Santa Rita* so that she wouldn't have to drive back to her village so late at night.

After the concert Jenny and I couldn't find Bernard anywhere. Jenny suggested he might have gone back to the yacht, but that didn't seem likely to me. I couldn't believe he would have left without saying anything. He had been standing beside me, and suddenly he was gone. We spent about an hour looking for him and then returned to the *Santa Rita*. It was past midnight. He wasn't on the yacht. I was frantic.

"Perhaps he's on Ann's yacht and has forgotten the time," Jenny said. "I saw them talking together a few minutes before we left the concert hall."

I ran over to Ann's yacht to ask if she'd seen Bernard. When I went below deck, I found Ann and Bernard, in a drunken stupor, slouched over her galley table. I had no idea where Robert was. Maybe he had gone to bed.

"Why are you here?" I blurted out. "I looked everywhere for you."

Bernard looked unperturbed. He didn't understand why I was upset. "Ann told me she had a great bottle of wine on the boat. It seemed less boring than making chitchat with that expat crowd after the concert."

I stormed off the boat and made my way back to the *Santa Rita*. It was the last time I spoke to Ann. I learned she and Robert divorced when they returned to Australia. I wasn't surprised. Good, I thought, though I was sorry for their twelve-year-old daughter.

I felt humiliated. Until then I had kept Bernard's drinking and the tension between us private. Now it was open season for the waterfront gossip brigade. I no longer spoke to Bernard. I stopped caring, making plans, coming up with ideas, or making meals. I hung out in cafés along the waterfront and came home to sleep. A week or so later, he finally noticed.

"How would you like to go for a sail?" he asked one morning.

In all the time we had been in Mallorca, he had refused to go anywhere with the boat.

I jumped at the chance to get out of Palma. "Sure," I said. I hadn't forgiven him, but I wasn't going to miss an opportunity for a change of scene.

Chapter 31

HOMEWARD BOUND

~~~~~~

Summer 1986: Spain/Montreal

> *If you do not change direction, you may*
> *end up where you are heading.*
> —LAO TZU

We sailed out of Palma on a sun-filled breezy morning under a brilliant blue sky. The *Santa Rita,* heeled to a perfect angle, and zipped through the water like a space ship towards infinity. I lost myself in sea spray and wind—my mind blank, my body alive to every nuance of the yacht's movement. It released some of the tension I'd been carrying with me since that night I found Bernard with Ann. Towards evening, while entering Palma's harbour, I noticed a well-dressed man in his thirties with a small, child-like woman beside him watching us from the water's edge. This didn't surprise me. The *Santa Rita* was a class act under sail. As we were tying up, the man asked if he could come aboard to see the interior.

He came down the companionway and stroked the teak pole that separated the salon from the galley as though it were a favourite pet.

"Teak, I like it," he said. "Are you willing to sell?"

Bernard gave him an outlandish price.

He didn't bargain. "I've business in Italy," he said. "I'll be back in two weeks with the money."

He then turned and left, with his little beauty scrambling behind.

"He'll never be back," Bernard said.

"Probably not," I mumbled. Bernard had no intention of selling, and I felt trapped.

Two weeks to the day, the buyer returned to the *Santa Rita.* Behind him was the tiny girlfriend carrying a leather briefcase. She placed the case on the salon table, and the buyer snapped it open to reveal more money than I had ever seen in my life. The bills, in American currency, were bound in neat little packets.

"Count," he said.

Bernard was mesmerized by the treasure before him. He counted the stacks.

Yes! I said over and over to myself.

Bernard could still back out, and I was a bit nervous. But to my relief he didn't.

"There's one problem," the new owner said. "I don't know how to sail."

"I'll give you lessons," Bernard said.

"I'd rather you take me to Sitges. I have a friend there who'll teach me."

I'd heard of Sitges, a small fishing village not far from Barcelona. I was excited about the prospect of going there. Once in Paris many years before our life on the *Santa Rita*, while strolling through Montmartre , Bernard and I looked in the window of a basement apartment where a small group of artists were about to share a pot luck lunch. The host invited us to join and later showed me a book of etchings by an artist friend.

"Miguel Conde?" I said to the host. "I've never heard of him."

"He's an American who came to Europe on a Guggenheim and stayed. He and his wife Carola settled in Sitges."

"I'd love to meet him," I said jokingly, never expecting it to happen.

"It's a small world," our host answered. "Who knows?"

The following day, the four of us set sail for Sitges. Once out on the sea, we learned that our buyer's girlfriend had been picked out of a line-up of prostitutes in Peru and that his business took him from Brazil to Miami, Las Vegas, Mallorca and Italy. He had a home in Las Vegas and a ranch in Brazil.

He then told us his friend in Sitges owned a bar. "He's a Brit," he said, "an ex-cop. After embezzling a large sum of money, he decided to move to Spain — no extradition between the two countries, you know. He bought the bar for his father who'd always wanted to own one."

Neither Bernard nor I answered. My mind was racing, wondering what we had gotten into. I was sure Bernard was having the same thought. The buyer then took out a good-sized bag of weed, rolled a hefty joint and offered us a toke. It shocked Bernard into action.

"Throw that stash overboard," Bernard ordered. "I could lose this boat if the Coast Guard comes aboard. Until we sign the papers this yacht is mine."

It was no secret that Mallorca was an easy place to buy pot, crack and cocaine. The stuff came in by boat and the area around the bay was closely monitored by the police. It dawned on me that our buyer might be in the business. That's why he came with cash instead of a cheque.

For once, Bernard and I were on the same page. We had no idea who this guy was. If we were stopped with him aboard, we worried about what might happen. And even though he got rid of the pot, we didn't know what else he might be carrying.

"As soon as we get to Sitges, we go to a bank before signing papers. This money could be counterfeit," Bernard whispered in the privacy of our cabin.

As though he had overheard our conversation, the next morning the buyer offered a suggestion. "Why don't you take the money to Andorra? I took it out of my account there, and you can open your own. My friend has a Mercedes. I can borrow it to take us up there. It's a good place. No taxes."

We decided to go along with his suggestion. Sitges was a small Spanish seaside village. Andorra was a country no more than a three-hour drive from Sitges. It was more likely we'd find a notary to handle paperwork in Andorra than in Sitges. There was also the added enticement of a beautiful ride through the Pyrenees to get there.

When we docked the *Santa Rita*, the buyer went looking for his friend and returned about an hour later with the Mercedes. He drove us to Andorra like an insane person. He lost the door handle of the car by scraping against something, and at one point it looked as though he'd lose the whole door when he started the car before it was shut. We said nothing.

We didn't trust this man but didn't want to anger him. He seemed crazy and irresponsible. In retrospect, I think he must have been high on something. I was so tense the whole way I could barely straighten out when I finally got out of the car. And I totally missed out on the mountain landscape. My eyes were glued to the back of the buyer's neck the whole way, willing the car to stay on the road, afraid that if I looked away, we'd go over the edge.

Bernard and I raced to the bank the soon-to-be-owner had suggested. Bernard opened an account. The teller counted the money. Everything went through without a hitch. Still, we wanted to get rid of this guy, and paperwork had to be done to transfer ownership. It was noon. Nothing would open again before 4 p.m. Bernard was frantic. In one legal office we found a secretary though the notary wasn't there.

"I speak Spanish," Bernard said. "Dictate to me what should go into the sales contract, and I'll write it. Then we only have to wait for the signature from the notary."

For some reason, she was willing. Bernard wrote the document. The moment the notary came in, we had him sign it. The deal was done. Now we had to get back to Sitges with that madman. He raced back with the same disregard for life and limb as when we went. I couldn't be sure we'd make it and marvelled that a friend could lend such an out-of-control person his car.

Once in Sitges and safely out of the car, we relaxed and shook hands. Now whatever happened to the yacht was his responsibility. I thought I'd enjoy the moment, but I didn't. I felt a heavy sense of loss. The *Santa Rita* had been my home and my refuge, and had kept my family safe. I recalled with a pang of nostalgia that awesome moment when I first saw her in the cradle at the Shin Hsing Boatyard. I still loved the *Santa Rita*, and hoped she was in good hands.

The new owner was all smiles and good will. "If you're ever in Sao Paulo, look me up," he said.

He gave me a card with his address. I played with the idea for a while. He had told us some wonderful stories about his ranch and the staff, and a dairy-loving boa constrictor that milked his cows until it was caught in the act. Then I let the idea go and threw away the card.

We rented a small beach house in Sitges, and I finally met Miguel and Carola. My introduction to Miguel was to mention the man in

Paris who had shown me the etchings. Carola and I became friends, and Bernard and I spent many evenings in their home eating gourmet meals cooked by Carola and drinking fine wine offered by Miguel. One of Miguel's posters is the first thing you see when you enter my apartment. An etching from his Guggenheim series hangs on my living room wall. We have a mutual friend in Montreal who married a girl from Barcelona whose father collected Miguel's work. When you travel the planet, it becomes a much smaller place.

During our stay, we received a post card from our buyer saying he managed to sail to Brazil on his own. He added that he liked the name *Santa Rita* and decided to keep it. The *Santa Rita* carried my name, and having watched her birth and lived with her so intimately over such a long period of time, I felt a part of me was out there with her, just as a part of her was with me. Wherever she sails, I am there. But I was also ready to move on. Bernard wasn't. He was adrift without the yacht. He had lost something very loved and with it, his identity.

"You can find another yacht, a smaller one that fits your exact requirements," I said. "There are a lot of used yachts for sale. And you can service other boats. You're good at that. A lot of yachties aren't." It was a conversation I'd already had with him several times before the sale of the yacht. I hoped he'd be listening this time.

I wanted to work out a compromise. I had let go of the sailing adventure, but I wasn't ready to let go of the marriage. I hoped Bernard would agree to a stable home where I could establish a life, and he could have his yacht. "I'll sail with you," I said, "but not live on the sea."

Bernard didn't respond to anything I said. His only communication was to mention his loss. Waking time was spent drinking. One day he woke and couldn't move his limbs. I finally got him to sit up and eventually to walk, but he moved around mechanically, detached from everything around him. Today I wonder if he had been having a mental breakdown — something I wouldn't have recognized then. And looking back, it makes me sad to remember that time and how little I understood of what the problem might be, though I wouldn't have been able to do much without his agreement.

Also, I had too many painful memories of my own to try to make sense of what was happening to him. I felt betrayed and misunderstood. I wasn't ready to take into account the stress of the responsibility he had carried or the number of years we spent cooped up with each other in a confined space. I was too close to the hurt.

As he slowly came out of his dazed stupor, his constant drinking and growing paranoia drove us further apart. He called me the spoiler of his dreams, the mate who deceived him. I was not the *Santa Rita*, and there would be no other. We left Sitges and returned to Montreal, but we fought constantly. He was bitter that he didn't have his boat, believed I was responsible for his loss, and was determined that I wouldn't have a home. He withheld most of the proceeds from the sale and lost it in poor investments. We couldn't bridge our differences, and eventually we divorced.

Subsequently, Bernard lived in many places and couldn't seem to settle anywhere. I re-established my life in Montreal. I liked the buzz of the city — the energy of its multicultural diversity, its creative edge, its indifference to unconventional lifestyles, and its multitude of coffee shops and outdoor cafés. Before my journey, I wasn't aware of how much I liked the city. It happened to be where I lived while longing for a better place, an idealized place. On my return, I was here by choice.

It wasn't easy in the beginning. I'd jerk awake every two hours preparing for my night watch. I'd unexpectedly feel the earth shift beneath me as though I was again on water. And I'd experience tension in my throat every time I saw a squall line and worry for those at sea, though curiously I didn't feel that anxiety when I was at sea. I had cut relationships with friends and colleagues. I now had to re-establish contact or build a new coterie of friends.

I couldn't fathom telephone answering machines. The first time I heard one, I slammed down the receiver. It was a long while before I would talk to one or bring myself to buy one. The birth of the computer was another shock. I forced myself to buy a huge, bulky thing that sat in a box in my bedroom for months before I worked up the courage to unwrap it. When I finally got someone to set it up for me, I was paralyzed in front of it.

I broke through my resistance by understanding that, if I wanted food on the table and a roof over my head, I'd better move with the times. There were no teaching positions available and no jobs for any-one without fluent French. I studied handwriting analysis through a correspondence course because I read in *Forbes Magazine* there was a call for it in the business community. I already knew about hand-writing analysis, having attended a lecture given by a nun in Mal-lorca, the church being a big proponent of the discipline with a num-ber of practitioners. I figured I'd find clients since so few laypeople were trained in this field.

I received a scholarship to continue my studies to become a Master Graphoanalyst, after which I set up a business for myself. I don't know if I would have had the courage to do that with no back-up support if I hadn't been tested at sea. Those adventure-filled years assured me of my capacity to overcome obstacles, adapt to changing circumstances, and survive whatever challenges came my way.

In spite of our divorce, Bernard and I never lost contact, our re-lationship cemented by those years at sea. They formed us, shattered us, and in the reconstruction of our separate lives brought us back into each other's lives, but with more humour, mutual respect and an appreciation of our differences.

Epilogue

COMING FULL CIRCLE

May 2016: Montreal

> *The personal life deeply lived always expands*
> *into truths beyond itself.*
> — ANAÏS NIN

When Bernard and I first explored the idea of going on this adventure, I didn't ask him to define his reason for his wanting to do it. I'm not sure he knew. I wasn't sure of mine. I only knew that anything that took me to a place I hadn't been was where I wanted to go. I had a restless spirit and a belief that somewhere else must be better than where I was.

We spent hours talking about finding our paradise, the perfect spot on the planet. We hoped to settle there and live an idyllic life. We thought Sri Lanka might be the place. Before that, when the kids were still little and Bernard and I lived in Mexico, we envisioned some remote island in the Caribbean where we'd build a home and plant our own food. That remote island never materialized. When we got to Sri Lanka, it was not the paradise we'd hoped for. No place was.

Instead I learned that people were the same everywhere. Whatever culture we were in, the fundamental needs and emotional responses of the people were the same. We all laugh at a bit of irony or a good joke. We all cry when tragedy touches our lives. We all become angry when we feel threatened, and we all want secure and stable lives.

The awareness killed any tendency I had towards seeing other people as different from me. It opened my heart and made me understand that whatever I was looking for would come from within. "*We* are like islands in the sea, separate on the surface but connected in the deep," wrote William James.

So when Bernard skyped me from Mexico and asked if I'd like to sail with him after so many years, I had to think about it.

"The yacht's in Tunisia," he had said. "The guy wants to sell, and I think the best market would be in Tahiti. We could do it again."

I thought back to the journey we had taken together so many years before. I found his proposition interesting. It was tempting. We'd be sailing on someone else's yacht with a purpose and time frame. We could repeat our earlier experience with less stress and from a totally different perspective — two seniors who had lived full lives since our parting and were coming together for a new adventure. Bernard told me the yacht was equipped with every convenience for an easy sail. I had no doubt we could do it.

But the more I thought about it, the less it engaged me. When we had first embarked on our adventure, I was searching for something outside of me. I had thought that what was out there was better, and that once I found my place, I'd find peace. I had to leave to come home to myself, and having satisfied my wanderlust, the urge was gone.

A vacation in Tahiti? Why not? Perhaps we could meet at different legs of the journey and do some day sailing. But in truth, I'm not a sailor. The *Santa Rita* had served as my launching pad — the base from which I could foray out into an unknown world. She served me well, but I've laid her to rest.

* * *

"I don't think so," I finally answer. "But maybe I could meet you there. You know, our voyage was an extraordinary journey, and given how much the world has changed since the eighties, far less possible today. I'd like to write about it."

"Do it," he says. "You're the writer."

"You might not like it."

"It doesn't matter," he answers. "It's your story."

Ithaka

Constantine Cavafy

As you start on your way to Ithaka
hope that the road is long and the way filled
with adventure and the widest knowledge.
Do not fear the Lestrygonians and the Cyclopes,
or angry Poseidon. Nothing will block your way
if your thoughts are high, if body and soul
are together touched by the finest feelings.
Neither Lestrygonians, nor any Cyclopes,
nor mad, seething Poseidon will check your way
if you refuse to harbour them in yourself,
if your soul does not set them down before you.

You must hope that the road is long.
Many summer mornings will come
when, with endless pleasure and joy,
you will enter eagerly new harbours.
You will tarry in Phoenician emporia
procuring their finest wares:
mother of pearl, corals, ambers, ebony,
and perfumes that will arouse you,
great profusions of provocative fragrances.
Many Egyptian cities will welcome you,
You will gain much from the learned ones.

Always hold Ithaka in your mind.
The goal of your journey is getting there.
But be calm, you need not go in haste.
Linger awhile, even for years, out there on the way.

The shores you seek are better reached in old age,
when you're filled by all you've gained voyaging.
Do not reckon that Ithaka will reward you in any way.

Ithaka gave you the marvelous journey.
Without her you would never have gone.
But now she has nothing left to give you.

If you find Ithaka austere, she has not deceived you.
Look what you've gained, so much wisdom and experience,
and at the end you will understand what all the Ithakas mean.

(TRANSLATED BY JOHN XIROS COOPER)

Acknowledgements

———

First and foremost, I'm hugely indebted to my wonderfully insightful critique group — Prue Rains, Claire Helman, Karen Zey, Veneranda Wilson, and the late Jim Lewis — all memoirists with their own stories and unique vision. Thanks also to my dear friend Jean Ambrosii whose passion for the written word and sharp eye for detail kept most of my grammatical slip-ups and redundant phrases to a minimum. And where would I be without the fine-tuned reading of Evelyn Matlin, who helped me pare down my story to its most important and poignant moments. And a special thanks to Pat Machin and Marilyn Mill who both read through the finished manuscript during its editing stage and gave me helpful comments.

I also want to acknowledge the Banff Centre for Art & Creativity for accepting me into the Wired Writing Studio program under the stewardship of Fred Stenson, where I was mentored by Curtis Gillespie, a consummate storyteller and truly nice guy whose own travel writing is a treat to read. His astute observation that my boat journey was a metaphor for my life's journey was an aha moment that shifted the focus of my story into something much richer than my original intent. All through my writing and into the editing of the manuscript, I tried to keep Curtis' vision of the memoir alive, and I believe it made *Seeker* a better book. Aside from being noteworthy writers in their own right, Fred and Curtis are special people. During my stay at Banff, I needed medical attention. Fred, in spite of his position, looked after me, and Curtis took time from his full schedule to drive me from one hospital to another. The best way I could thank them for their generosity and kindness was to make sure I completed this memoir.

I also want to say how grateful I am to John Xiros Cooper who permitted me to use his translation of *Ithaca*, a poem by Greek poet Constantine Cafavy. The poem so completely captured the voyage I made, and John's wonderfully interpretative translation made me feel I'd stumbled upon a soul mate.

And last but not least, a special thank you goes to my sons, Stefan and Jonah, who have enriched my life in so many ways and whose company on the journey made it a richer story. And Bernard, who let me tell his story through my eyes with no judgement.

About the Author

Rita Pomade, an intrepid nomad, hailing from New York, now lives and writes in Montreal. Her articles and book reviews have appeared in the ezine *Mexconnect,* and her monthly "Dear Rita" column was a regular feature in *The Chapala Review* during her last years in Mexico. Retired from teaching English as a Second Language at both Concordia University and McGill University, she now devotes herself to writing full time.